The Royal Museums of Fine Arts of Belgium

*A guide to the collections
of Ancient Art
& Modern Art*

The Royal Museums of Fine Arts of Belgium

A guide to the collections of Ancient Art & Modern Art

Ephrem

with collaboration
of the scientific staff
of the Royal Museums of Fine Arts of Belgium

Foreword by Eliane De Wilde
Principal Curator
of the Royal Museums of Fine Arts of Belgium

'ALICE
ÉDITIONS

The author and the Editor express their heartfelt thanks to
all who contributed to achieve this work, and particularly
Éliane De Wilde,
Principal Curator of the Royal Museums of Fine Arts of
Belgium,
her collaborators
*Anne Andriaens-Pannier, Pierre Baudson,
Véronique Bücken, Helena Bussers,
Véronique Coomans-Cardon, Brigitte de Patoul,
Catherine Heesterbeek, Frederic Leen, Thérèse Marlier,
André A. Moerman, Gisèle Ollinger-Zinque,
Françoise Roberts-Jones, Jacques van Lennep,
Sabine van Sprang* and *Brita Velghe*,
members of the scientific staff,
and *Régis Hespel*,
chief engineer.

They also thank
Chantal Pirlot,
Director of the Prométhéa Foundation,
and *Anne Vierstraete*,
chief agent of the Degroof Bank,
for their invaluable support.
The first edition of this guide
was made possible thanks to
the patronage of the Degroof Bank.

Translation and Adaptation
Steve Dept
Pre-Press
Olivier Vandenheuvel

Alice Éditions,
avenue Pré-des-Agneaux 27
B-1160 Bruxelles

Foreword

Each year, over a million art lovers tour the Royal Museums of Fine Arts of Belgium, making it the country's most visited museum. It is also the eldest museum, founded by First Consul Napoleon Bonaparte in 1801.

Visitors come from throughout the world to marvel at a unique collection of paintings and sculptures stemming mainly from the Belgian schools, though highlighted by a number of important complementary foreign accents. The collection ranges from the 14th century to present-day art.

Many of these visitors come several times, because the museum is so extensive and the amount of exhibits so large that it seems impossible to process everything at once, never mind actually seeing all the works. For years there has been a demand for a practical, well-illustrated guide written in a fluent, accessible language, intended for an enlarged public without neglecting high and rigorous scientific standards. This guide saw the light for precisely those eager readers: they can carry the book along as they stroll across the rooms, deciding for themselves about which exhibits they would like to learn a little more, i. e. the artist's life and context in art history, the importance of his œuvre within the collections and so on, often seasoned with the author's personal appreciation.

A number of priorities were set as requirements for the guide's design: a pleasurable legibility, visual attractivity and an outstanding presentation, three qualities to be found in our museum's rooms as well. It is the first time that the Museum of Ancient Art and the Museum of Modern Art are described together in one and the same book.

Partly thanks to some three hundred colour plates, this user-friendly guide will remain a delight for the eye after the visit and function as a personal *musée imaginaire* for the countless art lovers who want to investigate the matter more closely.

Éliane De Wilde
Principal Curator

Sum

THE GREAT MASTERS: A MUST

nary

How to us

Time Line.

Continous pagination
to which the index
entries refer.

Comment on a school,
a movement or a trend
of art history.

● Short biographical note,
or note about a
specific aspect of
art history

☐ Description of a work,
under the name and
surname of the artist

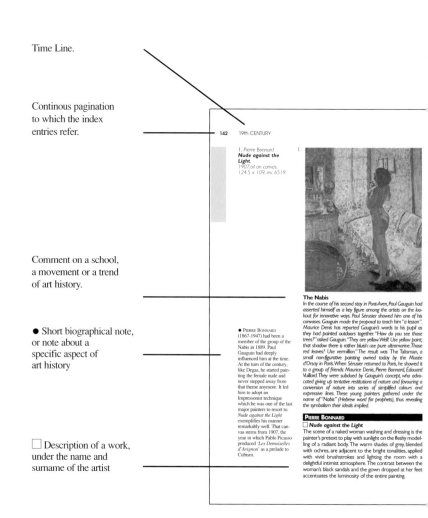

142   19th CENTURY

1. *Pierre Bonnard*
**Nude against the
Light**.
*1907, oil on canvas,
124.5 x 109, inv. 6519.*

1

The Nabis
In the course of his second stay in Pont-Aven, Paul Gauguin had asserted himself as a key figure among the artists on the lookout for innovative ways. Paul Sérusier showed him one of his canvases. Gauguin made the proposal to teach him "a lesson". Maurice Denis has reported Gauguin's words to his pupil as they had painted outdoors together. "How do you see those trees?" asked Gauguin. "They are yellow. Well! Use yellow paint; that shadow there is rather bluish: use pure ultramarine. Those red leaves? Use vermillion." The result was The Talisman, a small non-figurative painting owned today by the Musée d'Orsay in Paris. When Sérusier returned to Paris, he showed it to a group of friends: Maurice Denis, Pierre Bonnard, Édouard Vuillard. They were subdued by Gauguin's concept, who advocated giving up tentative restitutions of nature and favouring a conversion of nature into series of simplified colours and expressive lines. These young painters gathered under the name of "Nabis" (Hebrew word for prophets), thus revealing the symbolism their ideals implied.

● PIERRE BONNARD
(1867-1947) had been a
member of the group of the
Nabis in 1889. Paul
Gauguin had deeply
influenced him at the time.
At the turn of the century,
like Degas, he started painting the female nude and
never stepped away from
that theme anymore. It led
him to adopt an
Impressionist technique
which he was one of the last
major painters to resort to.
Nude against the Light
exemplifies his manner
remarkably well. That canvas stems from 1907, the
year in which Pablo Picasso
produced '*Les Demoiselles
d'Avignon*' as a prelude to
Cubism.

PIERRE BONNARD

☐ **Nude against the Light**
The scene of a naked woman washing and dressing is the painter's pretext to play with sunlight on the fleshy modelling of a radiant body. The warm shades of grey, blended with ochres, are adjacent to the bright tonalities, applied with vivid brushstrokes and lighting the room with a delightful intimist atmosphere. The contrast between the woman's black sandals and the gown dropped at her feet accentuates the luminosity of the entire painting.

e this guide

Reproduction of the
work in full, with
a number referring
to the key.

Colour of the circuit.

Caption, including:
• The artist's name and
surname,
• the work's tittle,
• its date, if known,
• the medium or material,
• its dimension in centi-
metres (height x width)
for paintings, height x
width x depth for sculp-
tures and, if required, Ø,
i.e. diameter),
• survey number

---

2. *Édouard Vuillard*
Two Schoolchildren,
1894, size paint on canvas, 214 x 98, inv. 6681.

EDOUARD VUILLARD

☐ *Two Schoolchildren*
Public Gardens was a generic title for a series of nine pain-tings of the same height with linked motifs. *Two Schoolchildren* belongs to that series, produced by Vuillard in 1894 for Alexander Natanson's town residence. Nowadays, three of these panels are in the United States and five are in the Musée d'Orsay, Paris.
Vuillard had joined the Nabis from 1890 to 1900 and had put Gauguin's lesson to practice. He had transposed the colours of reality to their deliberately unreal equivalents. Neither the green of the trees in the middle ground nor the beige shade of the dead leaves belong to nature. He combined a broad, flat application of matching, adjacent patches of colour with a treatment of depth inspired by Japanese prints.

VICTOR ROUSSEAU

☐ *The Secret*
This couple of young girls appear from the marble as if from the original tide, extolling the tenderness of the act of sharing. Between the two bodies that respond to each other without even touching, a narrow space is created by the echoed curves, a hardly perceptible space allowing for a play with light and shade, generating a subtle vibra-tion. The hairline and the ample draperies discreetly hint at Art Nouveau.

● VICTOR ROUSSEAU (1865-1954) already worked with his father and uncle at the age of eleven: they carved this stone on the yards of the Palais de Justice in Brussels. He started attending courses at the Academy of Fine Arts at the age of fourteen. He was twenty-four when he was admitted in Charles Van der Stappen's class. He was awarded the Prix de Rome at the age of twenty-nine. His precocious activity never slowed down, and his production was even more prolific due to the fact that he lived to be almost ninety a couple of years before his demise. Amongst the count-less sculptures he has left—ranging from monuments to a small ivory mask—*The Secret*, so full of graceful poetry, typifies this most cultured, refined artist who was fond of idealism.

3. *Victor Rousseau*
The Secret,
1916-1917, marble, 49 x 31.5 x 20.5, inv. 4335.

The Royal Museums of Fine Arts of Belgium

The history of the Royal Museums and their collections

Masterpieces seized for the Museum of the Louvre

Due to a peculiar diversion, the collections of the Royal Museums of Fine Arts of Belgium owe their origin to Bonaparte's cultural policy. The armies of the young French Republic evicted the Austrians from the Southern Netherlands in 1794. France first installed a Republican tenure, then imposed Napoleon 1st's Imperial rule from 1804 to 1815. In 1794, the Republic's commissioners stripped religious institutions of their possessions and selected masterpieces among their invaluable artistic treasures to fill out the collection of the Louvre Museum, created the previous year. Fifteen hundred paintings were gathered in Brussels, two hundred-seventy are sent to France. Four years later, director of the Brussels painting academy Guillaume-Jacques-Joseph Bosschaert selected hundred paintings among the works neglected by the French commissioners and founded an initial museum of which he was appointed as curator. It was located in the buildings of the old court of the Palace of Charles of Lorraine, where the present Museum stands.

A second phase thanks to the Vienna Congress

As a next step, Napoleon Bonaparte, First Consul of the French Republic, decided in 1801 to institute fifteen departmental museums to relieve the crammed Louvre; one of these was to be in Brussels, and over fifty works were sent from Paris over a period of ten years to complete the collection gathered by Bosschaert. The Museum's survey written up in 1811 enumerated three hundred and five works from various origins. After the fall of Napoleon, in 1815, the Vienna Congress forced France to recover the confiscated works. The future land of Belgium remained under Holland's domination for another fifteen years, and the Dutch King William I became the museum's first donor.

The main entrance of the Royal Museums of Fine Arts of Belgium, rue de la Régence, in Brussels. The building was designed by architect Alphonse Balat who also created the famous 'Serres de Laeken ' (Laeken greenhouse) in the gardens of the Royal residence. It was inaugurated on August 1ˢᵗ, 1880.

A Royal Museum

After Belgium had gained independence in 1830, the museum remained the city's property for sixteen years before it became the "Royal Museum of Painting and Sculpture of Belgium". The collection was henceforth increased through a number of acquisitions of which the prices are quite eloquent about the taste and fashion at the time: Petrus Christus's *Lamentation* was purchased for 4,000 francs in 1844 and Peter Bruegel the Elder's *Fall of the Rebel Angels* for 500 francs two years later. Of course, one should not forget that the painting was attributed to his son 'Hell' Brueghel at the time. But the same trend is exemplified half a century later, when *The Count of Bethlehem*, undoubtedly signed by Bruegel the Elder, was bought for 9,000 francs in 1902, while a painting by Alfred Stevens was paid 25,000 francs. Rogier van der Weyden's *Portrait of the Grand Bâtard de Bourgogne* was negotiated for 1,000 francs in 1861 whereas David II Teniers' *Flemish Kermesse* reached 125,000 francs six years later. The museum gradually acquired modern works as well and regularly welcomed group exhibitions, triennial exhibitions and other Salons.

The light well at Place du Musée, adjacent to Charles de Lorraine's palace, was designed by architect Roger Bastin.

Alphonse Balat's opus maius

The rooms became too cramped in spite of several extensions. King Leopold II's architect Alphonse Balat—to whom we also owe the greenhouses of the château of Laeken—then erected his major work in what is today the rue de la Régence, the building that became the Museum of Ancient Art and still is its most prestigious architectural element today. This Palais des Beaux-Arts, designed to welcome the capital's temporary exhibitions and artistic events, was inaugurated by the king in 1880 on the occasion of a huge retrospective exhibition of fifty years of Belgian art. Later, it hosted the official Salons and the renowned annual exhibitions of the Group of XX before it became the Museum of Ancient Art in 1887. From then on, the exhibitions of the art circles took place in the Museum of Modern Art, located in the old court buildings until 1959.

A museum for modern art

The significant increase of the collections of the Ancient Art section and even more so of the Modern Art section compelled the Museums to extend the available exhibition surfaces. Exceptional large-scale renovation works were executed during the twenty-three year long office

(1961-1984) of M. Philippe Roberts-Jones as Principal Curator of the Royal Museums of Fine Arts of Belgium. In 1964, the civil engineering works began at the Place du Musée. The first part of this project was completed in 1974, when fifty-three rooms that meet the standards of present-day museology were inaugurated in an extension of the Alphonse Balat building. Ten years later, the new Museum of Modern Art was finished: it is distributed over eight underground levels receiving daylight from a light well, in perfect harmony with the architectural conception of the Place du Musée; the new museum is linked to the Museum of Ancient Art on the one side and articulated to the entirely renovated building at the angle of the Place Royale on the other side. Henry Pauwels had been in charge of the department of Ancient Art under Philippe Roberts-Jones's tenure, and succeeded to his office from 1985 to 1989. He supervised the completion of the houses of the Rue du Musée, hosting the curator's administration.

A policy of acquisitions, bequests and a donation

The present Principal Curator Éliane De Wilde took office in 1989 and resumes the programme's achievement. The garden of sculptures and the gallery of sculptures have already been completed on one side of the Alphonse Balat building, and on the other side, the library and the Cabinet of drawings. On a long-term basis, the project should integrate the restoration of several other rooms, within the framework of the renovation of one of the Museums' wings and of the hotels at the angle of the Place Royale and the Rue de la Régence, in order to 'loop the loop' and close off the imposing, flawless quadrilateral block of the Royal Museums of Fine Arts of Belgium. Like her predecessors, Éliane De Wilde carries out an extremely dynamic policy of increase of the collections. Under her leadership, the Museums have benefited from a donation by the provincial government of Brabant, from the Alla Goldschmidt-Safieva bequest and from the Irène Scutenaire-Hamoir bequest, i. e. an overall total of four hundred thirty-five pieces among which over a hundred works by René Magritte (paintings and drawings). To this day, the combined collections of the Royal Museums of Fine Arts of Belgium, Ancient Art and Modern Art, count over twenty-thousand items altogether—paintings, sculptures, drawings and engravings—of which some two thousand five hundred are presented to the public. They are geared to the extremely fertile artistic development of the Belgian provinces, illustrated in parallel with a significant number of works stemming from foreign schools.

The Genie of The Arts, in embossed and gilded copper, has been sculpted by Guillaume de Groot in 1880 for the Leopold I memorial in Laeken. It was placed as a vane on the belvedere of the Museum of Ancient Art as soon as 1897.

Pratical information

The Royal Museums of Fine Arts of Belgium
combine the Museum of Ancient Art and the Museum of Modern Art under
the MRBAB-acronym.

MAIL ADDRESS

Musée royaux des Beaux-Arts de Belgique
Rue du Musée 9, B-1000 Bruxelles.
Tel. +32 2 508 32 11 Fax: +32 2 508 32 32.
Internet: http://www.fine-arts-museum.be
Info@fine-arts-museum.be

VISITORS' ENTRANCE

Rue de la Régence 3 (Museum of Ancient
Art) and, as from april 11, 2000,
place Royale 1-2 (Museum of Modern Art),
B-1000 Brussels.

Opening hours and days
From Tuesday to Sunday,
from 10 a.m. to 12 and from 1 to 5 p.m.
for the Museum of Ancient Art,
from 10 a.m. to 1 p.m. and from 2 to 5 p.m.
for the Museum of Modern Art.

Closing days
Every Monday, the 1st of January, the 2nd
Thursday of January, the 1st of May, the 1st
and 11th of November and
the 25th of December.

RECEPTION OF THE VISITORS

Visitors are welcomed in the entrance hall
of the Museum of Ancient Art by volunteers from the Association of Friends of the
Royal Museums of Fine Arts of Belgium.

DISABLED VISITORS

Wheelchairs are available for disabled
visitors and access facilities can be made
available upon request at the Education
Departments.
Tel. +32 2 508 33 50 (F) / +32 2 508 34 50 (NL).

ART SHOP

Located on the right hand-side of the forum
of the Museum of Ancient Art, the Art
Shop is open from 10 a.m. to 4.45 p.m. and
presents a great variety of guides, cata-
logues, art books, posters, postcards, slides,
video, child games and gifts.
Tel. +32 2 508 34 27.

AUDIOGUIDES

Walkmen that offer recorded guided tours
with comments on a selection of works
from the collections of Ancient Art can be
rented at the Reception.

AUDIOVISUAL

A non-stop audiovisual projection is presented to the public in the small auditorium
adjacent to the forum of the Museum of
Ancient Art; headphones are available
free of charge at the Reception.

CAFETERIA

A place for snacks, open from
10.30 a.m. to 4.30 p.m.
A reservation is required for groups.
Tel. +32 2 508 34 71

EDUCATION DEPARTMENTS

The Education Departments organise guided general or thematic tours, workshop-
tours and conferences, for adults as well as
for children. A number of these services
can be provided in foreign languages. The
programmes are published in the *Quarterly
Agenda*. For adult or school groups, please
fix an appointment.
Information: Education Departments
Tel. +32 2 508 33 50 (F) / +32 2 508 34 50 (NL)

QUARTERLY AGENDA

A *Quarterly Agenda* lists the programme of
all events related to the Royal Museums, the
new acquisitions and the museum life. For
information: Education Departments
Tel. +32 2 508 33 50 (F) / +32 2 508 34 50 (NL)

ASSOCIATION OF THE FRIENDS OF THE ROYAL MUSEUMS OF FINE ARTS OF BELGIUM

Gathered in a non-profit association, the
"Friends" support the activities of the Royal
Museums of Fine Arts of Belgium and take
on voluntary service performances in
various fields. The Friends of the Museums
benefit from several advantages.
Tel. +32 2 511 41 16.

THE 'MIDIS AUX MUSÉES ROYAUX'

The Royal Museums of Fine Arts of Belgium
welcome the "Midis de la poésie", the "Midis
de la philosophie", the "Concerts de midi"
and the "Midis du Cinéma" ('Poetry noon
hour', 'Philosophy noon hour', 'Noon
Concerts' and 'Noon movie') in the large
auditorium.
For information: Education Departments
Tel. +32 2 508 33 50 (F) / +32 2 508 34 50 (NL)

The collections of Ancient Art and Modern Art

The forum

The forum where the visitor of the Royal Museums is welcomed has been maintained just as it was conceived by Alphonse Balat, the architect of the edifice. King Leopold II inaugurated the monument in 1880 to celebrate the fiftieth anniversary of the Belgian nation. It was initially designed for temporary exhibitions but it was used to host the museum's permanent collections seven years later. The passageways to all the Museums' rooms depart from this majestic hall, circled by a covered walk on the first floor. Its imposing surface—fifty-five metres by eighteen—contributes to show several sculptures and four large-scale paintings to their advantage.

1

1. *Constant Montald*
The Boat of Ideal,
1907, oil on canvas, original state 535 x 525, present state 400 x 505, deposit by the Province of Hainaut.

● CONSTANT MONTALD
(1862-1944)
At the turn of the century, Symbolism's concern was to restore art's spiritual content; Constant Montald claimed to represent an 'idealist' fraction, ambitioning to illustrate the ideal model of a blooming society (cfr. p. 127). He produced the two monumental canvases facing each other in 1907. He had intended them to decorate this hall of the Royal Museums, but the purchasing authorities turned them down. However, the two compositions were generally hallowed when exhibited in Ghent, Brussels and Paris. After the artist's demise in 1944, each of the works went through a number of vicissitudes and encurred significant damages.

CONSTANT MONTALD
☐ The Boat of Ideal
Two young men are standing in the copse and marvel at a statuette. Three young women have silently approached them across the dormant waters, inviting them to take place in the boat so that they could lead them to the realm of ideal harmony.
A photograph of the original state of the work is shown in front of the canvas (at present the canvas is amputated of a one-metre strip at its base), enabling us to picture the entire composition.
The Fountain of Inspiration faces it: the youngsters drink from it in a similar setting. The gold of the treetrunks and the efflorescence's down bathe in the translucent atmosphere of a timeless utopia.

2

JAN VERHAS

☐ *The School Parade in 1878*

Leopold II was thirty years of age when he accessed the Belgian throne in 1865. By that time, he had been married twelve years with archduchess Maria Henrietta, daughter of archduke Joseph Habsburg of Austria, prince Palatine of Hungary. In August 1878, the country celebrated the royal couple's silver wedding. The ceremonies lasted four full days in Brussels and included this memorable march, performed by twenty-three thousand schoolchildren. This parade was a spectacular demonstration of the overwhelming success of the schooling policy, briskly implemented during the second half of the 19th century.

The following excerpt from a report on the festivities: "Let education spread and bear fruit, it will turn our boys into mature men and good citizens, our little girls into women, worthy of their husbands. [...] When casting the eye on those ardent groups, so full of spirit and fervour, one could only say: Look! There goes the 20th century!"

Jan Verhas was an artist and a most accurate chronicler: the photographic rendering of the event recreates it in an elating way. The sovereigns, the members of their family and the dignitaries of the Royal House attend the procession on the tribune in front of the palace, which, at the time, was not the same as today's). At the foot of the stairs, two crouching lions and four statues symbolise the liberties granted by the Constitution—freedom of worship, of education, of the press and of association. On the opposite side, burgomaster Jules Anspach, flanked by an alderman and the police superintendent, supervises the celebration.

MATHIEU KESSELS

☐ *Scene from the Flood*

The taut man who braces himself to save the woman and child from the waves personifies vigour. His tense features convey self-control during strain. The harmonious

2. *Jan Verhas*
The School Parade in 1878
1880, oil on canvas
241 x 423, inv. 2821.

3

3. *Mathieu Kessels*
Scene from the Flood,
c. 1830, plaster of Paris,
216.5 x 116.5 x 92.5,
inv. 507.

1

2

musculature of his body shows off his ease. The tightly linked group of the woman and groping child are his counterpart, appearing to be part of the fluidity of the element from which they have just escaped, rendered by the dress's flowing streamline and the body's curve. The gestures reply to one another like in a choreographer's arrangement. The child's legs, the woman's, and the push of her hand on her saviour's leg correspond to the traction he exerts. The way the forces balance each other out confers real-life dynamism and a sharp sense of urgency to the composition.

This original plaster cast (from which a marble statue was cast after the sculptor's demise) belongs to Mathieu Kessels' later style. He had been a supporter of orthodox Neo-Classicism (cfr. p. 102), but stepped away from the models of the Antique towards the end of his career and treated more sentimental religious subjects.

● JEF LAMBEAUX
(1852-1908)
was thirty-two years old when he presented *La Folle Chanson* at the Salon de Bruxelles in 1884. He achieved fame with *The Fountain of Brabo*, of which the museum's bronze reduction was exhibited before the monument was unveiled on Antwerp's Grote Markt. To mention only the major highlights of a very prolific œuvre, the relief of the *Human Passions* must be remembered as well: it was installed in 1899 in a pavilion Victor Horta had designed for this purpose and erected at Cinquantenaire Park.

JEF LAMBEAUX
☐ *La Folle Chanson*
A nymph delights a satyr with her foolish song, accompanying herself with castanets. The graciously spirited movement of the nymph's body surrounds the adipose, hairy mass of the hoofed creature. The lecherous satyr's lewd laugh replies to the sensuous, provocative expression of the young woman.

3

1. *Jef Lambeaux*
La Folle Chanson,
1884, bronze,
150 x 106 x 83,
inv. 4086.

2. *Jef Lambeaux*
Le Dénicheur d'aigles,
1890 or a little earlier,
bronze,
236.5 x 144 x 114.5,
inv. 11366.

3. *Antoine Bourdelle*
Heracles as an Archer,
1909, bronze,
243.5 x 240.5 x 110,
inv. 4607.

There is a complicity in the two characters' attitudes and a contrast in their respective natures, conveyed by the different textures: smooth and silky for the female figure, coarse and rough for the satyr. At the time, the strange voluptuous delight that stems from this association enthralled some and scandalized others.

☐ Le Dénicheur d'aigles (The Eagle Nester)

The hazardous venture of dragging a grown eagle from his nest requires extraordinary force and courage, depicted by the sculptor in this Promethean image. The body's powerful arabesque, the jutting out of the muscles, the sharp planes that build up the face and the wide open mouth giving a howl all combine to express the effort's violence.

Like his peer Antoine Bourdelle's, Jef Lambeaux's work foreshadows Expressionism, where every formal detail carries the same tension.

ANTOINE BOURDELLE

☐ Heracles as an Archer

Heracles, the Greek mythological hero, was put to the test: he had to perform twelve inordinate tasks—Herculean tasks. One of the assignments he had to carry out was to kill the man-eating birds of Lake Stymphalos. The formidable power of the piece stems from the full modelling of the musculature, tense with concentration and strain. The archer's gesture makes the action plausible for the senses. The bow's curve replies to the tension of the arms, hints at the string and almost materializes the arrow. This merely virtual presence of an arrow and an aim tones down the reference to the mythical narrative: it suggests a universal symbol of the superman.

● ANTOINE BOURDELLE (1861-1929) was Rodin's preferred assistant as soon as 1890. He learnt the expressivity of the modelling from him. His fondness of Idealist tenets, attested by his participation in the Salon de la Rose Croix (Rosicrucians' Salon, cfr. p. 127), motivated him to find inspiration in Greek mythology and in archaic forms. The synthesis of these two choices developed into the personal style he resorted to from 1900, whereof *Heracles as an Archer* (1909) is a masterpiece. He has produced almost nine-hundred sculptures and had a considerable influence.

Ancien
Art

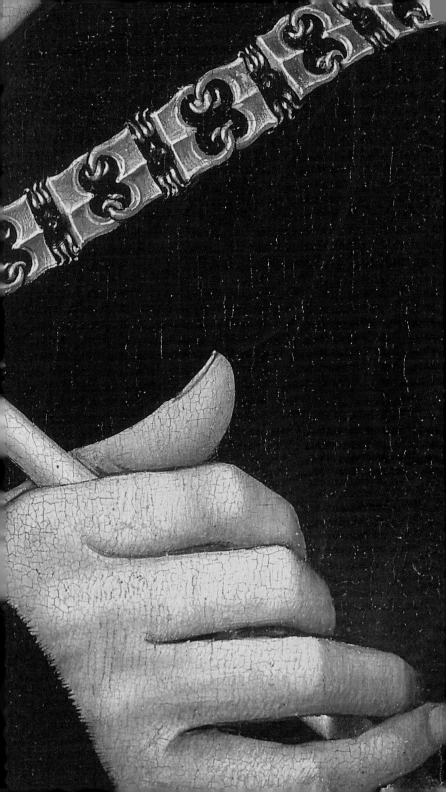

15th century

Philip the Bold's wedding with Marguerite of Mâle (1369) had linked Flanders to the Duchy of Burgundy.
His grandson Philip the Good, the Grand Duke of Occident, transferred his court to Bruges, then to Brussels in 1436.
Artists from the Southern Netherlands enjoyed the privilege of subsequent patronage by the palace and nobility: the goldsmiths and book illuminators were particularly favoured, whereas the nobles' interest for painting mainly focused on portraiture.
Prosperity and commerce, to which the port of Bruges largely contributed, favoured the growth of a wealthy upper middle class, from which the court appointed its high officials. Significant commissions stemmed from this increasingly powerful new class, including portraits, altarpieces—considered to be a patent display of wealth—and small devotional pictures for domestic use, in which the commissioners were represented in a devout attitude.

1

1. South Netherlandish School
Scenes from the Life of the Virgin,
*appr. 1400, walnut,
63 x 271, inv. 4883.*

● MASTER OF FLÉMALLE
(ROBERT CAMPIN?)
(c. 1375-Tournai 1440)
Experts assume the Master
of Flémalle to be the author
of some forty works,
and count him amongst the
founders of the new pictorial mainstream of the first
half of the 15th century.
Since he was contemporary
to Rogier van der Weyden,
he could well be Robert
Campin, the master from
Tournai. The name "Master
of Flémalle" stems from an
erroneous hypothesis dating
back to the end of last century, stating that three of the
works attributed to the painter originated from the
abbey of Flémalle, close
to Liège. It is known today
that there never was an
abbey in Flémalle at all.

SOUTH NETHERLANDISH SCHOOL

☐ *Retable of the Scenes from the Life of the Virgin*
The retable focuses on the Virgin's coronation: the
angels miraculously carry her away to the heavens,
where the Christ crowns and blesses her. On both
sides, key moments of her life are evoked: on the right,
the first encounter of her parents Joachim and Anne
in front of the Golden Gate. Her birth is pictured in
the second arcature, where St. Anne fondles a
newborn child with a girl's features, according to the
period's conventions. Expressions of sober tenderness
give the scene an intimist touch. On the right-hand
side, Mary presents Jesus at the Temple.
At an undetermined period, the panel has been amputated
of a fifth episode, that has been used as part of a cupboard,
which explains the broad plane scars. One can clearly identify
the cross-section of the pictorial matter on the edge of the
missing part: the artist drew upon a white primer, consisting
of chalk and glue, then applied thick, opaque layers of tempera.
This was the most usual medium for easel painting until the
15th century. This altarpiece was carried out at the dawn of
the century and shows the growing interest of painters for
the nature of the faces and the rendering of textures.

MASTER OF FLÉMALLE (ROBERT CAMPIN?)

☐ *The Annunciation*
The artist places the scene in a bourgeois interior. Every
familiar object is rendered with careful accuracy and
endowed with a symbolic meaning. The lilies, for example,
are a metaphor for Mary's virginity. The prayer book is
a traditional iconographical element of the Annunciation:
the Virgin is said to have been reading a biblical prophecy
announcing the Messiah at the very moment of the
Annunciation. St. Christopher is seen carrying the infant
Jesus on the woodcut on the mantlepiece: this will later
become Mary's role. The spiritual intensity of this
Annunciation is not solely expressed by the characters,
but by every detail in its unconspicuous beauty.
The Master of Flémalle shows here how accomplished he is
in the use of glaze, which lends such a marvelous density to
materials. He has not chosen the unique vanishing point
perspective familiar to the Italians: the vanishing lines of the

table, of the room's floor tiles and of the hall's floor tiles converge in separate points.

MASTER OF THE AIX ANNUNCIATION

☐ *The Prophet Jeremiah*
The artist has represented a humanist, glancing through a precious book in a corner of his study, rather than a jewish prophet. This representation introduces the Renaissance. To the rendering of details and to the portrait's nature, the Master of the Aix Annunciation has added a truly sculptural treatment of the silhouette and of the drapery. He stresses monumentality by placing the character on a base in a niche, painted in grisaille.

ROGIER VAN DER WEYDEN

Rogier van der Weyden's influence on the Flemish Primitives was stronger than that of any other artist of the 15th century.
☐ *Lamentation*
Rogier van der Weyden has articulated this Pietà around the slightly curved diagonal of the Christ's body. The parallel inclination of the Virgin's bust, as she embraces him in an ultimate kiss, is more than a stylistic choice of composition: It evokes the twofold passion of Christ and his mother. This privileged relationship is also hinted at by the light that illuminates them, whereas the other two cha-

2. *Master of Flémalle (Robert Campin?)*
The Annunciation,
oak, 58 x 64, inv. 3937.

3. *Master of the Aix Annunciation*
The Prophet Jeremiah,
obverse wood, 152 x 86, inv. 4494.

● MASTER OF THE Aix Annunciation. (Barthélemy d'Eyck?) (mentioned in Aix-en-Provence between 1444 and 1472). Schooled in the Netherlands, the Master of the Aix Annunciation was most probably linked to the court of a great lord, the Duke of Anjou, Count of Provence and King of Sicily, the "Good King René". He would have followed his patron to the Provence and painted the

Triptych of the Annunciation there between 1443 and 1445. The Prophet Jeremiah is the right panel of this work that made him famous. The centrepiece (Ste.-Marie-Madeleine church in Aix-en-Provence) was the Annunciation part, flanked by both prophets who had announced the advent of the Messiah: Isaiah (this panel is kept in the Boymans - van Beuningen Museum in Rotterdam) and Jeremiah.

● The use of oil as a binding medium for pigments, so specific to 15th century painting, had been applied and improved during previous centuries. This technique had become an accomplished mastership by then, enabling a smooth facture without brush strokes, and the use of glaze: extremely thin layers of paint that do not obliterate the underlying coat, but simply modify its colour.

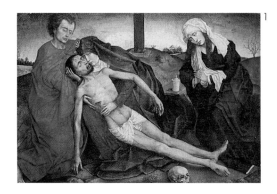

● ROGIER VAN DER WEYDEN
(1399/1400-1464)
Rogier de le Pasture was born in Tournai at the turn of the century. Twenty-seven years later, a certain Rogelet de le Pasture is listed there as an apprentice of the master Robert Campin, although no evidence has been found to support that they are one and the same person. Records also mention that Rogelet de le Pasture acquired his patent as a master in 1432. After working in Bruges for a certain time, he settled in Brussels, where he held the post of official painter to the municipality from 1436. That is probably when he translated his name to Flemish: Van der Weyden. The Burgundian Court was transferred to Brussels at the same time; and even though Jan van Eyck was the duke's painter and "varlet de chambre" (manservant), Rogier van der Weyden was commissioned for the portraits of Philip the Good, Isabella of Portugal, Charles the Bold and other eminent personalities. His fame spread throughout Northern Europe and as far as Italy, and numerous Flemish and foreign disciples streamed into his workshop. All of these followers pursued his work in one way or another. Rogier van der Weyden passed away in Brussels in 1464, where he was buried in St. Michael's Cathedral.

racters are crowned with a halo. They are St.-John the Evangelist, the favourite disciple, who has a gesture and a look of compassion for Mary, and the Magdalen, sharing their grief. The psychological element of the tragedy is stressed by the tight framing of the group. The restrained but distressed expression of the faces and the eloquent play of the hands convey an intense sympathy in sorrow. Van der Weyden's pathetic fervour tallies with the widespread spirit of devotion of this period, and may be considered as a key element of his success and of his influence upon his followers.

☐ Portrait of the Grand Bâtard de Bourgogne

It is startling to observe how Rogier van der Weyden has captured the essence of his model in this portrait of Anthony of Burgundy, the illegitimate son of Philip the Good. All elements combine so as to render his courteous pride: the haughty expression of the face, the tightly sealed lips, the gaze cast elsewhere, the collar chain of the Order of the Golden Fleece and even the elegant geometry of the hand clasping the arrow—perhaps the emblem of an archers' guild— strengthen the portrait's character.

The features are modelled by a play with light and shade—more or less dense at the bridge of the nose, at the jawbone and under the chin—that stems from the superimposition of glaze. The dignity of his carriage is heightened by the three-quarter view, a specialty of Netherlandish portraiture.

☐ Portrait of Laurent Froimont

This portrait is very different from the previous painting: a donor is pictured praying to the Virgin. This is indeed the right-hand panel of a diptych, the other half of which is the Madonna at the Museum of the City of Caen. Here again, Rogier van der Weyden perfectly combines the expressiveness of a face with that of the hands. The back of the panel, painted in grisaille, reveals a representation of the martyrdom of the model's patron, St. Lawrence, deacon of the Church of Rome in the 3rd century.

1. *Rogier van der Weyden*
Lamentation,
*oak, 32.2 x 47.2,
inv. 3515.*

2. *Rogier van der Weyden*
**Portrait of the Grand
Bâtard de Bourgogne**,
*oak, 39 x 28.5,
inv. 1449.*

3. *Rogier van der Weyden*
**Portrait of
Laurent Froimont**,
oak, 49 x 31, inv. 4279.

PETRUS CHRISTUS

☐ **Lamentation**

At the centre of the composition, the Virgin faints in the arms of St.-John and one of her half-sisters. Christ lies on a shroud, spread out at her feet by the Joseph of Arimathea, as the Nicodemus is tilting his body. On the right, the Virgin's other half-sister, with the Italian headdress, wipes her tears in company of her husband. On the left, the Magdalen emphatically expresses her grief. The postures and expressions are conventional. The costumes add a touch of theatrical pathos to reality. The characters seem to take part in a timeless performance of a medieval mystery; but the voluptuous colour scheme of this stagnant, peaceful scene is magnificently rich, with delicate shades.

Petrus Christus does not attain Van der Weyden's expressiveness or sense of unity. However, he succeeds in organising the layout of the group of monumental figures and integrates a superb landscape to the composition.

● PETRUS CHRISTUS
(c. 1410/1420-1475/76)
Petrus Christus was born a painter's son in the Southern Netherlands. He acquired freemanship in Bruges in 1444, where he was active from then on. He even became the dean of his guild. He may have travelled to Italy. He passed away in Bruges, most probably before 1475.

4. *Petrus Christus*, **Lamentation**, *oak, 101 x 192, inv. 564.*

1. *Master of Moulins*
Madonna adored by the angels,
oak, 38.5 x 29.5, inv. 3638.

2. *Hugo van der Goes' studio*
St. Anne Trinity with a Franciscan Donor
oak, 32.5 x 39, inv. 2748.

MASTER OF MOULINS

☐ *Madonna Adored by the angels*

The figures are silhouetted against gold ground. The Master of Moulins uses this archaism to stage the scene in the heavens, where the angels join the Virgin in her adoration before the son the Lord has given her.

HUGO VAN DER GOES'STUDIO

☐ *St. Anne Trinity with a Franciscan Donor*

In this painting, the elements of the setting are allegorical rather than real, and endow the work with a sense of poetry. The turf on the foreground, dotted with symbolic flowers, defines an unhallowed area on which the commissioner of the panel, a 15th century clergyman, is kneeling. The harmony between the adjacent hues of St. Anne's coat and dress and the subdued shades of blue of the Virgin's garment demonstrate the painter's expertise.

● MASTER OF MOULINS
(Jean Hey?)
(active in France between 1480 and 1500)
The Master of Moulins was most probably trained in the Southern Netherlands, but his name stems from the capital of the Duchy of Bourbon. He served both Duke Peter II and Duchess Anne of Beaujeu, tutors of Charles VIII, the young French monarch. He may also have worked at the King's court. A dozen works have been attributed to him, leading us to believe that he departed from Hugo van der Goes' manner to develop a personal style, leading him to become one of the major painters of his time.

● HUGO VAN DER GOES
(c. 1430-1483)
Hugo van der Goes is believed to be born in Ghent around 1440. His master is not yet known, but he was listed as a freemaster of the painter's guild at Ghent in 1467, where he was active for some ten years. He entered the Roode Klooster near Brussels shortly after 1475 as a donatus, a privileged lay brother. He was quite renowned at the time, and was summoned to Louvain as an expert when Dirk Bouts died, in order to eva-

luate the unfinished Justice panels (cfr. p. 10). Maximilian, the future emperor of Austria, dined with him during his stay in Brussels; and Tommaso Portinari, representative of the Medici's bank in Bruges, commissioned him for a major triptch, posthumously delivered in Florence. But Hugo van der Goes became subject to attacks of depression and melancholy, and passed away at Roode Klooster in 1482.

3

 4

CARLO CRIVELLI

☐ *Panels of the Montefiore dell'Aso Polyptych Madonna and St.Francis of Assisi*

The refined, soberly sensitive draftsmanship succeeds in endowing the Virgin with delicate, impassive beauty, a rather restrained tenderness as opposed to the Infant's spontaneous gleaming. The mannered style with which the hands were treated convey her serene sweetness and St. Francis' clenched expression of pain. He is branded with the stigmata of the Christ's Passion on the hands and chest, and he opens his frock to bring his wounds to light. His deep suffering furrows his brow as he participates in Jesus' agony. The Montefiore Polyptych consisted of twenty-three panels, arranged on three levels with different heights. At present, they are disseminated in some ten different places. *The Madonna* was its central panel and *St. Francis of Assisi* stood at its right-hand side. The overall width of the polyptych was 2.75 m.

DIRK BOUTS

Dirk Bouts is considered to be one of the major painters of the 15th century

☐ *Calvary*

In this work, the artist crucifies Jesus at the top of a stretched cross, rising to touch the sky. This language of symbols, such as expressing the nobility of sentiments by means of elongated shapes, a recurring element in the art of Dirk Bouts.

Although the drawing of this work is masterful, little can be said about its colours. The layers of tempera on canvas, have been deteriorated beyond restoration. However, this is an early example examples of this technique in Netherlandish Painting.

3. *Carlo Crivelli*
Panels of the Montefiore dell'Aso Polyptych, Madonna and St. Francis of Assisi,
Arched wood, 183 x 56.5 and 59.5, inv. 1485 et 1486.

4. *Dirk Bouts*
Calvary,
tempera on canvas, 181.5 x 153.5, inv. 8181.

● CARLO CRIVELLI
(c. 1430/1435-1493/1495)
Carlo Crivelli was the son of a Venetian painter, and he was particularly active in the Marches. We owe him several large altarpieces, among which this Polyptych he executed for the St. Francis Church in Montefiore dell'Aso. The panels of the polyptych are separated by a set of colonnettes supporting an arcature, a combination of Gothic elements, gold ground stemming from the Byzantine heritage, and a conception of volume and depth that typifies Renaissance style.

●DIRK BOUTS
(c. 1410?-1475)
He developed a stylistic synthesis of the respective influences of Jan van Eyck and Rogier van der Weyden, through which his work reached a rare spiritual intensity. He may well have been born in Haarlem between 1410 and 1420. One can only guess at the years of his training. His marriage with the daughter of a rich family in Louvain, none later than 1448, seems to indicate that he had already settled in this prosperous town that offered attractive opportunities to artists. He quickly became its most considered painter. Of his four sons, two also had a painter's career. Since he had been appointed by the town council to be Louvain's official painter, he was commissioned for important works; one of those was *The Judgment of Emperor Otto*, but its execution was interrupted by Dirk Bouts' death in 1475.

☐ *The Judgment of Emperor Otto*

Dirk Bouts was Louvain's foremost painter in 1468, when the town council commissioned him for two Justice panels. It was customary to decorate the courtroom of City Halls with an edifying picture of a notorious judgment. These panels represent a miscarriage of justice, as told by the *Golden Legend:* Otto III, ruler of the Holy Empire. Two episodes of *The Judgment of Emperor Otto* are represented on the panels.

The Wrongful Execution of the Count (left-hand panel). Otto listens as his spouse slanderously accuses a count of his court of having desired her. The unsuspecting emperor orders the execution of his courtier. The central scene pictures the innocent count wishing his dismayed wife farewell as he is led to his death. On the foreground, the beheading is treated as a solemn celebration of iniquity. The executioner presents the severed head to the countess, and she takes an oath to avenge his memory.

The Ordeal of the Countess (right-hand panel). The countess testifies to the innocence of her mourned husband by

Dirk Bouts
**The Judgment of
Emperor Otto
The Wrongful Execution
of the Count**
and **The Ordeal of the
Countess**,
*oak, 324 x 182 each panel,
inv. 1447-1448.*

appealing to Divine Justice: the red-hot bar of iron she holds in her hand proves that the Lord has intervened on her behalf. Stunned by his unrepairable false verdict, Otto condemns his own wife, who is seen burning alive at the stake in the rear of the picture.

As Dirk Bouts died, only the right-hand panel was completed. The left-hand panel was entrusted to his workshop. The differences are disclosed by a careful comparison of the relief and expression of the features and of the rendering of materials and drapery. However, the entire composition may be attributed to the master. It is an impressive feat to stage the narrative and stretch the slender figures within the constraining vertical frame. Likewise, the advantages Dirk Bouts cleverly draws from the gothic arcatures of the framework confirm his artistic maturity; In the median part of *The Ordeal of the Countess*, he has doubled them up with mock ogival arcatures, in order to define spaces and to divide time up as well. Beyond the throne hall, the Divine Judgment leads to its consequence, the capital punishment. And on the other hand, as if through a window, the symmetry of the ornamental "motif" projects the teaching into the 15th century courtroom, on this side of the frame.

● Hans Memlinc
(c. 1440?-1494)
Biographical elements of his later life lead us to the assumption that Memlinc was born at Selingenstadt on the Main between 1430 and 1440. As no documents concerning his younger years are available, the hypothesis that he has approached Cologne's masters and their work merely rests on stylistic analysis. He became a citizen of Bruges in 1465, where he was recorded as a burgess under the name "Jan van Mimmelinghe". His family originated from the village of Mömlingen, close to his town of birth, and he translated his name to Flemish himself. His first authenticated work dates back to 1467. His artistic reputation grew as his social status rose. In 1473, he was listed as a member of the "Onze-Lieve-Vrouw-ter-Sneeuw" confraternity, frequented by noblemen—amongst which the Duke of Burgundy, Charles the Bold—clergyman and wealthy burgesses such as William Moreel. Memlinc reached the peak of his career in the eighties, and died in Bruges in 1494.

HANS MEMLINC

☐ Portrait of a Man

The personality of this character with sealed lips and an enigmatic gaze is by no means disclosed by his face, although the accurate outline of the features and the rendering of the hair's detail carefully single him out. Memlinc's refined facture tends to idealise his characters; the distant suavity of the faces seems to make them unattainable. Memlinc was the first Netherlandish painter to set out the figures of his portraits against a landscape, thus acknowledging their kinship with the portraits of his Italian contemporaries.

☐ Portrait of William Moreel and his Wife

The praying posture and the three-quarter view of the characters clearly indicate that these portraits are the wings of a triptych. The lost central panel most probably pictured a Madonna. William Moreel, seigneur of Oostcleyhem, was an eminent official in Bruges, where had taken office as burgomaster. He also dealt in spices and represented the Bank of Rome there. It is accredited that this portable triptych, picturing him with his wife Barbara van Vlaenderberch, was commissioned in the early seventies.

This type of triptych was adapted by Memlinc from the devotional diptychs Rogier van der Weyden had introduced (cfr. p. 28: *Portrait of Laurent Froimont*). The background opens up on a scenery that must have stretched across the central panel.

☐ *The Martydom of St. Sebastian*

Sebastian was the officer of a praetorian cohort in Rome in the 3rd century. He was executed on the charge of assisting Christians. Obviously touched by the Divine Grace, the martyr's body and soul remain indifferent to the piercing arrows shot by elegant, impassive archers. The scene is staged in a placid world of mystical legend, far away from the city, thrust away in deep distance by an ingenious perspective.

1. *Hans Memlinc*
Portrait of a Man,
oak, 35.5 x 25.5, inv. 1358.

2. *Hans Memlinc*
**Portrait of William
Moreel and his wife,**
*oak, 37 x 27 and
37.5 x 28
inv. 1451-1452.*

3. *Hans Memlinc*
**The Martyrdom of
St. Sebastian**,
oak, 67 x 68, inv. 2927.

The minor masters from Bruges
*Towards the end of the 15th century, a number of anony-
mous minor masters from Bruges can be considered as
Memlinc's followers.*

MASTER OF 1473

☐ *Triptych of Jan de Witte*
This *Triptych of Jan de Witte* is the only known work of
the Master of 1473. It was painted in that year, probably
on the occasion of the marriage of its commissioner.
Rather than an ornamental altarpiece, this smaller triptych is more likely to have been a devotional object that
Mr and Mrs de Witte kept at home.

4. *Master of 1473*
**Triptych of
Jan de Witte**,
*1473, trefoiled oak
74.5 x 38.5 each
panel, inv. 7007.*

1.*Master of the Legend of St. Lucy* **Madonna with Saints,** *oak, 108 x 171, inv. 2576.*

2. *Master of the Legend of St. Ursula* **Madonna and St. Anne between St. Catherine and St. John the Baptist, St. Barbara and St. Louis,** *oak, 82 x 125, inv. 6719.*

3. *Master of the Legend of St. Catherine* **Nativity,** *oak, 78 x 50.5, inv. 10513.*

MASTER OF THE LEGEND OF ST. LUCY

☐ **Madonna with Saints**
The Master of the Legend of St. Lucy was active in Bruges between 1480 and 1501 and later.
The Madonna with Saints was placed in Notre-Dame in Bruges in 1489. The Madonna sits enthroned, fondling the Infant, surrounded by eleven holy women with expressionless features, all resembling each other. They can be identified thanks to the detailed rendering of their attributes. But today this work is appreciated for its scenic view of Bruges at the background.

MASTER OF THE LEGEND OF ST. URSULA

☐ **Madonna and St. Anne between St. Catherine and St. John the Baptist, St. Barbara and St. Louis**
The conventional name of the Master of the Legend of St. Ursula stems from eight small paintings, conserved in the Groeningemuseum in Bruges. This painting is organised around the Madonna, a recurring theme in his work.

The minor masters from Brussels
At the same period, Van der Weyden influenced a certain number of artists in Brussels, most of them anonymous masters.

MASTER OF THE LEGEND OF ST. CATHERINE

☐ **Nativity**
The Master of the Legend of St. Catherine, to whom we owe this *Nativity* with its bright glossy colours and some-what static style, may well be Rogier van der Weyden's son.

MASTER OF THE VIEW OF STE. GUDULE

☐ **Marriage of the Virgin**
The Master of the View of Ste. Gudule received his name from the fact that several paintings of his are embellished with portrayals of this church. However, the Marriage of the Virgin includes the southern portal of the transept of Notre-Dame-du-Sablon in its median part. The master's more mannered style is illustrated by the subtle play of curves outlined by the bearing of the figures, and the affec-ted posture of the hands with tapering fingers.

MASTER OF THE LEGEND OF ST. BARBARA

☐ *Scenes from the life of St. Barbara*
The Master of the Legend of St. Barbara's work of reference consists of two panels, dedicated to the holy woman; one of these is a part of our collection, whereas the other panel is kept in the Heilig-Bloedmuseum in Bruges. It is likely that both panels combined to form the central part of a triptych.

SOUTH NETHERLANDISH SCHOOL

☐ *Portraits Of Philip The Fair and Joan the Insane*
The Master of the History of St. Joseph has also been called Master of the Abbey of Affligem, by way of reference to the triptych originating from this abbey, a narrative of Jesus' and Mary's lives from Nativity to the Entombment. The triptych called "Triptych of the City Hall of Zierikzee" has been attributed to this master, and the Portraits of Philip the Fair, son of Maximilian of Hapsburg, and of his wife Joan the Insane, are its lateral panels.

JEROME VAN AKEN, NAMED HIEROYMUS BOSCH

☐ *Calvary with donor*
Bosch stages a genuine intercession procedure here. The humbly kneeling donor prays for his salute. By his side, St. Peter, bearing the keys of Heaven, presents his protégé to Mary with a gesture of the hand and speaks in his favour. John echoes his plea, and implores the Virgin to intercede for him before the crucified Christ. Set against a peaceful landscape including the town of 's Hertogenbosch on the horizon line, the Saviour's death is not treated as a mournful scene, but rather as a hope for the Redeeming of mankind.

4. Master of the View of Ste. Gudule
Marriage of the Virgin,
oak, 47.2 x 33, inv. 7559.

5. Master of the Legend of St. Barbara
Scenes from the Life of St. Barbara,
oak, 73.5 x 124.5, inv. 6149.

6. South Netherlandish School
Portraits of Philip the Fair and Joan the Insane,
oak, 125 x 48 and 124 x 47 inv. 2405-2406.

1. *Jerome van Aken,*
named Hieronymus Bosch
Calvary with
donor
oak, 73.5 x 61.3,
inv. 6639.

2. *Jerome van Aken,*
named Hieronymus Bosch
Triptych of the
Temptation of
St. Anthony *(replica), oak,*
arched at the top,
central panel
133.5 x 119.5,
each wing 131.5 x 53,
inv. 3032.

●JEROME VAN AEKEN,
NAMED HIERONYMUS BOSCH
(? - 1516)

Jerome van Aeken was born in a family, which originated from Aix-la-Chapelle. Both his father and grandfather were painters, settled in 's Hertogenbosch. That is where Jerome (Hieronymus in Latin) drew his new surname from. He remained in 's Hertogenbosch until his death. His standing was rather exceptional for a painter: he was one of the some three hundred sworn members of the exclusive Confraternity of Our Lady, reserved to scholars, noblemen and wealthy merchants. His work echoes the bourgeois mentality of the townsmen, at this turning point between the Middle Ages and the Renaissance. Departing from popular tradition, Bosch brands human deviance and delusion by means of his visionary's palette of innovative plastic expressions. This was the key to an immediate success and a significant influence on the 16th century.

☐ **Triptych of the Temptations of St. Anthony**

In the 3rd century A. D., Anthony, the son of a wealthy farmer from Upper Egypt, handed out everything he owned to the poor at the dawn of his twentieth year, and retired to the desert. He became the founder of monastic life in the Theban deserts and led a holy life; he lived to be a hundred and five years old. However, in the course of the first fifteen years of his retreat, he had to struggle against the evil visions of temptation which have become legendary. On the left panel of the triptych, Anthony is swept away into space by the demon, but his companions succeed in bringing him back to his shed. The right panel pictures the visions of greed and lust that divert his attention away from his reading. And the centre of the main panel shows the holy man lost in prayer, trying to escape the assaults of the fiendish hallucinations.

Unlike the previous painting, this triptych can be related to Bosch's characteristic manner. Save a handful of details, it is replica of the original work conserved in the National Museum of Ancient Art in Lisbon, of which twelve copies are known. The demand was obviously considerable; but nothing is known about the conditions under which the copies were executed or about the staff of the workshop of the Master of 's Hertogenbosch.

The German Masters

A number of German painters, mainly from the first half of the 16th century, are represented in the Museum's collection; Lucas Cranach the Elder undoubtedly asserts himself as their leading figure.

LUCAS CRANACH THE ELDER

☐ *Portrait of Dr J. Scheyring*

The inscription in the upper left corner of the painting, identifying the portrait as that of a famous theologian of the Reformation, Dr J. Scheyring, has been determined to be apocryphal. The model might just as well have been the astronomer Johann Schöner, whom Cranach is likely to have known, since he had been selected by Wittenberg's intellectual upper middle class—to which he himself belonged— as their regular portrayer. He has even portrayed Martin Luther several times. The thin, firmly pursed lips between determined furrows, the hollowed temples and the sharp, frowning look convey the character's intransigence.

The artist has dated and signed the painting with his personal mark, a dragon spreading its wings, at the level of the character's shoulder. The portrait's expressiveness is stressed by the very accurate line of the hair, beard and fur and by the black border outlining the paint.

3. *Lucas I Cranach*
Portrait of
Dr J. Scheyring,
1529, wood, 51.5 x 35,
inv. 2033.

● LUCAS CRANACH
THE ELDER
(1472-1553)
Lucas Cranach the Elder was born in Kronach, Franconia (where Bavaria is today), in 1472. He undertook the traditional journeyman's travel in 1500, and arrived in Nuremberg and Vienna, where he painted his first known works. In 1504, He was summoned to Wittenberg by Frederick the Wise, Elector of Saxony, patron and friend of the artists and humanists. Cranach remained at his court for almost fifty years, becoming a notorious painter, leading a very significant workshop. He was burgomaster of the town and counted scholars, artists and great reformers such as Melanchton and Martin Luther among his friends. He followed the court when it was transferred to Weimar, the town in which he passed away in 1553.

3

2. *Gérard David*
**Adoration of
the Magi**,
*oak, 83 x 66, inv.
740.*

3. *Gérard David*
**The Virgin
with the
Bowl of Soup**,
*oak 35 x 29, inv.
3559.*

1. *Lucas I Cranach
the Elder,*
Venus and Love,
*1531, transferred from
wood to canvas, 176 x 80,
inv. 4759.*

☐ **Venus and Love**

Cranach probably painted *Venus and Love* for his second patron, Elector John the Constant. Until then, he had chiefly treated religious subjects; but this high official commissioned him for a great number of mythological scenes and nude figures. This painting illustrates an idyll of Theocritus, ornamentally hand-written in the top corner: Cupid was stung by the bees whilst filching honey from them. But as he whined about it, his mother answered that the stings of love are far more painful.

The subject relates to the spirit of the Renaissance, spreading across Southern Europe at the time. But whereas Classical sculptures were used as models for nudes in Renaissance painting, Cranach's formal idiom stemmed directly from the Gothic heritage. Set against a black background, the contour of the almost static silhouette of Venus is an impetuous line of remarkable purity. The somewhat mannered gestures of the woman are complementary to her gracefulness; surprisingly enough, she wears a sumptuous headdress and a magnificent necklace, but her nudity is only covered by a transparent veil.

GERARD DAVID

☐ **Adoration of the Magi**

The numerous different attitudes and expressions of the main characters and of the various auxiliary figures on the middle ground of the painting enliven this scene with such a spontaneity, that this sacred representation acquires a popular dimension and relates closely to everyday life.

☐ **The Virgin with the Bowl of Soup**

In this painting, traditional religious iconology has become even more flexible: an element of secular intimacy has been worked into this famous work and the scene's extreme charm is touching. At the turn of the century, this fusion of human nature with the divine spirit hints at humanism, this wind of change imported from Italy.

3

● GÉRARD DAVID
(c. 1455-1523)
Gérard David was born in
Oudewater (close to
Gouda), trained in Haarlem,
and registered at the painters' guild of Bruges in
1484, exactly ten years
before Memlinc's death. He
succeeded Memlinc as the
official painter of the town,
and maintained the School
of Bruges' standards high
for a quarter of a century; he
was the School's last really
talented representative.

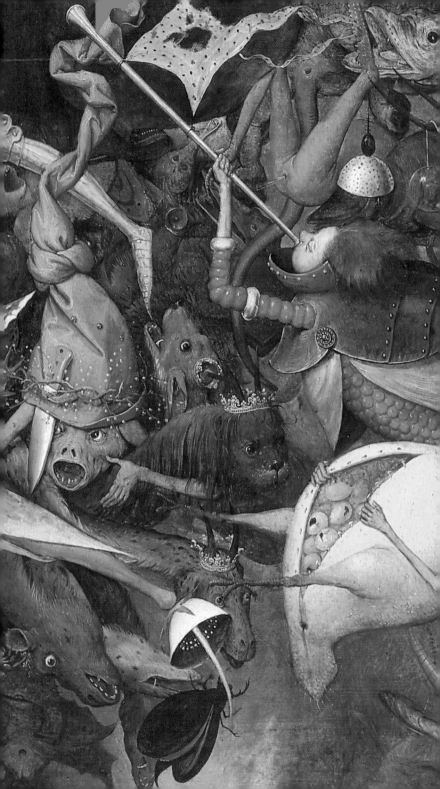

16th century

In the beginning of the 16th century, two concomitant factors influenced the development of South Netherlandish art simultaneously.
As a consequence of the bloom of Antwerp's economy, a great number of artists were commissioned and streamed into the country from all over Europe.
As a result of Italy's tremendous artistic attractiveness, almost everybody subscribed to the spirit of the Renaissance and allowed a new style to be introduced in the Netherlands.

● QUINTEN MASSYS
(1465/66-1530)
Quinten Massys was born in
Louvain in 1465 or 1466. He
was received as a freemaster
at the Antwerp Guild of St.
Luke in 1491, where he married and settled. He became
the first and foremost painter
of the School of Antwerp.
His work is immediately
linked to that of the Flemish
Primitives, but his close
contacts with the humanists
of his time brought him
close to the models of the
Renaissance. He died in
Antwerp in 1530.

● JOSSE VAN DER BEKE
(1480/1485 – ca 1541)
Josse van der Beke, known
as "van Cleve" after a town
in the North-East
Netherlands—where he was
presumably born around
1480-1485—was tempted by
Antwerp's prosperity. The
corporate books of the Guild
of St. Luke mention him as a
master in 1511-1512. At a
later stage, he was at the head
of a studio with five apprentices. Beside some evidence
that he passed away before
April 13, 1541, little is
known about this master,
whose style is representative
of the transition between
Antwerp Mannerism and
Italian Classicism.

QUINTEN MASSYS

☐ *Madonna Entroned*

Everything tends to date this work back to the painter's
earliest period. The Gothic architecture of the background, the frontal view of the characters and the deep
shadows of the drapery are reminiscent of Jan Van Eyck
and the School of Bruges.

☐ *Triptych of the Confraternity of St. Anne in Louvain*

This triptych was designed for the altar of this
confraternity in St. Peter's Church in Louvain and
finished in 1509. It stems from the artist's mature period
and shows the influence of Italian art. It tells the life of
the Virgin's mother according to the apocryphal Gospels.
Anne is said to have given birth to Mary after long years
of sterility. Once a widow of Joachim, she remarried,
became a widow again and then remarried for the
second time. Notwithstanding her great age, Anne gave
birth to a daughter each time. The central panel pictures
her descendants. The Virgin Mary and her mother stand
on either side of the Infant, flanked by their respective
husbands on the middle ground. On the foreground,
the Virgin's two half sisters play with their children; they
are also accompanied by their husbands.

The arrangement of the characters in three triangles around
the figure of the Infant is integrated in the Italianate architectural
pattern. At the dawn of the century, a turning point between
two ages, this painting hallows the triumphant entry of
Renaissance into Flemish art. Even the distant scenery is treated
after the manner of Leonardo Da Vinci, who also inspired the
suave drawing of these faces with slightly slanting eyes and
small mouths. Quinten Massys has a very personal manner of
graduating hues into fine shades, and he lends unity to the
picture by using the complementarity of colours to achieve a
perfect resolution of a harmony of shades.

The reverse side of the left wing pictures Joachim and
Anne as newlyweds offering a gift for the poor to the
temple. On the reverse side of the right wing, we see
Joachim as an aged man whose offering is refused by the
priest, believing that a man without descendants, incapable

3

1. *Quinten Massys*
Madonna Enthroned,
oak, 130 x 86, inv. 1497.

2.*Quinten Massys*
**Triptych of the
Confraternity of St. Anne
in Louvain**, *1509
oak, arched at the top,
central panel 224.5 x 219,
wings 219.5 x 91 and
220 x 92, inv. 2784.*

3. *Josse van der Beken,
known as van Cleve*
**St. Anne Trinity
with St. Joachim**
*Wood, arched at the top,
109 x 74, inv. 565.*

4. *Joachim Patinir*
**Landscape with
St. John the Baptist
preaching**
*oak, 36.3 x 45,
inv. 6178.*

of increasing the number of the chosen people, is under a divine curse. On the obverse of the left panel, an angel pays Joachim a visit—despair has driven him to retire among the shepherds—and announces that, notwithstanding her sterility, his ageing spouse would give birth to a daughter whom he should name Mary; The obverse side of the right panel pictures Anne on her deathbed, surrounded by her distressed daughters and receiving the blessing of her grandson Jesus.

JOSSE VAN DER BEKEN, KNOWN AS VAN CLEVE

☐ *St. Anne Trinity with St. Joachim*

The three main characters on this panel are the same as the main figures in the triptych by Quinten Massys. Anne carries the Infant Jesus in her lap. Her face is weary and betrays her great age as she looks at Joachim, her first husband. The latter can be identified by the richness of his garments and the purse hanging from his belt, in reference to his offering to the Temple, which was once turned down. His profile is sharp and bony; his face is withered by age but wreathed in smiles as he watches his male descendant. The beaming Virgin supports her sleeping child, but her meek smile reaches for angels.

St. Anne carries a twofold symbol: the apple in her hand announces the advent of a New Adam, the Christ. At the same time, the child is asleep and prophesises her oncoming death, which may perhaps account for the immense sadness in its grandmother's gaze.

JOACHIM PATINIR

☐ *Landscape with St. John the Baptist preaching*

This painting is representative of Joachim Patinir's manner. The religious topic is staged in a preponderant landscape. In fact, the scenery is not real at all, but is a microcosm in which every single element is pictured at the same scale, no matter how distant they are. The depth is determined by the sole tonality variation: from the shades of brown in the foreground, to the greens in the middleground and the blues in the background, fading endlessly.

● JOACHIM PATINIR (last quarter of the 15th century - 1524) Joachim Patinir was born in the Maas valley in the last quarter of the 15th century. It is not yet known where he was schooled, but he was made a member of the Antwerp painters' Guild of St. Luke. He was active in Antwerp during his entire career, and acquired a remarkable fame. On the occasion of a trip to the Netherlands in 1520 or 1521, Dürer met him, called him "the good landscapist" and drew his portrait. Patinir's main contribution was indeed that he developed landscape painting as an autonomous genre. He always represented a religious theme, but reduced it to a pattern he integrated in the whole.

1. *Aelbrecht Bouts*
Triptych of the Assumption of the Virgin
oak, arched at the top, central panel 185 x 107, each wing 185 x 47, inv. 574.

2. *Aelbrecht Bouts*
The Last Supper,
oak, arched at the top, 102 x 72, inv. 2589.

● AELBRECHT BOUTS
(active in Louvain from 1473-1549)
Aelbrecht was born in Louvain around 1460. He was Dirk Bouts' second son, and it is most likely that he was trained in his father's workshop. Dirk Bouts died in 1475, and we loose track of his son until 1479, when he is known to have been in Louvain again. He stayed there until his death in 1549, and was buried in Our-Lady-of-the-Dominican Friars, at his father's and his brother's side.

AELBRECHT BOUTS

☐ Triptych of the Assumption of the Virgin

The central panel of the triptych pictures the Assumption of the Blessed Virgin. The second episode, on the middleground, shows the funeral cortège. The twelve apostles gather round the open grave on the foreground. In the upper register, angels playing music surround Christ and the Holy Ghost, who are both leading the Virgin as she rises towards God the Father in glory. The landscape on the background spreads across the lateral shutters. On the left wing, two deacons—one of them wearing St. Peter's tiara—are complementary to the scene of the main panel. On the foreground, an angel assists the painter's father-in-law, kneeling in the devout attitude of a donor. On the middleground, Thomas, the unbelieving apostle, looks on as Mary is carried away to the Heavens. He does not seem to trust his eyes, so an angel hands him the girdle of the Virgin's coat as evidence. The couple of donors introduced by an angel on the foreground of the right shutter has been identified as the painter and his wife.

☐ The Last Supper

Aelbrecht Bouts pursues his father's manner, sometimes even referring to one of his works as a model. *Jesus in the House of Simon (inv. 2580)* for example, is a reversed replica of his father's painting, kept in the Berlin Museum. In The Last Supper, Aelbrecht Bouts plagiarises his father's opus maius—the central panel of the Altarpiece of the Sacrament of St. Peter's Church in Leuven.

MASTER OF 1518

☐ Triptych of the Abbey of Dielegem

This work has sometimes been called Triptych of the Magdalen. The central panel is a representation of the Gospel according to St. Luke (VII, 37). As Jesus is seated at the table of Simon the Pharisee, a sinful woman sneaks

3

4

3. *Master of 1518*
**Triptych of The Abbey
of Dielegem**,
*oak, arched at the top,
central panel 180 x 150,
wings
185 x 70 and 185 x 71,
inv. 329.*

4. *Jan Mostaert*
**Triptych
of Albrecht Adriaensz.
van Adrichem**,
*oak, arched at the top,
central panel 134 x 97.5,
wings
140.5 x45.5 and
139.5 x 45,
inv. 3466.*

in and weeps as she rubs his feet with perfume and dries them with her hair. The unnatural effects of perspective, the ornamental superabundance and the blatant expressiveness reflect the taste of the Mannerists of the beginning of that century. The left shutter pictures Lazarus risen from the dead, flanked by his sisters Martha and Mary. Jesus, having made his thanksgivings to His Father, shouted: "Lazarus! Come outside!" And the dead man came out (Gospel according to St. John, XI. 43). The Magdalen's rapture as the angels carry her away to the Heavens is part of *the legend of the life of the Magdalen.* The kneeling donor is a prémontré abbot.

JAN MOSTAERT

☐ **Triptych of Albrecht Adriaensz. van Adrichem**
This is a triptych on the Passion of Christ. *The Descent from the Cross,* on the centrepiece, is embedded in the altarpiece's frame, as Gothic masters traditionally did. It also reflects Van der Weyden's influence on North Netherlandish painting. The left shutter, Christ *Crowned with Thorns,* is closed by a Renaissance-inspired portal. Mostaert is dependent on the

● JAN MOSTAERT
(c. 1475-1555 / 1556)
Jan Mostaert was born in Haarlem in 1475, and listed as a painter in a document from his birthplace, dated 1498. Haarlem was the setting for the major part of his career, although he spent a period of several years as a court painter to Margaret of Austria in Mechlin, around 1520.

48

1. South Netherlandish School, first quarter of the 16th century
Small Girl with Dead Bird, *oak, 36.7 x 29.8, inv. 4434.*

2. Jan Gossaert
Venus and Cupid, *1521? oak, arched, 36 x 23.5, 41.5 x 30 with the reserved frame inside the panel, inv. 6611.*

3. Jan Gossaert
Portraits of two donors
(shutters of a triptych), oak, 70 x 23.5 each wing, inv. 4740.

● JAN GOSSAERT
(1478-1532)
Jan Gossaert is also know under the name of Mabuse, after the latin name of the town of Maubeuge, where his family originated from. He registered with the Antwerp Painters' Guild in 1503. When in 1508 Philip of Burgundy was sent on a special mission to the pope, Gossaert took on the task of copying the Antique, and accompanied him to Rome. That is how the tradition of the artists' journey to Rome was launched. At the end of 1515, Philip of Burgundy hired Gossaert to decorate his castle in Suytburg, on the island of Walcheren. That is where the first known examples of nude paintings in the Netherlands occur. Gossaert had imported essential Italianate elements that would rapidly lead to a boom. He passed away in 1532.

Primitives' tradition and at the same time he feels the urge of obeying to new tendencies. The obverse side of the right shutter is an Ecce Homo, when Pontius Pilate offered Jesus flogged to his accusers, hoping to soothe them with a compromise. When closed, the altarpiece pictures the Ascent to the Calvary with the donor Albrecht Adriaensz. van Adrichem, who was a municipal magistrate of Haarlem at the time. He is introduced by St. Catherine and St. Bavo, the patron of the church for which the work was executed.

ANONYMOUS MASTER
☐ Small Girl with Dead Bird
Nothing is known about this little girl, except that she is wearing an early 16th century dress. The style of the portrait is Netherlandish, and little can be said about this painter. But the lightness of the facture, the subtle refinement of the colours and the masterful modelling of the features are those of an accomplished painter, who has succeeded in conveying the unspeakable dismay of a child faced with death.

JAN GOSSAERT
☐ Venus and Cupid
The theme, taken over from classical antiquity, was quite fashionable in Rome at the time. Cupid was the son of Venus, and he reached the hearts by piercing them with his arrows. He is pictured with his mother reproving him, as she strongly opposes to his ventures. "You insolent son", quotes the couplet painted on the frame, "you who are accustomed to torment people and gods, you do not even spare your own mother. Lest you be more considerate with her, you will perish."
Gossaert draws the attention to the dynamic attitude of the figures, by decentering the architectural elements and by stressing the bodies' relief through a play with light and shade. He transgresses the classical rules of symmetry and stability.

☐ Portraits of two donors
These portraits are the two wings of a triptych, the dramatically reduced central panel (a Madonna) of which is currently in the Chrlyser Museum in Norfolk, Virginia. The architectural elements of the wings are continued in that central panel. Gossaert's work is typified by the relief of the faces and the classicism of the background of these two very beautiful portraits.

BERNARD VAN ORLEY

☐ *Triptych of the Virtue of patience*

This triptych is the major work among the different Van Orley paintings in the Royal Museums. His motto "ELX SYNE TYT" ("Elk zijn tijd", each in his own time) can be read on the left pillar, on the foreground, and indicates that the artist valued it: it comes over like a manifest of his commitment to that period. The date is mentioned at the bottom of the same pillar: 1521. Margaret of Austria had commissioned this work to offer it to her counsellor Antoine de Lalaing. The open triptych is a representation of the Book of Job, after the Old Testament. Job was a wealthy man, life treated him well and he was respectful of God. Satan defied the Almighty to put his faithful subject to the test: their dialogue can be seen on the upper part of the left shutter, and on the lower part, the series of calamities pouncing on Job: his sheep are struck by lightning; his camels, his oxen and his asses are stolen. The central panel pictures the family feast attended by his entire descendancy; the roof of the banqueting hall falls in and all are annihilated in a flash.

The sovereign influence of Renaissance canons is attested by the architectural structure, enlivened with an ornamentation that is a mere product of the artist's fantasy, and with its single vanishing point perspective. But the demons blowing a raging storm on the upper part of the scene intrude on this unity: this sudden onset of the powers of gloom is reminiscent of the medieval spirit, and disturbs the element of balance implied by Renaissance. The entire dramatic tension of the scene is conveyed by this interference. The verticallty of the pillars is treated as counterpart of the oblique arrangement of collapsing columns and foreshortenings by which the characters are thrust towards the onlooker. The background illustrates further details of the story. On the left-hand side, Job makes an offering on behalf of his children; on the right, he is surrounded by his wife and musicians as he is struck by lepra.

On the right wing, Job's friends ask him to intervene on their behalf, now that he has been sanctified by the ordeals. The reverse sides of the shutters tell another: the parable of the Rich Man and Lazarus.

4. Bernard van Orley
Triptych of the Virtue of Patience, *1521*
oak, arched at the top, central panel 176 x 184, each wing 174 x 80, inv. 1822.

● BERNARD VAN ORLEY (c. 1487/1488-1541) Bernard van Orley was born round 1488. His father was a painter and probably trained him. His first known work dates from c. 1512; it is the Triptych of the Carpenters and Coopers of Brussels, of which two of the wings belong to the Museum (inv. 1436-1435). He was at the service of Margaret of Austria, Queen Regent of the Netherlands, from 1515, and was appointed official painter to the court in 1518. He was in charge of a significant workshop. He achieved fame in the field of painting and through his cartoons for stained glass and fine tapestry. His essentially decorative work was highly praised. Due to his sympathy for the Protestant community, van Orley fell into disgrace; but he was reengaged five years later by the new Queen Regent, Mary of Hungary. He passed away in Brussels in 1541.

1. Bernard van Orley
The Haneton Triptych,
oak, central panel
187 x 108.5, each wing
87 x 48,inv. 358.

2. Bernard van Orley
**Portrait of Joris van
Zelle, Physician**, 1519,
oak, 39 x 32, inv. 1454.

3. Jan Massys
Susanna and the Elders,
1567, oak, 162 x 222,
inv. 2548.

● JAN MASSYS
(? - 1575)
Jan, son of Quinten Metsys,
was accepted as a master at
the Antwerp Guild in 1531.
At first, he concentrated on
faithfully perpetuating his
father's work. He was char-
ged with heresy and banned
from Antwerp in 1544. He
stayed in Italy during the fifteen years of his compelled
absence. The kinship of his
later style with that of the
School of Fontainebleau
induced historians of art to
assume that he stayed there
as well. He returned to
Antwerp when he was
reprieved in 1558 and
worked there until his death
in 1575.

☐ **The Haneton Triptych**
The commissioner of the work was Philip Haneton, first
secretary to the Private Council of Charles V, and he is
pictured with his family on the wings of the triptych. The
intensity of the Lamentation on the central panel isdue to
the expressiveness of the faces and the dense composition, the characters closely centered at half-length, entrapped in the resolutely archaic gold ground.

In this masterful painting, van Orley combines a very personal,
mannered style with elements from the Flemish Primitives and
from Albrecht Dürer.

☐ **Portrait of Joris van Zelle, Physician**
The artist was familiar with the model, who was his neighbour in Brussels. The border of the tapestry states that
he was aged twenty-three at the time and portrayed by
van Orley in 1519. The handshake motif attests a close
relationship between the painter and the physician, an
interesting humanist type in his consulting-room.

JAN MASSYS

☐ **Susanna and the Elders**
In the course of his second Antwerp period, Jan Massys
was particularly fond of picturing attractive young women
involved in indecent situations. Susanna and the Elders
quotes an excerpt from the Book of Daniel. Jan Massys
uses the biblical narrative as a pretext to play the unwor-
thy old judges' concupiscence against Susanna's innocence as she is about to bathe.

The lightness of this mannered work stems from the rotating
movement formed by the chain of expressive gestures of the
figures surrounding Susanna. In his characters, in the ornamental
sculptures of the garden, in the landscapes with abundant architectural elements, Jan Massys sums up and shows off the results
of his Italianate training, as in a Romanist manifest. To the painter's
vivid imagination, the Bible's reference to the incestuous inter-
course between Lot and his daughters (inv. 2549) suggested a
garden of perverse delights, set against the background of the
cataclysm of Sodom.

4. *Jan Sanders van Hemessen*
The Prodigal Son,
oak, 140 x 198, inv. 2838.

5. *Pieter Aertsen*
The Cook,
*oak, 127.5 x 82,
inv. 3744.*

JAN SANDERS VAN HEMESSEN

☐ *The Prodigal Son*

One cannot help focusing on the evocative descriptions of the debauchery in which the prodigal son was led astray, on the foreground. The architectural elements and the costumes are characteristic of Renaissance, but the characters themselves are typically Flemish. Far behind the colonnade, the evangelical scenes of repentance and the return home seem to be a concession the artist felt compelled to make.

The monumentality of the figures, so expressive that they approach caricature, endows the representation with overwhelming strength.

PIETER AERTSEN

☐ *The Cook*

Proudly standing in front of the fireplace where she is about to roast a skewer with poultry, the cook prevails. Aetsen was fond of colourful scenes in which vegetables, venison and cooking utensils enable him to work with superbly contrasting hues.

The artist stages this ancillary theme and towering character with jubilation, foreshadowing the Baroque spirit that painters such as Snijders and Jordaens would develop in the course of the following century.

● JAN SANDERS VAN HEMESSEN
(c. 1500-c. 1556)
Jan Sanders van Hemessen was born in Hemiksem, close to Antwerp, where he was admitted as a freemaster a little earlier than 1524. A great number of his works treated religious themes and staged the most exuberant characters.

● PIETER AERTSEN
(1507/1508-1575)
Pieter Aertsen was born and died in Amsterdam, but he became a freemaster in Antwerp in 1535. He also acquired the right of citizenship and was active there for thirty years, achieving considerable success. His wife's nephew, Joachim Beuckelaer, became his pupil. He has left us his genre paintings, religious works and still lifes.

● JOACHIM BEUKELAER
(1533-1573)Joachim
Beuckelaer is assumed to
have been born in Antwerp
in 1533. He became a mas-
ter in 1560, but can be
considered as his uncle
Pieter Aertsen's epigone. He
specialised in still lifes with
pantry details and market
scenes.

● PIETER BRUEGEL
THE ELDER
(1527/1528-1569)
In 1551, "Peeter Brueghels"
is registered as a master at
the Antwerp painter's guild.
He made the journey to
Italy in 1552 and 1553. For
a period of over ten years,
he produced countless drawings for the Antwerp
engraving workshop "De
Vier Winden" (The Four
Winds). Jerome Cock, the
master of that workshop,
distributed engravings after
works of Hieronymus
Bosch, from which Bruegel
drew inspiration for a number of his drawings. The
first painting that can positi-
vely be attributed to him
dates back to 1559. That is
also when he decided to
drop the "h" from his surname and to sign "Bruegel".
He married and settled in
Brussels in 1563. From then
on, he dedicated the better
part of his life to painting.
Pieter Bruegel the Elder
passed away in Brussels in
1569, and was buried in the
church of Notre-Dame-de-la
Chapelle.

☐ *Christ at Martha's and Mary's*
The story of this visit is told in the Gospel according
to St. Luke. Jesus had dropped by a woman named
Martha. Her sister Mary sat down at his feet to listen
to him, and Martha moaned about having to take up
the household duties alone. The housewife on the
foreground is clearly emphasized. Aertsen cleverly
plays out the patrician-looking group surrounding
Christ against the character of Martha's, wearing
working clothes.

JOACHIM BEUCKELAER
☐ *Christ at Martha's and Mary's*
Beuckelaer treats the identical theme as his
contemporary, stressing the domestic aspect even
more by focus-ing on the kitchen. He displays a
dazzling talent for rendering the texture of the food
and the play of light on the kitchen utensils and the
drapery. In the meantime, Jesus' visit takes place in
the distance of another room of this splendid
Renaissance residence.

3

PIETER BRUEGEL THE ELDER

Pieter Bruegel had a key influence on sixteenth century art, the tenor of his art as well as its innovative technique both kindled. He did not subscribe to the models of Italian Renaissance; he was not interested by the picturesque side of the common people. His art conveys with radical originality how essential the value of the human factor is within society.

☐ The Fall of the Rebel Angels

The scene is taken from the Apocalypse: at the centre of the painting, archangel St. Michael appears out of celestial brightness wearing a golden armour, his wings spread out, the wind unfurling his turquoise cloak. Angels dressed in white robes assist him as he runs the fallen angels through. Other angels sound the trumpets and bugles, hailing his purifying action. The corrupt angels turn to hideous hybrid creatures and are thrust into infernal empty space.

This nightmarish but fascinating nether world still belongs to the Dark Ages, are reminiscent of the spirit of Hieronymus Bosch. But the painting is clearly linked to Renaissance by this sky, streamlined by a centrifugal composition based on the radiance of the sun. This whirling construction is an application of the principle according to which the sun is the centre of our system, as the Polish astronomer Nicolas Copernicus (1473-1543) had demonstrated some twenty years before. Bruegel was resistant to the fashionable italianate imagery of that period, but was probably the artist of the middle of the century who most adequat-ely assimilated the heritage of his own time. The fact that the painting is dated and signed is also rather new. It bears the following inscription in the lower left corner: M.D.LXII BRVEGEL. 1562 was the end of the painter's Antwerp period.

1. *Pieter Aertsen*
Christ at Martha's and Mary's,
1559, oak, 140 x 196.5, inv. 3754.

2. *Joachim Beuckelaer*
Christ at Martha's and Mary's,
1565, oak, 113 x 163, inv. 3934.

3. *Pieter Bruegel the Elder*
The Fall of the Rebel Angels,
1562, oak, 117 x 162, inv. 584.

1. *Pieter Bruegel the Elder*
The Fall of Icarus,
*canvas, 73.5 x 112,
inv. 4030.*

● Peter Bruegel the Elder uses a technique that is subservient to the Flemish Primitives. But he invents an entirely new style, openly neglecting the accuracy of the rendering, the subtlety of glaze, and the delicacy of the relief: he has a swift and joyous stroke, whereby his characters gain this forceful expressiveness, and their postures this overwhelming truthfulness. The pictural matter itself obtains a very direct power of expression through Bruegel's absolute simplification of technique. The often apparent white of the primer illuminates the painting. But the sense of volume and matter is particularly well conveyed by means of a simple, straightforward modulation of the tonalities.

□ **The Fall of Icarus**
This painting was inspired by an excerpt of the Metamorphoses of the Latin poet Ovidius. Daedalus was imprisoned in the labyrinth he had designed for Minos, king of Creta. So he had imagined to escape from the island with his son Icarus by means of gluing feathers together with linen and wax to make wings. But Icarus was so thrilled by the flight that he boldly approached the sun instead of following his father. The heat melted the wings' wax and Icarus fell. Hurled towards the earth like a meteor, the boy's corpse crashes headlong in the sea, only a few metres away from the shore. No more can be seen than the legs, his hand, and a few feathers hovering above the splashes. Neither the peasant behind of his plough nor the fisherman casting his line are aware of the tragedy. A dream vanishes under the setting sun's gleaming indifference.

The scenery seems to evoke by the Strait of Messina, that Bruegel may have drawn on his journey to Italy, during which he closely studied nature. Although the questions raised by the attribution of this painting to Bruegel the Elder are quite tricky due to the poor state of conservation of the canvas, this landscape is definitely a product of Bruegelian inspiration.

□ **The Enrollment of Bethlehem**
An illustration of the account of the birth of Christ by the Gospel according to St. Luke: "In those days a decree went out from Caesar Augustus that all the world should be enrolled [...]. And all went to be enrolled, each to his own city [...]." That is why Joseph travelled to Bethlehem with his pregnant wife Mary.

In this transposition by Bruegel, Judea has become 16th century Brabant, and Joseph, a Flemish carpenter carrying a saw on his shoulder and a brace at his belt. He is leading his donkey towards the inn where the tax collector of King Philip II of Spain is holding office. Bruegel thrusts the Gospel's narrative against the reality he is faced with: to pay the tithe was far from easy for the Brabantine peasants. However, the village where the scene is staged is not real: Bruegel departed from realistic elements to create a synthetic image of mankind, resignedly attending to daily tasks and submitting to the precariousness of fate.

PIETER BRUEGHEL THE YOUNGER

□ **The Struggle between Carnival and Lent**
The subject of this composition originates in mediaeval literature. Carnival is the chubby character in the foreground, sitting astride a barrel, wearing a terrine for

2. *Pieter Bruegel the Elder*
The Enrollment of Bethlehem,
*1566, oak, 115.5 x 163.5,
inv. 3637.*

3. *Pieter Brueghel the Younger*
The Struggle between Carnival and Lent
*Oak, 121. 3 x 171. 5
inv. 12045.*

helmet and waving a spit at his opponent like a spear. Opposite, a monk and a nun drag the gloomy, raw-boned Lent: the beehive on his head refers to the honey of the Lent fast, and he brandishes a shovel with two herrings on it. The clash depicted here opposes feasting to days without meat, popular revelling to pious dryness, and the inn's regulars to churchgoers. However, misery takes its toll on either side. The numerous characters and scenes displayed on the square lend themselves to allegoric interpretation and relate *The Struggle between Carnival and Lent* to the famous *Proverbs,* through which Bruegelian style acquired a dimension of critical reflection on society in its time.

Again, this work by Pieter Brueghel the Younger is a straight borrowing of one of his father's works. However, the striking beauty of this scrupulous copy, and the crispness of its colours, rule out disdainful reduction of the son's status to that of an impersonal copyist. Unlike some of his other paintings, which are largely due to his studio, the painterly quality of this work and the careful rendering of every detail hint at the sole hand of the master, and a very talented master indeed.

☐ Another very significant painting by Pieter Bruegel the Elder belongs to the Delporte Bequest (cfr. p. 62): The Bird Trap (*Winter landscape with skaters and bird trap*).

1. Pieter Brueghel the Younger
The Massacre of Innocents,
oak, 120.5 x 167,inv. 361.

2. Maerten de Vos
St. Paul at Ephesus,
1568, oak, 125 x 198, inv. 4310.

3. Paul Bril
View of a Port,
canvas, 105 x 150, inv. 4936.

● PIETER BRUEGHEL
THE YOUNGER
(1564-1638)
Pieter Bruegel the Elder died in 1569, leaving two young sons: Pieter, known under the name of Pieter Brueghel the Younger, and Jan, also known as 'Velvet' Brueghel. Pieter Brueghel the Younger registered as a freemaster in Antwerp's corporate books in 1584. For the years to come, the same books list nine apprentices as being registered at his workshop, which gives a fair idea of how significant it was. The workshop produced a large number of paintings, to a great extent copies of Bruegel the Elder's work. Although he had been too young at the time of his father's demise to benefit from his teaching, he drew inspiration from his colorist's technique with an obvious sense of light and matter. But he never quite equalled his father's genial, innovative and impulsive style. Apart from his numerous copies, he left a number of more personal works—genre paintings, country landscapes—mostly derived from the manner of Pieter Bruegel the Elder.

1

☐ **The Massacre of Innocents**
This is one of the works Pieter Brueghel the Younger has painted after one of his father's. It is staged in 16th century Brabant and allows an ambiguous interpretation like the Enrollment of Bethlehem. In the Gospel according to St. Matthew, when King Herod realised that he had been tricked by the wise men, who would not reveal where the "King of the Jews" was born, he was in a furious rage "and he sent and killed all the male children in Bethlehem and in all that region who were two years old or under". On the middle ground, on the right, the king's herald proclaims the king's edict from his horse; children are torn away from their mothers, people are running for a hiding-place as doors are broken down, under the ruthless watch of a posse of horsemen, forming an impassable iron fence with their spears.

MAERTEN DE VOS
☐ **St. Paul at Ephesus**
This painting, executed in 1568, was one of five for which he was commissioned by a wealthy merchant due to an intervention by Abraham Ortelius, the cartographer. Maerten de Vos was well acquainted with the Antwerp Humanists. The theme stems from the Acts of the Apostles: Paul's preaches had miraculous consequences At Ephesus, he converted exorcists and magicians. "Many of those who were now believers came, confessing and divulging their practices. And a number of those who had practiced magic arts brought their books together and burned them in the sight of all" (Acts, XIX. 18-19). On the foreground, another story is told: on the right, Paul is being restrained by a disciple as citizens of Ephesus hurl abuse at him and invoke the greatness of their idol Artemis (Acts, XIX. 30-32).
The lively composition is constructed on either side of the diagonal that leads the eye to the stake. The bright, lustrous hues fade down to blurred pink shades on the background. The architectural elements are set sharply against the sky, blending Roman heritage and imaginary building projects. This work is representative of the predominance of Romanesque taste in Flanders during the second half of the 16th century, shortly before Rubens' Baroque overruled it.

4. Jan Provost
St. Jerome's Penitence,
*oak, 68.5 x 52.5,
inv. 10817.*

PAUL BRIL

☐ **View of a Port**
This is an accomplished example of Paul Bril's maturity. The composite scenery is reminiscent of Bruegel the Elder. However, the human bustle around the moored sailboat does not have the value of a metaphor or reference intended to add a meaning to the painting. The Mediterranean sunset just invites the onlooker to take delight and share the sense of fulfilment radiating from this world that opens up on the infinity of a dazzling sea. Paul Bril's art stems from the cosmic Flemish art scene, but is deeply permeated with Italian atmosphere, foreshadowing the classical 'ideal' landscapes of Claude Gellée (Le Lorrain) and Nicolas Poussin.

JAN PROVOST

☐ **St. Jerome's Penitence**
(HEULENS-VAN DER MEIREN DONATION)
St. Jerome, father of the Church of the 4th century, is especially known for his Latin translation of the Scriptures, the Vulgate. The painting pictures a number of episodes from

● JAN PROVOST
(c. 1465-1529)
Jan Provost was born in Mons around 1465, but seems to have settled in Bruges from 1492 on. It is more than likely that he became acquainted with the work of Memlinc and of Gérard David. He was

commissioned by the town councillors as well as by the religious authorities. We are mainly familiar with his portaits and his paintings with a religious theme, but he was also a decorator and an occasional cartographer. He passed away in Bruges in 1529.

● MAERTEN DE VOS
(1532-1603)
Maerten de Vos was born in Antwerp in 1532. He travelled to Rome in 1552, maybe together with Pieter Bruegel the Elder. He was admitted as a freemaster at the Antwerp Guild of St. Luke in 1558, and became one of the most appraised and prolific painters of his time. He passed away in Antwerp in 1603.

● PAUL BRIL
(1554-1626)
Paul Bril was born to a family of painters in Antwerp in 1554. He stayed in Lyon when he was twenty, then joined his brother Matthijs in Rome, where he eventually settled and had a brilliant career. His scenic views of the Eternal City were scattered throughout Europe and inspired a significant number of painters. It is known for a fact that he was in touch with 'Velvet' Brueghel during the latter's journey to Rome. Paul Bril died in Rome in 1626.

● The Heulens - Van der Meiren donation.
In 1988, Irene Heulens - Van der Meiren donated the collection that her husband had gathered together with patience and discernment to the Royal Museums. This collection includes twenty-three paintings dating from the end of the 15th to the 18th century, and a great number of drawings, sculptures, objet d'art's and furniture, totalling a hundred and eleven pieces of the highest quality.

the history of the Saint's life, blending facts and legends together. St. Jerome had retired into the desert, inflicting constant self-punishment to his body.

He is seen pounding against his chest with a stone. He has stripped of the scarlet mantle and the cardinal hat, traditional iconographical attributes of St. Jerome, just like the lion laying at his feet. The lion refers to an excerpt from the Golden Legend: at the time when Jerome was an abbott of a monastery in Bethlehem, a lion limped towards him. Jerome welcomed him and cured his injured paw, as pictured on the right-hand side of the middle ground. The lion remained with the friars as a pet, escorting and guarding the monastery's donkey. One day, as he had fallen asleep, a merchants' caravan travelling through Bethlehem stole the donkey. Much later, they happened to be in that neighbourhood again, and the lion chased them away. He then brought the camels and the donkey back to the monastery by beating on the ground with his tail. That is the scene pictured on the left.

ANONYMOUS MASTER FROM THE SOUTHERN NETHERLANDS
☐ *Anthropomorphic Landscapes*
(HEULENS-VAN DER MEIREN DONATION)

Both of these spellbound landscapes reveal the features of a face. The greenish hill of the one also appears to represent the face of a peaceful woman lying down. On the other, a steep hillock draws a masculine profile, set against the sky. But every feature of these faces is also a scenic element: the man's goatee is also a thicket on a logan, while the woman's chin is a smooth rock.

The numerous little folk scenes, rendered with spontaneous liveliness, situate this master in the second half of the 16th century, in Bruegel's footsteps. His manner relates him to Abel Grimmer, who also painted series on the four seasons' theme; it is very likely that these two panels were part of such a series: the feminine landscape would represent the spring while the other one would

2

celebrate the summertime and the agricultural labour.

This parallel the artist draws between man and nature is far more than a phantasmagoria; it expresses the entire new spirit of a period in the course of which empirical observation had overwhelmed the knowledge of human anatomy, a time when one attempted to explain the cosmos through the human microcosm. "Man has a frame of bones supporting the flesh", wrote Leonardo Da Vinci, "the world has a frame of rocks to support the earth; man withholds a lake of blood in which, when he breathes, the lungs expand and draw together, the earth's body has its own ocean, rising and falling every six hours as the world breathes."

DENIS VAN ALSLOOT

☐ *Winter Scene with View of the Château of Tervueren*
(HEULENS-VAN DER MEIREN DONATION)

This landscape is quite typical of the painter's manner. He combines aerial perspective with a significant difference in the scale of representation, stresses the sense of depth, and uses a subtle play with light variations to confer amplitude to the atmosphere of this vast, motionless expanse.

● DENIS VAN ALSLOOT
(c. 1570-c. 1626)
Denis van Alsloot was active in Brussels, where he was appointed as official painter to the court of the Archdukes Albert and Isabella around 1600. His œuvre—consisting of landscapes and historical themes—is quite representative of the turning-point between both centuries.

The Delporte - Livrauw Bequest

In 1974, the Royal Museums of Fine Arts of Belgium inherited an invaluable legacy: the two hundred and twenty-nine pieces of the private collection of Dr Franz Delporte-Livrauw and his wife Marguerite Livrauw. These art lovers' refined eclecticism added its most ancient South Netherlandish work to the Museum's collection, a panel dating back to the beginning of the 14th century, as well as one of the wings of a Catalan altar-piece of the 15th century. The collectors had gathered a great number of Flemish paintings, among which a masterpiece by Pieter Bruegel the Elder, and—in an entirely different field—a portrait of the Fayoum, French and African sculptures, a tapestry, furniture, chinaware, etc.

1. South Netherlandish School - around 1300 **Calvary and Ressurection** *(obverse),* **St. Dominic** *(reverse), wood, 137 x 90, inv. 8733.*

SOUTH NETHERLANDISH SCHOOL

☐ Calvary and Ressurection and St. Dominic

On the obverse side of this painting, two episodes of the Passion have been superimposed: the Calvary and the Resurrection. The iconology of the Calvary is particularly well developed here. On either side of the Cross, Mary, assisted by two holy women as she faints, and St. John the Evangelist share one and the same grief. But they are flanked by two prophets, wearing the Phrygian cap, who express quite a different feeling. Their presence is related to that of the Sun and the faint Moon above the scene of the Crucifixion. The dull tonality of the Sun reminds us of the eclipse that plunged the whole Earth into darkness, as mentioned in the Gospel according to St. Luke; the prediction of such an eclipse can be found twice in the Old Testament's Prophetic books: "And on that day, says the Lord Yahweh, I will make the sun go down at noon, and darken the earth in broad daylight", prophesies Amos. Isaiah also refers to the moon: "The sun will be dark at its rising and the moon will not shed its light." The Evangelist, echoed here by the medieval iconology, refers to those texts in ordrer to assert that the Scriptures are fulfilled through the Passion of Christ. In the Resurrection pictured on the lower register, Christ sits upon his grave, risen from the dead and flanked by a couple of angels. Leaning against the Holy Sepulchre and dozing off, the Roman sentries are dressed as armsmen of the 13th century, wearing a coat of mail, bearing spear and shield.

The superimposition of the two scenes and the contrasting hues of bright red and pink, set against a lapis lazuli background, remind us of the medieval art of stained-glass panes and enamels. The very accurate drawing is stressed by a white line in order to emphasize the undulating rhythm of the figures, and can clearly be assimilated with the mannered style of International Gothic.

The reverse side of the painting is dedicated to St. Dominic, founder of the order of the Preaching Friars in the 13th century. By means of a perfectly even and plane representation of the features, the artist places all the face's elements next to each other, including the ears, with an exceptionally free handling of the line. The frontal treatment of the face and the strict demarcation of the coloured zones remind us of the South Netherlandish wall paintings of the beginning of the 14th century.

PERE LEMBRI

☐ Fragment of the altarpiece of St. Michael and St. Peter

The upper right panel refers to the Acts of the Apostles: Peter granted a baptism to the Roman centurion Cornelius and to his family. Below right, a traditional representation of the risen from the dead on Judgment day. Above left, St. Michael, the archangel.

According to the *Golden Legend*, the waters surrounding the Mont-Saint-Michel would open to yield a passage to pilgrims on the Saint's day. One day, the tide rose swiftly, and everyone ran towards the shore, save a pregnant woman who was about to deliver and unable to run. But the archangel kept her out of harm, and she gave birth to a son and nursed him amidst the raging waves. The inferior left panel also illustrates a narrative from the *Golden Legend:* Plague was decimating The Roman population. On Easter day, pope Gregory ordered a procession with a statue of the Holy Virgin to wander through the streets of the city. Wherever she would pass by, the air was purified. Above the fortress of Crescence, St. Gregory caught sight of the archangel St. Michael, sheathing a bloodstained sword. Since that day, the fortress is named Castello Sant'Agneli. This series of four panels is only a fragment of a monumental altarpiece, of which some ten panels are known, but disseminated. Eminent Catalan painting specialistsattribute this work to Pere Lembri, who was active in the diocese of Tortosa, between Valencia and Barcelone, from 1400 to 1420.

2. Pere Lembri
Fragment of the altarpiece of St. Michael and St. Peter,
wood, 205 × 168,
inv. 8755.

2

1. *Pieter Bruegel the Elder*
The Bird Trap,
*1565, oak, 37 x 55.5,
inv. 8724.*

PIETER BRUEGEL THE ELDER

☐ *The Bird Trap*

Unlike the composite landscapes such as that of the *Enrollment of Bethlehem*, the village pictured by Pieter Bruegel in this renowned composition is a typified Brabantine village. That microcosm is the setting he uses to stage an allegoric narrative on the unawareness of mankind. On the foreground, at the right, a bird trap is set up to catch the careless birds that might alight there. But they don't seem to worry about it. The skaters aren't concerned about the brittleness of the ice on which they horse about. However, the interpretation of the painting should not prevent the onlooker from contemplating the winter scene, bathed in a golden haze, unfurling around the wide bend of the frozen river. Far behind, at the blurred boundary between the sky and the huge snowy areas, the mirage of a city seems to rise from a dazzling infinity. This painting has been the laboratory of one of Bruegel's innovative experiments. Reducing the diversity and the impact of the local shades, blending the atmospheric tonalities into one camaïeu, he foreshadowed a technique that will later be used by numerous 17th century Dutch landscapists.

PIETER BRUEGHEL THE YOUNGER

☐ *The Village Wedding*

This is one of the most popular themes of all times. As the most boisterous villagers eagerly dance to the music of a couple of bagpipes, others chat and drink. The gleaming bride is seated in front of a drapery fixed up between two trees. She receives the traditional bridal gifts of the time. A 16th century engraving has attested that Bruegel the Elder was the creator of this scene, but the original painting has vanished. It goes to the son's credit that a more or less true copy of the father's work has eventually reached us.

2

2. *Pieter Brueghel the Younger*
The Village Wedding,
*1607, oak, 38.5 x 51.5,
inv. 8725.*

1

● JAN BAPTIST BONNECROY
(1618 – after 1665)
Born in Antwerp, Jan Baptist
Bonnecroy was admitted as
a freemaster in the Guild of
St. Luke in 1645. Twenty
years later, he was a registered member of the Brussels
painters' guild. His fame
mainly rested on his urban
landscapes picturing
Brussels and Antwerp.
Panoramas were in fact an
autonomous painting genre
with an essentially documentary vocation: there is no
vividness in those pictures,
not a living soul in those
cities.

JAN BAPTIST BONNECROY

☐ *View of Brussels*
This is a bird's eye view of Brussels dating back to
about 1664, seen from a mound on the territory of
Molenbeek. The surrounding wall was fortified, and
seven gates gave access to the town. Only one still
stands today: the Porte de Hal, silhouetted far right
on the canvas. The layout of Brussels' inner boulevards is that of the city wall pictured here. Behind the
ramparts, the minutely detailed monuments,
churches and public buildings fit into clusters of ste-
reotype houses. Close to the centre of the picture,
one can recognise the City Hall and its towering bel-
fry, topped by Saint Michael, the archangel. Farther
left, the cathedral's spires show on the horizon line.

ANTOON SALLAERT (STUDIO)

☐ *The Infanta Isabella Shooting down the Bird at
the Match of the 'Grand Serment'*
Isabella, daughter of King Philip II of Spain, and her
husband the archduke Albert governed the Southern
Netherlands since 1598. Throughout her rule, the
archduchess knew how to secure the sympathy of
her subjects. She was concerned about their fate and
took part in their pageants. Thus, in the month of
May, 1615, she participated in a shooting contest
organised at the Sablon by the 'Grand Serment', the
Oath of the Brussels Crossbowmen. The aim was to
shoot the *papegaï*—a wooden bird attached to the
spire of the Notre-Dame. The archduchess wins the
shooting and is solemnly proclaimed "Queen" of the
'Grand Serment'.

● ANTOON SALLAERT
(before 1590 –1650)
Antoon Sallaert was born
and trained in Brussels, and
admitted as a freemaster in
1613. His native town was
the setting of his entire
career, where he was com-
missioned to paint numerous
works. His prolific oeuvre
included historical paintings,
religious and mythological
subjects, and he designed
cartoons for the Brussels
heddle setters.

1. *Jan Baptist Bonnecroy*
View of Brussels
Oil on canvas, 169 x 301.5
Long-term loan by the
Baudouin Foundation

2. *Antoon Sallaert (studio)*
**The Infanta Isabella
Shooting down the
Bird at the Match of
the 'Grand Serment'**
Oil on canvas, 180 x 340
inv. 172.

3. *Antoon Sallaert (studio)*
**The Archdukes Albert
and Isabella attending
the procession of the
Maids of the Sablon**
Oil on canvas, 180 x 339
inv. 173.

☐ **The Archdukes Albert and Isabella attending
the procession of the Maids of the Sablon**
In memory of this festivity, the Infanta opened a fund
with a view to granting, year after year, a perpetual
annuity of 200 florins to six young girls from indigent
families. In addition, she ordered that the young virgins
would have to take part in a procession at the Sablon,
on Whit Monday, for two consecutive years. Of course,
this was more of an honour than a constraint.

The twelve virgins are wreathed with bindweed and dressed
up in Marian colours. The previous year's chosen ones come
first, wearing heir hair up, followed by the newly chosen
maids, with loose hair. Immediately after them, the musicians
march before the miraculous statue of Our Lady, surrounded
by representatives of the parishes' guilds. Behind them, a
mitred prelate bears a cross. The court's dignitaries and the
archdukes bring up the rear, on foot.

17th century

The 17th century was compelled to assimilate the consequences of the great religious upheavals of the previous century. Since 1545 and for the twenty long years that the Council of Trent had lasted, the Roman Catholic Church had devised strategies of reconquest to hold the Reformation in check.

However, the Counter-Reformation has only been partly victorious. Europe was to remain divided: Protestant in the North, Catholic in the South. This dividing line ran straight through the Netherlands: the mostly Protestant northern provinces separated from the Catholic southern provinces. The Calvinist stronghold of the North formed the Union of the Seven Provinces, whereas the southern provinces became the Spanish Low Countries, infeodated to Spain for another century. The provinces under Spanish dominion were caught in the merciless warfare the occupier had waged against Protestantism since 1570. An armistice was concluded with the Union of the Seven Provinces in 1609; it lasted twelve years and offered the Netherlands an opportunity to rise again from their ashes.

1. *Roelandt Savery*
**Landscape
with Birds**,
*1622, wood, 28 x 42,
inv. 4941.*

2. *Josse II de Momper*
Mountain Landscape,
*oak, 121.5 x 186.5,
inv. 7615.*

3. *Osias Beert*
Still Life with Lobster,
bois, 71 x 105, inv. 6591.

The Flemish School

In the early 17th century, Flemish painting was at the crossroads of the previous century's two main trends. The native tradition and the influence of Italian painting overlapped.

ROELANDT SAVERY

☐ *Landscape with Birds*

Roelandt Savery (1576-1639) was faithful to his heritage of great accuracy in the rendering of detail and was also a masterful colourist; his attractive paintings radiate Edenic poetry, as we experience with this *Landscape with Birds*, or with the *Landscape with Animals* (inv. 4824).

JOSSE II DE MOMPER

☐ *Mountain Landscape*

Josse II de Momper (1564-1635) belonged to a family of landscapists who were very active in Antwerp in the 16th and 17th centuries. He unfurled the landscape in a series of ample curves, conveying a feeling of aerial calm to his slanted views. De Momper's representation of mountains is marvellously accurate, which seems to imply that he had crossed the Alps and probably travelled to Italy. The tiny characters that decorate the scenery are by another artist: since the Renaissance, it was common practice to rely on a fellow painter, who specialised in figures, to enhance the landscape.

OSIAS BEERT

☐ *Still Life with Lobster*

When Osias Beert (1580-1623/24) placed these objects and this food side by side on a table, apparently without worrying much about a homogeneous composition, and when he devoted himself to render the rare textures and materials with extreme minutiae, his only obvious concern was sensual delight.

In the course of the 16th century, Still Life had become a distinctive genre within Flemish painting. It had absorbed the Naturalist accuracy of the Van Eyck brothers. Still Life became increasingly popular in the 17th century.

3

JAN I BRUEGHEL, NAMED 'VELVET' BRUEGHEL
☐ Still Life

Jan I Brueghel seems to have gathered the ornaments and finery of a young bride: two necklaces in the jewelry casket, a pendant and three rings spread out on the table, and on the far left-hand side, a golden hairpin on which a pearl is mounted. The composition is dominated by a gleaming Renaissance style goblet with splendidly rendered glints of gold. A glistening wreath is delicately balanced upon that cup, a garland of roses, carnations, cornflowers, lilies of the valley, anemones and others, intertwined with the symbolic forget-me-nots.

'Velvet' Brueghel may have learnt the rudiments of his incomparable technique from his maternal grandmother, a former miniature painter. The lush consistency and the vigour of the flowers is obtained by means of a very accurate juxtaposition of the strokes of the thinnest brushes.

● JAN I BRUEGHEL, NAMED 'VELVET' BRUEGHEL (1568-1625)
Jan, the second son of Pieter Bruegel the Elder, has detached himself from his father's manner. He was a very versatile artist, displaying his skill in genre paintings as well as in allegories or mythological scenes. He was an innovative landscapist and a particularly outstanding flower painter. From 1606 on, he became—with Rubens—the favorite painter of the Archdukes Albert and Isabella at their court in Brussels; and one of the most significant artists of the first quarter of the century.

*4. Jan I Brueghel,
named 'Velvet' Brueghel*
Still Life
*1618?, wood, 47.5 × 52.5,
inv. 5013.*

4

1

1. *Hieronymus II Francken*
Jan Snellinck's Art Shop,
*1621, wood, 94 x 124.7,
inv. 2628.*

HIERONYMUS II FRANCKEN

☐ *Jan Snellinck's Art Shop*

Hieronymus II Francken (1578-1623) belongs to a whole dynasty of painters who were mainly active in Antwerp from the end of the 16th century till the middle of the 17th century. His brother, Frans II, had become a specialist of an entirely new genre at the time, the depiction of "Cabinets of Amateurs", highly favoured in Antwerp's upper middle class. Generally, a character was represented with his real or fictitious collection. Jan Snellinck's Art Shop is a variation of this genre. Jan Snellinck, who was a painter himself, ran an art shop in Antwerp. It is assumed that he is the bareheaded figure holding a miniature, at the rear of the painting, on the right. The scene takes place in 1621 (the date is mentioned on the stained glass) and gives us a fair idea of the taste of the art amateurs of the beginning of the 17th century. At the centre of the room, a clerk unveils a massive table on which antiques are displayed. On the left foreground, books, a globe and a few collector's items are presented to the customers.

Of all the exposed paintings, only Frans Floris' Adam and Eve has been identified beyond doubt, above the splendid Renaissance-style chest. On the floor in the foreground, a Madonna with a flower garland and a large still life are representative of genres that became widespread and increasingly popular in 17th century Netherlandish painting.

The Baroque

In 1585, the vast strategy of Catholic reconquest, developed by the Council of Trent within the framework of Counter-Reformation, included the implementation of a huge urban renovation plan of Rome by Pope Sixtus V. Departing from St. Peter's Square, a network of boulevards were to link the Holy Places to each other and to the gates of the Eternal City. The capital of Christianity would henceforth "radiate" on the rest of the world; at the same time, Rome would become the spatial paradigm of Baroque. When Louis XIV settled in Versailles a century later, in 1682, the royal estate echoed an identical conception: from the Château's gate, facing the Sun-King's apartments, three different highways would radiate towards the French provinces. In the 17th century, the sovereigns of the great monarchies and the Supreme Pontiff distinguished them-selves in very similar ways. The bombastic expressions of their authority convey their common concern: to glorify the power, to startle the people in order to gain their support. Plastic art was used to back up their tenure as well, inspired by the Holy See's attempt to mobilise and unite dissident trends under its rule. Breaking away from the restrained art of the Renaissance, Baroque painting (from Portuguese barocco, "uneven pearl") stirred passionate sensibility by means of lively, forceful compo-sitions, structured around spirals and obliques, resorting to spe-cial effects and illusions to set up a form of communication bet-ween the earth and the heavens, and hence to substantiate the Catholic vision of the supernatural.

PETER PAUL RUBENS

Rubens has asserted himself as a leading genius of Baroque art in Europe in his own time. He has achieved a striking synthesis of the heritage of Flemish painting—the underpinning of his training—and of Italian art, with which he had become acquainted in his younger years.

☐ *Four negro Heads*

The model for study has seemingly been identified in seve-ral of Anthony van Dyck's and Jacob Jordaens' paintings as well. The port of Antwerp welcomed vessels from all over the world, even from the Portuguese trading posts on the Angolan coast, creating oppor-tunities for painters to become acquainted with African models. In order to render the complexion and modelling of these faces, the artist plays with a limited palette of whites, ochres and blue-tinged greyish hues, accentuated with a touch of red. The layout of the heads alongside a single main dia-gonal and the suggested surroun-ding space enhance this study of expressions with the cohesion of a well-structured work.

2. Peter Paul Rubens
Four negro Heads,
transferred from wood to canvas, 51 x 66, inv. 3176.

2

1. *Peter Paul Rubens*
**The Martyrdom
of St. Ursula**,
wood, 49 x 39, inv. 1198.

1

☐ The Martyrdom of St. Ursula

This painting is a modello stemming from the beginning of the painter's maturity, around 1617. The theme refers to the Golden Legend. In the 5th century, Ursula, a Christian princess from Brittany, had gathered eleven thousand virgins together, coming from various regions. She converted them and led them all to Rome. Two Roman army officers felt uneasy about this pilgrimage's tremendous success, so they asked the leader of the Huns to wipe them all out when they would head back. The ultimate moment of the massacre is pictured here: Ursula is between the hands of her executioners. The skies open up and an angel appears, bearing the crowns of beatitude and martyrdom.

The feat of skill Rubens accomplished here is to only show a handful of the thousands of characters, suggesting an apparently neverending flow of intertwined corpses of martyrs. The preparation of Rubens' paintings went through a number of sketches. The modello was the very last of these stages, and included more or less detailed indications of the colour scheme.

☐ Twelve Sketches for the decoration of Torre de la Parada
The Fall of Icarus

In 1636, four years before his demise, Rubens was commissioned for the decoration of the twenty-five rooms of Torre de la Parada, a royal hunting lodge of King Philip IV on the outskirts of Madrid. Rubens entrusted the execution of most of the final canvases to a group of assistants, one of them being Jacob Jordaens. The master reserved only a few of the paintings for himself but achieved all the sketches, totalling a hundred and twelve. These were delivered with the paintings, two years later. Most of these were covered with subjects drawn from Ovid's Metamorphosis. Some forty paintings and fifty sketches of this huge undertaking have reached us, and twelve of these sketches are in this Museum. This truly dazzling painter's swansong is a very significant review of his masterliness: the artist's entire work appears to us through the visible strokes of his brush.

The wooden panel was first prepared with a white prime coat. This primer was then sanded down with agate pumice and coated with a thin layer of light ochre, applied with broad brushstrokes that remain visible. This was the apprentices' task. The master would then draw the main figures with darker earth, directly with the brush. He would either stress the outlines by accentuating the line, or he graduated the shades, sometimes adding a touch of grey; or he would apply thin layers of fluid, almost transparent matter. He marked areas that were to reflect the light by means of white impasto's. The background was only hinted by tonality indications to be interpreted by the painter of the final version.

2. Peter Paul Rubens
The Fall of Icarus,
wood, 27.3 x 27,
inv. 4127.

2

● PETER PAUL RUBENS
(1577-1640)
Peter Paul Rubens was born in Siegen (North-Rheinland-Westphalia) in 1577. Ten years later, his mother became a widow and returned to Antwerp. He took Latin courses there, and when he had completed his artistic apprenticeship in 1598, he was admitted as a freemaster in the Antwerp Guild of St. Luke. He undertook a journey to Italy in 1600 and remained there for eight years. At the time of his return, in 1609, an armistice of twelve years was concluded between Catholics and Protestants, enabling the clergy of the Counter-Reformation to rebuild churches and religious edifices. The artists benefited from this and were commissioned for a tremendous amount of works. The same year, Rubens was appointed as official painter to the court by the Archdukes Albert and Isabella, and he married Isabella Brant. One year later, he bought a sumptuous house in Antwerp (today's' Rubenshuis'). One of his many assistants was young

Anthony van Dyck, who worked for him from 1618 to 1620. From 1620 on, he obtained and took on a number of commissions, through which he acquired a European level, such as the thirty-nine ceiling paintings of the Church of St. Charles-Borromeo in Antwerp, the twenty-five paintings about the History of the Life of Mary de' Medici for the French Court, nowadays exposed in the Louvre, the cartons for a series of tapestries for the Archduchess-Infanta Isabella, several paintings for Charles I of

England. He lost his wife in 1626, but remarried Helena Fourment in 1630, who was then sixteen years old and became his constant model; she is known to us through a number of portraits. He acquired the estate of Steen, near Elewijt in Brabant, in 1635, and that is where he spent most of his later years. His ultimate major work, executed between 1637 and 1638, is the series of sketches for the hunting lodge of King Philip IV of Spain, Torre de la Parada. Peter Paul Rubens passed away in Antwerp in 1640.

1. *Peter Paul Rubens*   1
**The Carrying of
the Cross**,
*arched canvas, 569 x 355,
inv. 163.*

2. *Peter Paul Rubens*
**The Martyrdom
of St. Lieven**,
*canvas, 455 x 347,
inv. 161.*

☐ **The Carrying of the Cross**
This highlight of Rubens' religious work was probably completed round 1636, just before he undertook the sketches of Torre de la Parada. He achieves a synthesis between the religious priorities of Counter-Reformation and the artistic values and canons of the Baroque. The acceptance of Christ to suffer for the greater glory of God is perfectly integrated in the solemn procession of the Church.

This exaltation is expressed by the ascending diagonal movement in the composition. The eye is attracted upwards due to a technique in which Rubens has attained unequalled perfection: to suppress local shades and to let adjacent tonalities alter the shades: take a closer look at the two thieves flanked by two soldiers at the bottom of the painting: the carnation of their torso reflects the colour of the girdle around their waist. The same applies to the man helping Christ to bear his cross: his legs are shaded by the red reflection of Jesus' garment. This can be observed on the faces of Christ, of Mary and of John. At the top of the canvas, the pink shade of the banner blends with the sky's slate grey. In a restless motion, every coloured plane thrusts the eye towards the next plane.

2

The Martyrdom of St. Lieven

This painting dates back to approximately 1636/37. Lieven, bishop of Ghent and a legendary evangelist of 7th century Gaul, was tortured to death by thieves. One of them throws the martyr's ripped out tongue to the dogs. But two angels appear from the clouds and the murderers are suddenly struck dead. The horses are thrown in disarray, and the armed men flee in panick, driven mad by this prodigy. A couple of putti bring the crowns of martyrdom and eternal beatitude.

Rubens has structured this dazzling composition around a spiral movement with a perfect mastery of colour. The eye departs from the central vermillion headdress and whirls towards the translucent tunics of the angels, blending with the clouds.

2

3

● FRANS SNIJDERS
(1579 – 1657)
After training under Pieter
Brueghel the Younger, Frans
Snijders became a master in
1602. He visited Italy in
1608-1609, and then returned
to Antwerp. He excelled in
still-life subjects, such as
flowers and fruits, and in
painting hunting scenes.
In 1628, he was the dean of
the Romanists and quite
renowned: most of
Antwerp's wealthy art lovers
included works by Snijders
in their collection. Rubens
himself owned four of his
canvases. His innovative
compositions are Baroque
variations—clearly Rubens'
heritage—on the more
descriptive still-life paintings
of his peers.

☐ The Adoration of the Magi

This painting can be dated from 1618 by means of stylistic analysis. In a majestic setting closed by a monumental
column, a few wisps of straw are all it takes to suggest the
Infant Jesus' crib. Kneeling at the Saviour's feet, one of the
Magi, wearing a gleaming red cloak and surrounded by
acolytes bearing presents, celebrates a solemn liturgy.
That was the task for which the Baroque artist was commissioned: a transposition of the Gospel's narrative into
the triumphant Roman Church's pomp and ceremony.
Rubens has organised this composition around the canvas' two
diagonals. The face of Jesus is at their intersection. On the foreground, the harmony of the shades literally explode the mantle's golds, in which transparencies blend with firm impasto's
catching the light. The onlooker's eye is immediately attracted
by the centre of the painting, by the Infant who draws all interest towards him.

FRANS SNIJDERS

☐ The Pantry

Departing from the unfurled outline of a swan, Frans
Snijders divides the composition into several planes, level-
led in both depth and vertically. The parallel lines of the
table and of the red pegboard at the top determine the
painting's horizontality. A vertical rhythm is given by the
slices of salmon and by the suspended venison at the
right—a symmetric counterpart to the maid's silhouette.
On the right foreground, a grocery basket defines the origin of a diagonal that goes straight through the basketful
of fruit on the left before disappearing in the patch of blue
sky cut out by the window in the corner.
These structures draw the eye through manifold shapes,
although Snijders does not attain genuine stylistic homogenei-
ty. He combines horizontal and vertical lines with the obliques,

4

the underpinnings of the Baroque's formal idiom. Neither does he achieve this modulation of the shades that is so dazzling in Rubens' work: he uses the mere juxtaposition of well differentiated local shades to make the heaps of food gleam.

JAN FYT

☐ The Dogcart

The display of the hunt's game on the dogcart enables Jan Fyt to stage the planes of his painting in several levels, and to introduce two live dogs in the scene. The composition is constructed around a form of spine, determined by the curved line of the peacock. Like jewels mounted in a setting of subdued shades, the cockscomb, the peacock's neck and the eyes on its feathers, a few white blazes and the dimmed vividness of featherings twinkle and scintillate, whereas the landscape on the background lightens the canvas and creates a peaceful, dusky atmosphere.

This synthetic element of composition and the use of a perfectly accomplished tonal unity are two assertions of a well-processed Baroque influence. Jan Fyt's superiority is revealed by his treatment of the furs and feathers of game, rendered with minutiae by an overwhelming diversity of techniques.

CORNELIS DE VOS

☐ The Artist and his Family

This group portrait is dated 1621. The painter's family is represented in a lavish interior that is supposedly his own. The three unities of Classical theatre are present. Every element hints at a well staged scene in which each character plays his role. This work brilliantly echoes the upper middle-class' desire to assert itself and, as this is a self-portrait, how important the fact to be part of that class is to the artist.

Every one of the faces expresses a different emotional touch, observed with subtlety. The play with the hands enlivens the painting and gives it cohesion. The rendering of complexion, of the delicate shades of the hair and of the sumptuous materials is particularly impressive.

● JAN FYT
(1611 – 1661)
Born in Antwerp, Jan Fyt studied with Frans Snijders before he was admitted as a master at the Antwerp Guild of St. Luke, in 1629. From 1632 onward, he spent some ten years travelling in Italy, in France and, more briefly, in Holland. He eventually returned to his native town, where he made an outstanding career and even chaired the Romanists. He excelled in flower pieces, still lifes and hunting scenes, which were highly valued in his time. His innovative contributions to genre painting included a refined palette of attractive hues and a very personal way to impregnate his compositions with élan.

1. *Antony van Dyck*
**Portrait of Porzia
Imperiale with
her daughter
Maria Francesca**
*canvas, 184.5 x 134,
inv. 6115.*

2. *Antony van Dyck*
François Duquesnoy, *(?)
canvas, 77.5 x 61,
inv. 3928.*

3. *Antony van Dyck*
Rinaldo and Armida,
*oak, 56.5 x 41.5,
inv. 3781.*

ANTHONY VAN DYCK

*Van Dyck was right at Rubens' side at the pinnacle of the
Baroque School of Antwerp. Although he lacked Rubens'
sovereign genius, his refinement and precocious talent
justified his international fame, acquired in the course of
a brief career and sanctioned by history.*

☐ Portrait of Porzia Imperiale with her daughter Maria Francesca

At the age of twenty-two, after a short sojourn in
England, van Dyck undertook a six year long journey to
Italy. He stayed over a year in Genoa, a prosperous
trading centre where commissions were abundant. This
Portrait of Porzia Imperiale with her daughter Maria Francesca
stems from that period. The low angle view enforces
the Lady's majesty. In this rather bombastic staging, the
somewhat withdrawn but charming young woman is an
element of discreet appeal. The influence of Rubens is
very obvious in this superb portrait.

The painting is built around a diagonal and cleverly plays out
two colour areas against each other: the deep black of the
mother's dress on the one side, and the iridescent tonalities
of the young woman's portrait on the other, set out against
a bronze-coloured background, hinting at lavishness.

☐ François Duquesnoy (?)

Van Dyck met the sculptor François Duquesnoy in Rome
during his Cisalpine journey. It is very likely that this sober
representation familiarly portrays him, with psychological
shrewdness instead of pompous display. The overall tonality
is rather dark, and privileges the sensitive features with the
alert gaze and the elegant hand presenting a satyr's head.

4

4. *Anthony van Dyck*
**Jean-Charles
della Faille,**
*1629, canvas,
130.8 x 118.5, inv. 6254.*

● ANTHONY VAN DYCK
(1599-1641))
Son of a wealthy merchant
and an artist mother,
Anthony van Dyck was
admitted as a master at the
Antwerp Guild of St. Luke
at the age of nineteen. He
then worked for two years in
Rubens's workshop. He painted few mythological or historical representations, his
paintings' themes were more
often religious. But he
achieved fame through his
official portraits: his models
were the rulers and outstanding figures of the European
aristocracy. His career led
him to travel from Antwerp
to London, to Italy, to the
Hague, to Brussels, to Paris.
He became the first painter
to the King of England and
eventually died in London at
the age of forty-two, a
famous man. He was buried
there in the choir of St.
Paul's Cathedral. Rubens
had passed away just one
year earlier.

☐ **Rinaldo and Armida**

Van Dyck has executed the painting for the King of England
in 1629. The theme is taken from Torquato Tasso's
Gerusalemme liberata, a long epic poem of the previous century,
narrating the feats of arms of Rinaldo the crusader. The
enraptured Armida has found her sleeping lover at last.
This grisaille is two years younger than the painting at the
Museum of Fine Arts in Baltimore and is an accurate and faithful
copy thereof. Van Dyck painted it himself as a model for an
etching; engraving was the only means of distributing paintings
at the time, implying a transposition of the colour scheme to
an idiom of grey values. We can observe here how the artist
initiated this translation to a camaïeu of greys and beige. The
composition is still reminiscent of Rubens' manner, but van Dyck
moderated the Baroque exuberance with a touch of Classicism,
which also illustrates his somewhat distant character.

☐ **Jean-Charles della Faille**
(DELLA FAILLE DE LEVERGHEM DONATION)

Van Dyck painted this portrait of Reverend Father della
Faille of the Society of Jesus in 1629. As he returned from
Italy, he was appointed painter to the Court of Archduchess
Isabella. He had reached the peak of his career and the
pinnacle of his talent, and achieved over-whelming fame
and success. As a theologian and a mathematician, professor
at the Imperial College of Madrid, as a geographer, a
counselor of Philip IV for military architecture, and as tutor
of the Infant of Spain, Father Jean Charles della Faille was
a leading intellectual figure.
The cartographer's instruments, painted in bronze, determined
the character's status. The hand clasping the compasses links
the scientist's attributes to the stern and noble silhouette of
the religious figure, haloed with a subtle luminosity, set out
against an immaterial space. The fine, slender face under the
imposing biretta—focal point from which the entire brightness
of the painting seems to radiate—asserts itself through the
spiritual and intellectual power emanating from it.

● The donation of Count
Georges della Faille de
Leverghem.
In 1942, Count della Faille
de Leverghem donated
thirty-seven paintings
stemming from the 16th to
the 19th centuries to the
Museum.
Three of these were
portraits by Sir Anthony
van Dyck.

1. Jacob Jordaens
**Satyr and
the Peasant**,
*ca. 1640/1645, canvas,
130 x 172, inv. 588.*

2. Jacob Jordaens
**Satyr and
the Peasant**,
*ca. 1620/1621, canvas,
188.5 x 168, inv. 6179.*

3. Jacob Jordaens
**Allegory of
Fertility**,
*canvas, 180 x 241,
inv. 119.*

4. Jacob Jordaens
The King Drinks!
*canvas, 156 x 210,
inv. 3545.*

JACOB JORDAENS

Jacob Jordaens remained the most illustrious and significant representative of the Antwerp Baroque after Rubens' and Van Dyk. demise The Royal Museums own the master's most beautiful set of works.

☐ Satyr and the Peasant

Among the numerous Jordaens paintings kept in the Royal Museums, we find these two interpretations of the notorious fable by Aesop. The satyr is sitting at the peasant's table, and the latter first warms his hands by blowing upon them, then cools his soup by doing the same. The satyr refuses to remain in the house of a man who is blowing warm and cold with one and the same mouth. This form of sententious wisdom perfectly met the moral standards of that period's middle-class. Jordaens was very fond of such themes, with which he encountered success and appraisal, and they became recurrent in his work.

The two paintings have been executed at twenty years' interval. The 1620 version clearly acknowledges the influence of Carravaggio: common people were chosen as models, and *chiaroscuro* effects were used to stress the contrast. Jordaens was under thirty at the time, but he obviously had discovered what would remain his main objective: exaltation of light. In the second version, the group displays a goodhearted, easy going mood and is haloed by a cleverly distributed dusky light.

☐ Allegory of Fertility

In 1623, Jordaens painted one of the highlights of his œuvre, bursting with sensuality and blissful tenderness. The nymphs and the satyrs gather to make their offerings to Pomona, a Roman goddess who possessed an unequalled art of cultivating fruits and tending gardens. The marvellous abundance of fruit from the earth and the gorgeous splendour of the bodies unite in a pagan celebration of life, a praise of the lavishness of light.

The horizontal composition is distributed on either side of the

● JACOB JORDAENS
(1593-1678)
Jacob Jordaens was born in Antwerp in 1593, to a dealer in linen and textiles. He completed his apprenticeship in 1615 and was admitted as a master into the Antwerp Guild of St. Luke. From 1619 on, Jordaens was at the peak of his mastery, and the better part of his work was produced in the decades 1620-1640. He was a most versatile artist, and indiscriminately painted religious works, historical subjects, genre scenes or portraits, depending on the commissioners' desire. In 1635, under Rubens' supervision, he took part in the decorations for the 'Joyous Entry' of Cardinal-Infant Ferdinand of Austria into Antwerp. Two years later, he participated in the execution of the canvases for Torre de la Parada (cfr. p. 72), for which Rubens had painted the *modello's*. This was the first time he was commissioned by a royal house. Jordaens would henceforth enjoy a highly considered position in the Antwerp artistic sphere. He increased the number of his assistants, and his personal wealth grew: he had a superb house with a huge workshop built in Antwerp, and lived there until his very last day. In 1642, after Rubens' and van Dyck's demise, an even greater amount of orders came streaming in, and a more significant part of the work was entrusted to his collaborators. He lived for another thirty-six years, during which he devoted all his time to the sheer joy of painting. He died in 1678, on the same day as one of his daughters who lived with him, both stricken with the plague. As professed Calvinists, they were buried in the Protestant cemetery of Putte, beyond the Dutch border.

perpendicular axis of the nude nymph, seen from the back and drawing attention at first. The eye is then guided towards the exquisite modelling of the anatomies by the play with the highlights and the graduated shades. The crouching satyr on the left is an impetuous masterpiece of Jordaens' virtuosity at its best.

☐ *The King Drinks!*

This is a representation of the traditional "King's feast" on the day of the Epiphany, still celebrated in Flanders nowadays, although in Jordaens' day, this celebration implied gargantuan banqueting. The painter is more than familiar with this wealthy merchants' social sphere, as he stems from that circle and shares its customs.

The distribution of the figures within the overloaded composition of this tight congregation brings Jordaens' amazing know-how to the fore. On either side of the central figure of the 'king', two opposite, inverted right-angled triangles determine the painting's structure. The joyous exuberance of the mimicry and hands is a counterpart for the strict geometry, constraining the characters and stifling their gesticulation. Intruding from the right, the light models the faces' relief, gives the space its depth and transforms materials as it makes them glisten with sheen and reflections.

1. *David II Teniers*
The Flemish Kermesse,
*1652, canvas, 157 x 221,
inv. 1841.*

2. *David II Teniers*
The Card Players,
wood, 28 x 40, inv. 6515.

● DAVID II TENIERS
(1610-1690)
David Teniers the Younger
stemmed from an artists'
family in Antwerp, and was
admitted as a master in
1632. Five years later, he
married Anna, the daughter
of 'Velvet' Brueghel. He
showed little concern for the
Baroque trend that had
reached its peak in Flanders
at the time. He was attached
to the Flemish tradition of
genre painting. He was
appointed official court
painter to the Archduke
Leopold-William, then
Governor of the Low
Countries, in 1651. His
career was crowned with
success and he lived to be
eighty years in agreeable
material comfort.

DAVID II TENIERS

☐ The Flemish Kermesse

Scenes of peasants rejoicing have often been depicted in
Flemish painting. David Teniers owes the better part of his
fame to representations of such festivities. In this very
beautiful Flemish Kermesse, his acute sense of observation
enabled him to stage individuals with genuine gestures, totally
engrossed in the present moment. On the foreground, four
aristocratic figures have just come off a stage-coach to join
the party. The painter may well have pictured his own likeness,
accompanied by his wife, and the manor set out against the
glistening golden sunset sky may be "De Drie Torens", the
residence he had acquired thanks to his brilliant success.

☐ The Card Players

This is one of the recurrent themes in 17th genre painting.
Teniers deals with it with overwhelming mastery of the
psychology of the faces and the realism of the postures, and
particularly for his study of the light. A soft light falls straight
on both players, modelling their features, detailing the drapery
of the costumes, skimming the ledges of the furniture and
brushing a reflection on each object of the setting. The
fireplace is a second source of light, giving depth to the painting.

ADRIAEN BROUWER

☐ Flute player

Never mind the reason for which the flute player interrupts
his music to gaze at us with that impudent grin: all anecdotal
elements aside, the character's expression definitely takes
the spectator aback.

☐ Seated Drinkers

By moving the seated drinkers away from the traditional
cabaret where one would expect to encounter them and
transferring them to an indefinable setting, Adriaen
Brouwer turns a genre painting into an enigmatic
composition. What is the squalid shack where uncouth

4

5

characters take to cheerless drinking? Perhaps a farmyard? Moreover, what is the role of the elegant man, whose cloak and hat reflect the setting sun's warm hues, the only patch of light in the dull harmony of this dreary landscape? Instead of describing the situation in a picturesque way, Brouwer has chosen to express a form of disenchantment through his small painting.

PEETER NEEFS THE ELDER

☐ *Interior of Antwerp Cathedral in daylight*
The two different versions of the interior of the Antwerp cathedral are outstanding examples of the work of Pieter Neefs the Elder, an eminent representative of the Antwerp School of the first half of the 17th century. He specialised in architectural painting and was the foremost church interior painter of his time. The scenes he depicted also constitute a very accurate documentation on the cathedral's daily life. One can see the ceremonial the priest observes as he brings the Eucharistic species to a bedridden person. In the nave, a group of passers-by have come to attend a low mass; one of them is a housewife with her shopping basket. On the right-hand side of the foreground, a bunch of beggars and lame ask for charity.

The figures are outlined with a crafty brush and have expressive attitudes. But the representation of the faces lacks detail, the characters are mere walk-ons. The building has been rendered with far greater minutiae. The faithful perspective—aim of this pictorial genre—increases the sense of depth, almost to vertigo.

3. Adriaen Brouwer
Flute player,
*copper, 16.5 x 13,
inv. 3464.*

4. Adriaen Brouwer
Seated Drinkers,
oak, 25.5 x 21, inv. 2854.

5. Peeter Neefs the Elder
Interior of Antwerp Cathedral in daylight,
wood, 59 x 84, inv. 1355.

● ADRIAEN BROUWER
(1605/06-1638)
Probably born in Oudenaarde, Adriaen Brouwer is assumed to have been a pupil of Frans Hals during his sojourn in Haarlem and Amsterdam, at the age of twenty. He was the painter of the inns and of the common people, with whom he always mingled, and he drew his inspiration from Bruegel's characters. But he

asserted his individuality very soon. His sense of observation gained finesse, and he became one of the most penetrating witnesses of the human soul. He was a highly educated man, a member of the Rhetoric's Chamber, renowned and appreciated by his peers: Rubens owned seventeen of his paintings, Rembrandt eight, and van Dyck portrayed him in a proud and dignified attitude.

He returned to Flanders in 1631 and settled in Antwerp, where he was registered as a freemaster. But either because he had incurred too many debts, or because he was suspected of intelligence with the Union of the Seven Provinces, he was imprisoned in 1633. When he was released, he became dependent of a number of fellow artists. He died at the early age of thirty-three.

1. Jan van Goyen
View of Dordrecht,
1644 and 1653, canvas,
97 x 148, inv. 2823.

2

● JAN VAN GOYEN
(1596-1656))
He was born in Leiden to a
cobbler and amateur painter,
and completed his appren-
ticeship at the age of twenty-
two.His first known work is
a landscape, dated 1620. He
devoted himself to this genre
for his entire lifetime, and
his work is a significant link
in the development of
Netherlandish landscape
painting. Besides his artistic
career, he ventured in diver-
se commercial speculations
that led him into severe
material inconveniencies.
But this did not prevent him
from leaving a considerable
graphic œuvre of about nine
hundred paintings.

● JACOB ISAACKSZ.
VAN RUYSDAEL
(1628/29-1682)
Jacob van Ruysdael was born
in Haarlem, where he was
registered at the Guild of St.
Luke. He was the nephew of
the renowned landscapist
Salomon van Ruysdael and
was marked by his strong personality. He settled in
Amsterdam in 1656, as the
opportunities for artists occurred more frequently there
than in his native town. He
never became really wealthy
but succeeded to live off his
art rather comfortably, as his
painting was quite respected.

The Dutch Golden Century

The seven Northern provinces of the Netherlands broke loose from the Spanish yoke and achieved independence with the Union of the Seven Provinces. This new democratic and Protestant republic soon flourished and attained commercial prosperity. As the Calvinist doctrine did not tolerate the presence of religious images in places of worship, Dutch artists found their commissioners in the recent circles of the wealthy upper middle-class merchants. They mostly ordered easel paintings, such as portraits, genre scenes, still lifes and landscapes.

JAN VAN GOYEN

☐ *View of Dordrecht*

Jan van Goyen painted this View of Dordrecht in 1644, at the peak of his talent. It was his favourite subject: if we only count the paintings, we find that he has treated it thirty-seven times—with a number of variants—during the last eighteen years of his life. These paintings followed drawings on this motif, and were free interpretations of reality. The requirements of the composition determined his choice of the details and their layout. What these works had in common was the development of a very low horizon line, three quarters of the painting's surface being occupied by cloudy skies. In this view, Van Goyen succeeds in conveying a sense of depth by an astute graduation of the perspective levels of the characters, the crafts on the river and the edifices on the land. The composition's rhythm and structure are partly dependent on the light patches the clouds define on the water, with a broad, dark strip on the foreground.

JACOB ISAACKSZ. VAN RUYSDAEL

☐ *Landscape with River*

Jacob van Ruysdael exclusively painted Holland, and the better part of his work was devoted to water landscapes. In this *Landscape with River*—where the figures were painted by A. van de Velde—the artist cleverly plays with dusky light to accentuate volumes and model the clouds.

3

4

2. *Jacob Isaacksz.van Ruisdael*
Landscape with River,
canvas, 135 x 179, inv. 1177.

3. *Jacob Isaacksz.van Ruisdael*
Seascape,
canvas, 55 x 65, inv. 1794.

☐ **Seascape**
In this *Seascape*, the force of the elements is dramatised by the large part of the painting occupied by a densely overcast sky. On the foreground, the wharf is beaten by the frothing waves. Staged on the middle ground, on the horizon, the boats are rocked and buffeted by the raging winds, an eloquent image of the precarious destiny of the populations that live in unison with the sea and are so dependent on its mood.

FRANS HALS

☐ **Three children and a cart drawn by a goat**
This painting is the separated right part of a larger horizontal canvas. The wider left part belongs to a British collection. A couple and its seven children are depicted here, familiarly sitting on the ground in front of a shrub. When assembled, these two canvases constitute a family portrait, staging three more children coming back from a walk to join their family, gathered before the painter. The upper middle-class governed the Northern Netherlands and was particularly fond of family portraits. They ostentatiously echoed their wealth and power, and at the same time celebrated the family virtues such as fertility and faithfulness. Frans Hals had not reached the age of forty when he painted this group, but he was already regarded as the foremost portrait painter of Haarlem's middle-class. His talent brilliantly comes to right as he depicts the lavish bliss of these children at their sunday best.
The whole is dominated by the overall darker hues, highlighted by the crimson cheeks, the ruff's whites and the delicately sheared lace of the headdresses. Other noticeable elements are the harmonious combination of subdued tonalities in the boy's costume and the subtle accuracy of the rendering of the billygoat's fur, crowned with flowers.

4. *Frans Hals*
**Three children
and a cart
drawn by a goat**,
*canvas, 152 x 107.5,
inv. 4732.*

● FRANS HALS
(1582/83-1666)
Frans Hals was born in Antwerp in 1582 or 1583. His family emigrated to Haarlem three years later, where Frans Hals was a member of the Guild of St. Luke in 1610. His first marriage was celebrated in that same year, and his first acknowledged work dates from the following year. Thanks to an exceptionally long lifetime—he lived to become eighty-four years old—his career was spread across more than half of his century. He was the favourite portrayer of Haarlem's burgess, but aimed to achieve a more condensed expression in his later work, which hauled him up to the level of his illustrious peer: Rembrandt.

● REMBRANDT
HARMENSZ. VAN RIJN
(1606-1669)
Harmen Gerritszoon van
Rijn, a miller in Leiden, had
ten children. His ninth child
was born on 15 July 1606,
and he named that son
Rembrandt. As he was particularly gifted, he attended
Latin school and then registered with the University of
Leiden at the age of fourteen. But he soon gave up
his studies to become the
apprentice of a painter of his
native town. He seemed to
have started working for his
own account from the age
of nineteen. He settled in
Amsterdam in 1631, where
he became a highly valued
portrait artist very soon,
quite appreciated by the
middle class. This by no
means prevented him from
dealing with historical painting, religious themes and
mythology. He was at the
peak of his career when he
purchased a luxurious residence in the Breestraat. He
developed his original creativity for another thirty
years, underpinned by an
accomplished craftsmanship
blended with incomparable
spiritual depth. He passed
away in 1669.

☐ **Portrait of Johannes Hoornbeek**
This likeness of Johannes Hoornbeek, who has just been
appointed as a professor in Theology at the University of
Leiden, is a work that stems from Frans Hals' mature period, as he was aged sixty-three.
In this painting, he demonstrates his accomplished skill in his dea-
lings with blacks and greys, due to which the hand and face assert
themselves. With a deliberate scarcity of means, he concentrates
the entire psychological strength of his model there.

REMBRANDT HARMENSZ. VAN RIJN

☐ **Portrait of Nicolaas van Bambeeck**
Rembrandt portrayed this wealthy merchant from
Amsterdam as well as his wife (the latter is kept at
Buckingham Palace) in 1641. He was at the peak of fame
and the famous Night Watch of the Rijksmuseum of
Amsterdam was in preparation. The character is standing
in three-quarter view, his right arm bent in a posture of
quiet self-assurance without display, his gaze firm without
being arrogant. The artist leans his model's elbow on the
crosspiece of a frame which simultaneously defines a realistic and an immaterial space; within this space, a subtle
play with light envelops and models the subject.
The facture handles the felt's lightness and the hair's impalpable
texture with delicate accuracy. The carnation is rendered with
finesse and the artist resorts to the finest draftsmanship to ite-
mize the lace's precise point. Rembrandt fully achieves the
sober realism that typified Northern Netherlandish portraiture at the time, but in addition he had the genius to halo his
models with a particular light that seems to radiate from the
likeness itself.

3

NICOLAES MAES

☐ *Dreaming Old Woman*

Nicolaes Maes (1634-1693) lingers on the face of this elderly woman with a form of affection. She has put her lacemaker's cushion aside to read a book, but then removed her spectacles and abandoned herself to sleep or to reverie. Beyond the anecdote, this scene of genre painting is emblematic of the art of living many elderly people have attained through a daily practice of spirituality. And indeed, even though we cannot identify the open book on the woman's lap nor the volumes on the shelf, it is definitely a bible that is opened next to her lacework.

Nicolaes Maes remains a subtle portrait and genre painter. This painting reveals that he was a pupil of Rembrandt's. The generous stroke and pictorial matter set the characters out against a somber overall tonality. The light plays with the chiaroscuro effects, but is more dependent upon reality than Rembrandt's light was. It clearly outlines the carried shadows and highlights the interesting areas with great accuracy.

French and Italian 17th and 18th centuries

1

2

1. *Simon Vouet*
The Entombment,
*canvas, 108 x 119,
inv. 4531.*

2. *Simon Vouet*
**St. Charles Borromeo
praying for the plague
victims of Milan**,
*canvas, 360 x 260,
inv. 298.*

● SIMON VOUET
(1590 -1649)
Though born in Paris in
1590, Simon Vouet stayed
in Italy from 1612 to 1627,
mainly in Rome. He had
achieved fame by the time
he returned to Paris, where
he remained until his demise in 1649. He was commissioned for a vast number of
works in the course of those
twenty-two years and was
valued as one of the most
significant artists of his
time. The better part of his
work consists of larger allegoric or religious
compositions.

The French School

SIMON VOUET

☐ *The Entombment*

The burial of Christ's body has been entrusted to a couple
of angels, assisted by the Magdalen. This very free adaptation
of the Gospel stresses the relationship between Jesus and
the Magdalen, and that sinners are the first to be concerned
by Redemption. As he intended her to symbolise sinners,
the artist has conveyed a very sensuous image of the
Magdalen here. The Virgin and St. John remain inconspicuous
in the semi-darkness on the left, and the holy woman kneeling
at the right only plays a secondary role in this scene.

The overall tonality of this painting is rather subdued, but a luminous diagonal of light colours crosses the picture with a versatile series of curvaceous forms, from the Magdalen's dress to the
unfurled wing of the angel at the top right-hand side. This outspokenly Baroque structure is maintained within the framework
of the canvas. French painting succeeded to blend lyricism with
a certain moderation, as this work masterfully illustrates.

☐ *St. Charles Borromeo praying for the plague victims of Milan*

This painting is exposed in the staircase at the exit of room 50.

This superb composition depicts a particularly popular
episode of the life of St. Charles Borromeo. He had been
the Archbishop of Milan and an important figure of the
Counter-Reformation, and was canonized in 1612. St.

3

3. *Philippe de Champaigne*
Presentation to the Temple,
1648, canvas, 257 x 197, inv. 25.

Charles, encouraged by a gesture of the angel accompanying him, kneels and implores the Heavens. Surrounded by putti, Christ and the Virgin appear in a cloud in order to answer his prayer and command the exterminating angel—seen on the middle ground—to sheathe his sword.

This play with contrast between the verticality of the columns and the diagonal by which the bishop is linked to the celestial world, between the static layout of the architectural elements and the motion of the enlivened characters was a widespread pattern in 17th century Baroque.

PHILIPPE DE CHAMPAIGNE

☐ Presentation to the Temple

The scene echoes a passage from the Gospel according to St. Luke:"Now there was a man in Jerusalem, whose name was Simeon [...]. The Holy Spirit had told him that he should not see death before he had seen the Lord's Christ [...]. And when the parents brought the child Jesus [...], he took him up in his arms and blessed God and said:'Lord, now lettest thou thy servant depart in peace, according to thy word; for mine eyes have seen thy salvation.' [...]. And there was a prophetess, Anna [...]. And coming up at that very hour she gave thanks to God, and spoke of the child to all who were looking for the redemption of Jerusalem." Philippe de Champaigne pictures Simon has he gives thanks to the Lord, carrying the Child in his arms. On the right-hand side, the prophetess points at Jesus. Mary is on the left, while Joseph brings the two turtledoves for the ritual sacrifice.

When Philippe de Champaigne painted this canvas for the high altar of the St. Honoré Church in Paris, he had reached his full maturity. The faces and gestures of Simeon and the group on the right may be reminiscent of Flemish painting, but those references are well processed within the coherence of a style. This applies to Raphael's obvious influence on the ample composition, unfurled around the median axis of the painting. Philippe de Champaigne has offered his well-balanced Classicist art to serve Counter-Reformation.

● PHILIPPE DE CHAMPAIGNE (1602-1674)

Philippe de Champaigne was born in Brussels in 1602. He had been an apprentice to several South Netherlandish painters, but refused to enter Rubens' workshop in 1621. He then took on a journey to Italy, but halted in Paris, where he was appointed for the decoration of the Palais du Luxembourg. In 1628, he took office as "ordinary painter" to he Queen Mother Mary de' Medici and as a manservant to king Louis XIII. As Richelieu's favourite painter, he was commissioned for religious works for churches and religious orders, so that he became a specialist of sacred art, but he was also highly valued as a portrait artist by the French aristocrats. Led by his natural inclination towards spiritual austerity, he became involved with the Jansenists of Port-Royal from 1646 on.

● Claude Gellée,
named Le Lorrain
(1600-1682)
Claude Gellée was born in 1600 in Chamagne, near Toul in Lorraine, and that is where his surname originated from. He stayed in Rome very early, between his twelfth and twentieth year, first as a servant, then as a pupil of the painter Agostino Tassi. He stayed in Rome until his demise in 1682, and has asserted himself as one of the foremost masters of classicist landscape painting.

● Hubert Robert
(1733-1808)
Born in Paris, Hubert Robert arrived in Rome at the age of twenty-one and lived there for eleven years. He became acquainted with Giovanni Paolo Pannini—a famous painter of views of Rome, blending fantasy and reality—and with his fellow countryman Jean Honoré Fragonard, with whom he often practiced his draftsmanship. He brought a number of sanguine sketches of ruins and gardens back to Paris in 1765, and based himself on these drawings for his paintings of the next ten years. In his later work, he drew inspiration from the scenery of Paris or from French antique monuments.

1. *Claude Gellée, named Le Lorrain*
Aeneas Hunting Deer on the Libyan Coast,
canvas, 112 x 157.5, inv. 1480.

2. *Hubert Robert*
Fountain and Colonnade in a Park,
1775, canvas, 244.3 x 216.8, inv. 7021.

CLAUDE GELLÉE, NAMED LE LORRAIN

☐ *Aeneas Hunting Deer on the Libyan Coast*
The painting depicts a passage from Vergilius' Aeneid. Aeneas, the Trojan prince, managed to escape when the city was seized by the Greek. During his long quest for a new land, his ships were thrust against the Libyan shore by a storm. In order to feed his companions of adventure, Aeneas killed seven deer. A pale sun gives the painting a subtle, diffused light, against which the rocks and trees are set out sharply, on either side of the vista leading to the pacified sea beyond the cove in which the ships are sheltering. With a serene sense of poetry, the scene illustrates restored harmony between man and nature.

The Legend of Aeneas was one of the favoured themes of Le Lorrain's commissioners. He executed this painting in 1672 for his latest generous patron, a Roman prince named Paolo Francesco Falconieri. Aged seventy-two, the artist was still at the peak of his talent.

HUBERT ROBERT

☐ *Fountain and Colonnade in a Park*
The shrubby growth under which the shabby entablature of an imposing colonnade vanishes does not prevent the late afternoon light from soothing the remains of its one-time splendour. Opposite the ruins, the lively jet of water of the fountain contrasts with the ramshackle architecture. The tiny figures engrossed in silent dreams or conversations play a minor part in this graceful scene, whereas the monumental setting focuses most of the attention.

4

3. *Carlo Maratta*
**Apollo Pursuing
Daphne**,
*1681, canvas,
221.2 x 224, inv. 269.*

4. *Luca Giordano*
Nativity,
*canvas, 187.5 x 278,
inv. 11633.*

The Italian School

CARLO MARATTA

☐ *Apollo Pursuing Daphne*

Since one of Cupid's arows had pierced him, Apollo had no further concern than his fiery love for the nymph Daphne. But she had taken the vow of chastity and fled his zealous advances. Apollo joined her just as she reached the Peneas river, of which her father was the tutelary divinity. He changed his daughter to a laurel in order to save her. The artist depicts the moment when the nymph's feet become the laurel's roots and her fingers are transformed into branches. Cupid hovers above the scene, apparently satisfied to be behind this metamorphosis.

Carlo Maratta (1625-1713) entered Andrea Sacchi's workshop at a very young age and remained there until his master's death in 1661. This circle, with which Poussin was also familiar, led him to develop a concept of painting based on classicism and tinted with intellectualism. This canvas perfectly illustrates this, filled as it is with references to Antique sculpture and to litterature. Maratta painted it in 1681, commissioned by Louis XIV, which attests that his fame had crossed the frontiers. He included more Baroque trends in his later work, and this synthesis made him one of the most significant Roman painters of the end of the 17th and the beginning of the 18th centuries.

LUCA GIORDANO

☐ *Nativity*

On the right side of the painting, within the triangle determined by the diagonal continued by the ox's backline, the crib's characters are gathered in ascending order. The flight path of the angel—bearing the scroll to the glory of God—is parallel to that diagonal, and this line produces the painting's impetus. The delicate blue and grey shades of the angel's tunic contrast with the glittering splashes of celestial gold, flinging the composition open upon infinity. Though outspokenly Baroque, this work cleverly balances the sense of intimacy of the Nativity group against the majesty of the angel, surrounded by a cohort of putti appearing through the clouds.

● LUCA GIORDANO
(1634-1705)

Luca Giordano was the son of a Napolitean painter, and he travelled all over Italy, as his predecessors had traditionally done. He developed an outstandingly masterful style and became one of the most renowned decorators of the late Baroque. He achieved overwhelming success in his own lifetime, in Italy as well as in Spain, where he was active for about ten years. Some three thousand works have been attributed to Giordano, including easel paintings and fresco's. This considerable output implies that he had to resort to a number of assistants, who have shown unevenness in the quality of their collaboration.

1

2

1. *Jusepe de Ribera*
Apollo Flaying Marsyas,
*1637, canvas, 202 x 255,
inv. 3445.*

2. *Giovanni Francesco
Barbieri, named Il Guercino*
**Giuseppe Gaetano
Righetti (?)
presented to the Virgin
by Four Saints**,
*canvas, 309 x 192,
inv. 266.*

● JUSEPE DE RIBERA
(1591-1652)
Jusepe de Ribera left
Spain—his native coun-
try—very early and never
returned. After staying in
Rome for some time, he
settled in Naples in 1616
and remained there for the
rest of his days. His fame
grew steadily. At first he
worked after Caravaggio's
manner, particularly fond of
sharp light effects in somber
backgrounds. His palette
became lighter from 1635,
and he introduced more
momentum in his composi-
tions. Ribera is one of the
major figures of the
Baroque.

JUSEPE DE RIBERA
☐ *Apollo Flaying Marsyas*
According to Ovidius' *Metamorphoses*, the satyr Marsyas
had cheekily prided himself on playing the flute even better
than Apollo played the lyre. The latter had defied him in a
contest, which he had obviously won, and Marsyas was
condemned to be flayed alive. The god is shown as he
serenely skins his shrieking victim, lying in pain with
outstretched arms. At the right, under a branch from which
a flute is dangling, his fellow satyrs sympathise with their
tortured peer. The contest's instruments lie abandoned on
the left foreground, but the antique horn aulos has been
replaced by a recorder and the classical Greek lyre has
become an Italian *lira da gamba*, still used in Baroque music
at the time. Apollo is crowned with a laurel wreath in
remembrance of Daphne.

Two predominant aspects of Ribera's manner are combined in
this accomplished work, stemming from the painter's maturity.
The satyr's tortured body is rendered with almost unbearable
realism and highlighted with a fine series of *chiaroscuro*-effects,
reminiscent of Caravaggio. However, the painter's more dynamic
trend is illustrated by Apollo's slender luminous figure, draped in
the garment's red arabesque.

GIOVANNI FRANCESCO BARBIERI, NAMED IL GUERCINO
☐ *Giuseppe Gaetano Righetti (?)
presented to the Virgin by Four Saints*
Four saints are calling a kneeling young man to the Madonna's
attention; he is wearing luxurious clothes, but he cannot be

3

3. *Giovanni Battista Tiepolo*
The Three Theological Virtues,
*octogonal canvas,
38.1 x 38.8, inv. 6869.*

identified beyond doubt. Behind him, probably because he is the donor's holy patron, St. Joseph goes down on bended knee. The bishop wearing a mit reis likely to either be St. Nicholas, or St. Augustine. On the middle ground, we recognize St. Francis of Assisi, opposite St. Louis, the king of France, who emphatically attempts to draw the onlooker's gaze towards the celestial apparition.

Il Guercino (1591-1666) has painted this canvas for the Church of Sant'Agostino of his native town Cento, probably in 1616. He demonstrates his subtle masterliness of composition by balancing both major areas on either side of an ascending oblique, linking the heads of St. Joseph and St. Francis. Every single character acquires an own relief through individual lighting, sharply contrasting with the overall ambient light scheme. In certain places, as for instance on the band of angels, he vividly accentuates the play with light and shade. Il Guercino became one of the masters of Italian Baroque due to his expressive talent, well typified in this representative work of his earlier period.

GIOVANNI BATTISTA TIEPOLO

☐ The Three Theological Virtues

Faith seems to soar above the other two theological virtues with gleaming, airy drapery and cloud-like haze. Her face is veiled, and her blind certitude links her to the heavens, as well as her unconditional engagement to the cross. Charity, fondling a grateful putto, raises her eyes in a spirit of offering; she still belongs to this world here below, her shades are more subdued. This applies to Hope as well: her attribute is a ship's anchor, replacing the vessel with all sails unfurled that was often used to symbolize Christian Hope.

In 1754, Tiepolo was commissioned for three fresco's in the new church of Santa Maria de l'Ospedale della Pietà in Venice, a hospital where Vivaldi had been teaching music to young orphans. He had made this dazzling sketch as a *modello* for the project of the medallion of the Three Theological Virtues he wanted to present to the commissioners. Brisk, lively strokes were used to apply the the light shades, contrasting with the more accurate draftsmanship of the darker group. The whole melts into an eloquent plastic idiom where metaphysical meaning transcends the decorative aspect.

● GIOVANNI BATTISTA TIEPOLO
(1696-1770)
Giovanni Battista Tiepolo was Venetian by birth and by culture, and he was to lead the Serene Republic's decorative art to its utmost representation. His earliest major fresco's date back to 1725, when he was twenty-nine years of age. Henceforth his reputation grew throughout Europe: He was summoned to decorate the imperial room and the grand staircase of the palace of the Prince-Bishops of Würzburg on the Main around 1750. When he returned to Venice towards the end of 1753, he undertook several major achievements in Italy, among which the fresco's for the church of Santa Maria della Pietà. He responded to the king of Spain's demand in 1761 and went to work in Madrid until his demise.

1

● Giuseppe Maria Crespi (1665-1747)
Crespi was one of the foremost painters of the Bolognese School. Aside from several paintings with religious and mythological themes, the better part of his work was devoted to representations of daily life.

● Francesco Guardi (1712-1793)
Francesco Guardi was born to a family of Venetian painters in 1712. He was active in his elder brother's workshop until the age of forty-eight; the latter's demise marked the beginning of his independence. He was famous for his views of Venice and of the backwaters of the lagoon, which occupied the major part of his life and work. But he is also the painter who first discovered how much very moist air would refract light and fade the contours of shapes. He conveys the almost immaterial aspect of his *vedute* by litterally capturing luminous vibrations.

GIUSEPPE MARIA CRESPI

☐ *The Trojan Women tearing Polymnestor's Eyes out*
During the Trojan war, Hecuba, king Priam's widow, had entrusted her youngest son and the city's treasure to her son-in-law Polymnestor, King of Thrace. But he had seized the treasure, murdered the young boy and thrown his corpse in the sea. When she was informed, Hecuba set a trap for the traitor. She is depicted as she tears his eyeballs out, assisted by another Trojan woman.

The painter brilliantly demonstrates his masterly sense of composition: he balances the figures on either side of the canvas' diagonal and gives them the fierce impetus of violent action, though the character's size is almost equal to the height of the painting. He sustains the sense of motion by imprinting movement to the draperies as far as the background, where the folds dissolve in the shadow. The light sharply sets the figures out against the somber, vaguely defined setting, and the entire scene is staged with expressive intensity. The subtle, refined hues and the delicate rendering of the materials strangely contrast with the cruel agressivity of the action.

FRANCESCO GUARDI

☐ *Doge Alvise IV Mocenigo appears in the Basilica of San Marco, 1763*
In 1763, Venice celebrated the coronation of doge Alvise IV Mocenigo. Between 1766 and 1770, Francesco Guardi executed a series of 12 Venetian Festivals after the etchings of the engraver Brustolon to commemorate the event. After the lengthy election procedure, the new doge is being led to the basilica of St. Mark, where he takes the oath before he is presented to the Venetian citizens from the top of the southern Chair. Guardi depicts the enthusiasm of the crowd that has gathered in the church. The people are everywhere: in the arcades, in the nave, in the aisles and standing on the columns' bases.

Guardi endows the basilica's atmosphere with a sense of unity by melting ochres and roses in a gold light. He renders the omnipresent swarm of characters with unequalled mastery by means of series of abundant, sparkling and vivacious brushstrokes.

3

JACOPO ROBUSTI, NAMED IL TINTORETTO

☐ **St. Mark's Body carried away by the Christians**

Mark, the Evangelist, is said to have been converted by the apostle Peter and to have been summoned to develop a Christian community in Alexandria. In the course of his assignment, he was arrested by the pagans, and according to the Golden Legend, "he was dragged through the streets of the city like an ox being led to the slaughterhouse. His flesh was limply hanging down to the ground, his blood watered the pavement." He was thrown in gaol, and passed away on the following day, when the torture was repeated. "And when the pagans wanted to burn the martyr's body, the air blurred out, it started raining hailstones, the thunder rolled and lightning bolts flashed, all this to such an extent that all had to flee, leaving St. Mark's body unattended; and the Christians hurriedly abducted the corpse and buried him as a holy man in his own church.

This sketch was probably made at the same time as the series executed for the Scuola di San Marco, but it does not seem to have introduced a finished canvas. The painter has indeed dealt with the same subject in a larger painting—presently kept at the Galleria dell'Accademia in Venice—whereby a lengthy architectonic perspective replaces the raging flood which almost drowns the square in this version. The technical freedom enabled by the sketch gives the scene additional dramatic dynamics, accentuated by the black outline of the figures. The light radiating from the martyr focuses the attention on him.

● JACOPO ROBUSTI, NAMED IL TINTORETTO (1518-1594)
He was the son of a Venetian dyer, and that is where his surname stemmed from: 'Tintoretto' means 'the dyer's little one'. Tintoretto was an autodidact who developed his own style and achieved fame. Between 1562 and 1568, he painted a series of three huge canvases for the Scuola di San Marco. From 1564 to 1588, he achieved his greatest work: the decoration of another major Venetian institute, the Scuola di San Rocco. His output remained evenly significant until his death, and placed him right at the peak of Venetian Mannerism.

Modern
Art

19th century

The French Revolution has brought about a number of significant institutional upheavals that have branded the 19th century. Liberalism, democracy and national awareness have replaced the values of the Old Régime.

Within this entangled set of phenomena, the rise of the middle-class—quite eager to take the place of aristocracy—exerted a decisive influence upon artistic development. New commissioners appeared, other patrons, prompted by new ideas.

Trends, movements and aesthetic doctrines succeeded one another at the same frenzied rate as society was overwhelmed by changes. Neoclassicism referred to the Antique, producing ideological models to which the French Empire could relate.

Romanticism drew its inspiration from local legends and from highlights of mediaeval history, and its development was simultaneous throughout Europe. It urged emotional values and supported patriotic struggles.

Realism tallied with the economic growth of industrial society and its concomitant proletarianization. It asserted itself towards the middle of the century, radically breaking away from the Romantic concept of heroic art inspired by remote history. Realism focused on man and on his daily life, and nature painting was applied to real and existing things.

Impressionism developed around 1872, considering itself as a merely aesthetic continuation of Realism, denying any ideological link.

Symbolism appeared throughout Europe in the course of the two last decennia of the century. Unlike the artists of the previous trends, having worked out a style, Symbolists rejected every aesthetic dictate or technique and attempted to convey their own poetic intuitions.

1. *Gilles-Lambert Godecharle*
Jeanne Catherine Offhuys, wife of Gilles-Lambert Godecharle,
vers 1807, plaster of Paris, 65 X 40 X 29, inv. 2723.

● GILLES-LAMBERT GODECHARLE (1750-1835) Godecharle was born in the middle of the 18th century and became a pupil of Laurent Delvaux, supporter of the Baroque aesthetic dictates, who undoubtedly had a permanent influence on him. From 1772 on, the empress Mary-Theresa of Austria —who ruled over the Southern Netherlands at the time— allocated a grant to the sculptor, enabling him to be active in Paris, in Berlin, in London and in Rome. He returned to Brussels in 1780, when his training was completed, and was commissioned for a significant amount of works. His two versions of *Justice rewarding virtue, protecting weakness and chasing vice away* (inv. 450-451), clay reductions for the fronton of the Palace of the Sovereign Council of Brabant (nowadays Palais de la Nation, in Brussels) attest his masterliness. The Southern Netherlands were annexed by France in 1792. Godecharle, who had achieved great fame, was overworked with private commissions. He then became Napoleon's sculptor, and found the time to execute his wife's bust. He later became William I 's official sculptor, when Holland took over Belgium's tenure in 1814 (inv. 3509). In the Southern Lowlands, Godecharle's work represents the transition between the Baroque and kindred styles of the *Ancien Régime* and Neoclassicism.

1

GILLES-LAMBERT GODECHARLE

☐ **Jeanne Catherine Offhuys, wife of Gilles-Lambert Godecharle**

This lively, engaging young woman had been the sculptor's companion before she became his wife, and it is no wonder that she captivated a husband thirty years older than she was. Godecharle was an outstanding portrayer, though still closely linked to the artistic dictates of the 18th century; this image of his spouse is full of charming sensitivity. The cheeky smile, the headdress with kiss curls and the plunging neckline call the *Empire*'s upstarts to mind, as they have been caricatured by Victorien Sardou in his famous comedy, *Madame Sans-Gêne*.

Neoclassicism

Towards the middle of the 18th century, the exuberance of Rococo aroused a deep-seated dislike, to which Johann Joachim Winckelmann, an archaeologist from Saxony, drew up a theoretical framework. He published his famous History of the Art of the Ancients in Rome in 1764. Throughout Europe, young artists appropriated his decided views: one must draw an ideal vision of beauty from nature; the ancient Greek did this spontaneously because they were not confused by cultural patterns, and that is why they were the best of all models. To express this ideal of beauty, art ought to be serene and restrained. Twenty years later, Jacques-Louis David painted the Oath of the Horatii (Paris, Louvre). This composition, inspired from the Antique, privileges a static vision, confirms the superiority of draftsmanship above colour, and shows scrupulous concern for the realism of the rendering. It acquired the status of a sort of manifesto of Neo-Classicism. The movement expanded, asserted itself in most of Europe and as far as the United States. In France, Neoclassicism was used to convey the Revolution's ideals before it became the Empire's official artistic doctrine; from 1830, it finally gave way to Romanticism.

JACQUES LOUIS DAVID

☐ **Death of Marat**

Jean-Paul Marat was a brazen, radical revolutionary. He was nicknamed "l'Ami du Peuple" after a controversial newspaper of which he was the editor. In 1792, He was elected to represent Paris at the Convention, at which he seated in Danton's and Robespierre's group of the *Montagne*. Together with them, he played a decisive role in the exclusion of the opposing party of the *Girondins*. Charlotte Corday supported republican ideas but was a follower of the *Girondins*. She decided to have Marat assassinated because she considered

2

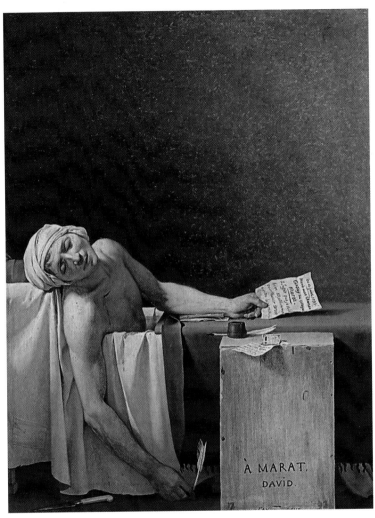

him to be the instigator of the massacres that seemed to lead the Revolution astray. On July 13, 1793, ushered into his house under pretext of disclosing information on a group of Girondins, she stabbed him to death. David was appointed to organise the funeral's pomp and to execute a memorial painting of Marat. As he suffered from a pruritus only a bath could relieve, Marat often worked in his tub. His head has collapsed now, his right hand has dropped to the ground, still clasping a quill. The painter has placed a letter written by his murderess in his left hand: "...my deepest Grief is all it Takes to be Entitled to your benevolence". A warrant and a note of Marat's hand lie on the chest he used as a working

2. *Jacques Louis David*
Death of Marat,
1793, oil on canvas,
165 x 128, inv. 3260.

1. *Jacques Louis David*
Venus disarming Mars,
*1824, oil on canvas,
308 x 265, inv. 3261.
Currently exhibited
at the forum*

● JACQUES LOUIS DAVID
(1748-1825)
Jacques Louis David was
born to a tradesman in Paris
in 1748, who died when he
was only nine. He received
the better part of his apprenticeship in Joseph-Marie
Vien's studio, then won the
Prix de Rome in 1774: a
sojourn in the French
Academy in Rome.
Subdued by the masters of
the Italian 17th century, by
Nicolas Poussin, and particularly by the growing artistic movement that departed
from Winckelmann's theo-
ries, he stayed there for five
full years. When he returned
to Paris in 1780, David had
reached the peak of his
maturity and fully determined the path of his career.
During the Revolution, he
became involved in the political struggle and offered his
talent to support his convic-
tions. As a member of the
Convention, he voted the
execution of Louis XVI in
1792, together with Marat.
As Superintendent of the
Fine Arts, he was also
nominated as the Master of
Ceremony of the revolutionary festivities. In 1815, the
second Restoration banished
all the regicidal members of
the Convention. David went
into exile in Brussels, where
he could count on a number
of admirers. He stayed there
until his demise in 1825,
and openly deviated from
his former aesthetic principles: he devoted his later
years to magnificent por-
traits and large paintings
inspired by mythology and
ancient litterature.

1

table: "You will give this warrant to that mother of five
children, whose husband died for the defense of our country."
Before this painting, David had selected his models in the pan-
theon of classic mythology. But this time, he chose to depict a
hero of contemporary history whose virtues he extolled and
whose ideal he shared, as ascertained by the dedication on the
foreground, intended as a signature. David had not been commissioned for this canvas—he donated it to the Convention—which
was a sort of memorial to his comrade in the struggle for the
Revolution's ideals. This martyr-like figure, bleeding from a wound
at the chest, is obviously reminiscent of Christ's sacrifice for the
sake of mankind. We feel compelled to focus on the character by
both the dull chromatic range, barely touched by the faint diffused
light, and by the unaffected austerity of the composition. In this
most powerful work, David idealized the hero within the stern framework of faithful realism. This painting marked the beginning of
the artist's long period of political involvement, which even lasted
during the Imperial tenure, right until Napoleon's fall.

☐ Venus disarming Mars

The entire scene is situated in the clouds of Mount Olympus.
Helped by Cupid and by the Three Graces, the goddess
strips Mars of his warrior's attributes to crown him with
flowers and offer him the rapture of nectar and the bliss of
love. During his exile in Brussels, the painter resigned from
political action and reverted to Ancient art. But the models
he drew from the Antique were not representative of Stoic
morals or civics anymore: he restricted himself to paint
superficially hedonic scenes.

With the help of several assistants, David worked on this large
painting—his ultimate work—from 1821 to 1824. He was still
fond of faithful, realist accuracy, and the models after which he
painted this canvas did not stem from the heritage of ancient
sculpture but from the stage of the Théâtre de la Monnaie. The
characters are charming, though a little dreary, and they are
indeed staged in a theatrical setting with dull and pretty colours.

2. *François-Joseph Navez*
**Portrait of the Painter
Louis David**,
*1817, oil on mahogany,
74.5 x 59.5, inv. 3262.*

3. *François-Joseph Navez*
**de Hemptinne Family
Portrait**,
*1816, oil on canvas,
150 x 127, inv. 3362.*

FRANÇOIS-JOSEPH NAVEZ

☐ Portrait of the Painter Louis David

This portrait is a slightly altered version of the one belonging to the Museum of Fine Arts of Valenciennes: David had not been satisfied with it because the flaw on his left cheek appeared to clearly. Navez has complied with the painter's wish, portrayed him anew and offered this likeness to him.

As in the majority of his portrayals, Navez' expertise rests on a sharp psychological observation of his model and on the keen and even craftsmanship he had acquired under David.

☐ de Hemptinne Family Portrait

This group portrays the artist's very close friends, who were also faithful patrons. The composition is centered around the little girl, and the succession of gestures stresses the couple's moral integrity. They clearly belong to the high society, as ascertained by the wealth of the fabrics and the distinguished attitudes. A variety of objects such as books, minerals and shells flatteringly hint at the commissioners' intellectual and aesthetic concerns.

Navez painted this family portrait when he returned from Paris with David, in 1816. Following his master's example, he ventures to resort to an entirely immaterial brownish background in order to focus all the attention on the figures. The characters' delicately differentiated expression, the perfect rendering of the draperies and the daring juxtaposition of green and blue in the centre of the composition turn this somewhat severe canvas about family virtues into a very beautiful achievement. The painting encountered immediate success and made Navez' reputation as a portrait artist. He was soon rewarded with quite a number of commissions.

● FRANÇOIS-JOSEPH NAVEZ (1787-1869) François-Joseph Navez was born in Charleroi in 1787, where his father was deputy mayor. He was a student at the Brussels Academy of Fine Arts from 1803 to 1808, where he was a pupil of P. J. C. François, who was an outspoken supporter of the Neoclassic dictates, even though he qualified his opinions. In 1813, Navez was impregnated with these ideas as he went to pursue his apprenticeship in Jacques-Louis David's workshop in Paris. He followed the latter back to Brussels when he went into exile in Brussels in 1816, but completed his training in Rome between 1817 and 1822. He then returned to Brussels (in 1822) and opened a workshop where he welcomed several pupils. Year after year, he accumulated honours and occupied important official positions, such as director of the Brussels Academy of Fine Arts. He passed away in 1869. The better part of his work consists of portraits, with which he had gained recognition from the beginning, and of huge compositions inspired by the Bible or by Ancient art. In the style he developed, Navez achieved a synthesis of his master David's teachings and of the purism of Jean-Auguste-Dominique Ingres and of the Nazarenes he had met in Rome. The evolution of taste had first placed him at odds with the upholders of Romanticism, then with the supporters of Realism towards the end of the century.

2   3

1. *François-Joseph Navez*
**Agar and Ismael
in the Desert**,
*1820, oil on canvas,
221 x 171, inv. 144.*

2. *François Rude*
**William 1, King
of the Netherlands**,
*1819, bust, bronze,
81.5 x 56 x 28.5,
inv. 2258.*

3. *Mathieu Kessels*
**The Discus
Thrower**,
*1822 ou 1823, statue,
plaster of Paris,
182 x 108.5 x 70.5,
inv. 484.*

4. *Jean Auguste Dominique
Ingres*
**August listening
to the Aeneid**,
*c. 1819, oil on canvas,
138 x 142, inv. 1836.*

● If the name of François
RUDE (1784-1855) sounds
familiar to every art lover, it
is due to the *Marseillaise*,
the high-relief at the base of
the Arc de Triomphe at
l'Étoile in Paris. It was
unveiled in 1836, a high-
light in the sculptor's career
when he was fifty-two
years of age.

☐ **Agar and Ismael in the Desert**
The theme stems from the Book of Genesis: Abraham's
wife Sarah had not borne him a child, so she offered that
he should perpetuate his name through Agar, her
Egyptian servant. That is how Ismael was conceived.
Fourteen years later, when Sarah was ninety, she was visited by Yahweh and conceived Isaac. She then cast Agar
and Ismael out, for "the son of this slave woman shall not
be heir with my son Isaac", she claimed. Abraham fired
them and they wandered off through the desert. When
they ran short of water, Agar "cast the child under one of
the bushes. Then she went and sat down [...] about the
distance of a bowshot, for she said, 'let me not look upon
the death of the child'." It is known that Yahweh saved
Ismael and made his descendants to a great nation. Agar
is pictured lost in the immenseness of the desert, staring
at the empty goatskin as she is about to abandon her
exhausted son.
Navez painted this canvas in 1820, during his stay in Rome,
where a group of German painters known as the Nazarenes
lived at the time. Their aim was to revive the idealism of the
quattrocento's Italian painters. Both their influence and David's
can be identified here. The graceful, simple line, the pallor of the
shades, the relief's attenuation and the static image combine
into an aesthetic transposition of the idea of maternal love. But
nothing compels us to share this mother's heartrending dilem-
ma at this tragic moment. However, Navez showed concern for
the realist representation his master had taught him and
remained scrupulous in his reconstitution of the costumes.

FRANÇOIS RUDE

☐ **William 1, King of the Netherlands**
After the Fall of the French Empire at Waterloo in 1815,
Brussels came under the authority of King William 1 of
Holland, and welcomed a great number of Bonapartists,
outlawed in France. Besides Jacques-Louis David, at the

4

peak of fame, one of them was an unknown young sculptor, François Rude. In order to assert himself in exile, the latter ventured to portray the king. This proved to be very difficult, because two renowned sculptors coveted that honour, and both had sculpted the ruler's bust: Gilles-Lambert Godecharle and Jean-François Van Geel. Rude started hanging about in all the places where he could catch a glimpse of William I, particularly the temple where he attended religious service on sunday morning. He would observe his model, then sketch him from memory. After a few months, he moulded a rough sketch and had it presented to the queen. She was enthralled and convinced the king to grant three posing sessions to the artist, who then had the privilege to carry out his project.

MATHIEU KESSELS

☐ The Discus Thrower

This original plaster cast was directly inspired from ancient sculpture and rigorously complied with Neoclassical dictates. It was hallowed enthusiastically. Kessels has produced a marble statue from it, and two bronze versions were cast long after his death; one can be seen near the Royal Museums, in the gardens of the Palais des Académies.

JEAN AUGUSTE DOMINIQUE INGRES

☐ August listening to the Aeneid

Vergilius devoted the last ten years of his life to the Aeneid, a great epic poem to idealize Roman national virtues. This tallied well with August's imperial policy, and he had the poem recited to him as its composition progressed. It is said that the emperor's sister Octavia fainted when the poet came to recite the passage depicting the death of her young son Marcellus.

● MATHIEU KESSELS
(1784-1836)
Mathieu Kessels originated from Maastricht, studied in Paris, then with an artist from Antwerp who had settled in St. Petersburg. He lived in Rome from 1819, where he became an assistant to Thorvaldsen. During the next fifteen years, he produced work of a refined facture, at first in the strictest spirit of Winckelmann's theories, then later loaded with a little more emotion (cfr. p. 20). He was very highly valued. After his demise, the Belgian Government acquired the whole series of works he had left in his Roman studio.

● JEAN AUGUSTE DOMINIQUE INGRES
(1780-1867)
Ingres was still very young when he became a pupil of David's. He undertook the traditional journey to Rome in 1806 and remained there for the next fourteen years, building up a faithful clientèle. This painting dates back to the end of that sojourn. Like his master, Ingres drew a great number of preliminary sketches from live models whom he asked to take on the inspired poses of ancient statuary. But the purity of the line typifies his work even more than the sculptural modelling of the anatomies. He considered the line to be superior to colour and balanced the momentum of his figures in a timeless equilibrium.

1. *Eugène Delacroix*
Apollo vanquishes the serpent Python,
c. 1850, oil on canvas, 137.5 x 102, inv. 1727.

2. *Théodore Géricault*
The Beheaded Man,
oil on canvas, 40.5 x 49.5, inv. 3725.

3. *Henri Leys*
The Spanish Fury in Antwerp,
1832-1836, oil on canvas, 91 x 160, inv. 3644.

● EUGÈNE DELACROIX (1798-1863) exhibited *The Massacre at Scio* (Paris, Louvre) at the Salon of 1824, asserting himself as a leading Romantic painter, a counterpart to Jean Auguste Dominique Ingres and the champions of Classicism. At the peak of glory from 1850 to 1861, he produced three major decorative works: one was the fresco on the central ceiling of the Louvre's Gallery of Apollo. The above painting is a sketch thereof, with remarkable freedom of colour and animation.

● THÉODORE GÉRICAULT (1791-1824) stands where the main trends of his time meet: between Jacques Louis David, whom he worshipped, and Eugène Delacroix, seven years his junior. His work, classicist like in *Nude studies* (inv. 6373), or passionately Romantic, as exemplified by *the Beheaded Man*'s (inv. 6373) morbid realism and *The Wreck*'s (inv. 3558) violence, was interrupted by an early death.

Romanticism

Romanticism appeared in England in the middle of the 18th, initially occurring in literature. It implied a fundamental break with Rationalism by allowing emotion to prevail. Under the Empire, French Romantic painters glorified the heroism of Napoleonic armies. Théodore Géricault and Eugène Delacroix introduced the pre-eminence of the vulnerability of man—thrust in the midst of present-day events—above the olympian serenity of ancient heroes. Romanticism asserted itself in Belgium with the advent of national independence, glamorized by Gustaf Wappers.

EUGÈNE DELACROIX
☐ *Apollo vanquishes the serpent Python*
Python, a monstrous serpent born from the flood, terrorised Delphi. When Apollo killed it, the city came under his yoke, enforced by the priestess who interpreted his oracles, the Pythia of Delphi. Apollo's blazing chariot appears in the dazzling sunlight, triumphantly crossing the clouds. Python, pierced by arrows, spits flames as he writhes in agony.

THÉODORE GÉRICAULT
☐ *The Beheaded Man*
Géricault's opus maius—*The Raft of the Medusa* (Paris, Louvre) — was inspired by a gruesome event that had occurred in 1816: hundred forty-nine castaways boarded a raft when the ship was wrecked, but only fifteen survivors were picked up after drifting for twelve days with neither food nor water. The artist's preparation of this huge canvas included numerous sketches and studies of details: he had

4

3

4. *Louis Gallait*
**Antiocha taken in by
the Crusaders**,
*1843, oil on canvas,
75 x 133.5, inv. 2717.*

● HENRI LEYS (1815-1869),
was a historical painter,
whose interest focused on
the events that had occurred
in Antwerp. This sketch
stemmed from his earlier
years, when he still gave
way to narrative vehemence
that was subdued in his
accomplished works. In his
thirties, emotions were overruled by documentary accuracy and static, scrupulous
minutiae. He was acknow-
ledged and appraised but
never had any followers.

observed hospitals' patients, and purchased corpses on
which post mortem examinations had to be performed.
He had obtained this head of a guillotined thief from a
doctor of Bicêtre. It is said that he kept it for two weeks
in order to follow the progress of decay.

HENRI LEYS

☐ The Spanish Fury in Antwerp
A paroxysm of the population of the Lowlands' eighty
year war against the occupying Spanish tenant: on
November 4, 1576, the Spanish military looted Antwerp,
killing over six thousand people and setting fire to five
hundred houses and to the Town Hall.

The painter has adopted a Baroque composition here: the
horizontal impetus of the fighters and of the buildings on the
right middle ground collides with the diagonal on the left
foreground, creating the overall sense of depth and the
dynamics of the painting. The vigorously shaded volumes and
the vivid brushstrokes of the sketch—in which the finishing
of detail has been neglected—animate this canvas with a
heroic spirit that relates it to Romanticism.

LOUIS GALLAIT

☐ Antiocha taken in by the Crusaders
Antiocha, founded in Asia Minor in the third century
B. C., had always been a prevalent city. A bastion of
Christianity, the Arabs occupied it for many years. The
Turks took Antiocha from Byzantium in 1084, but the
armies of the First Crusade took it back in 1098, on
their way to free Jerusalem. To the painter, this theme
was a pretext to unfurl picturesque exoticism.

● LOUIS GALLAIT
(1810-1887) When Louis
Gallait painted this canvas,
he was aged thirty-three and
had just acquired a steadily
increasing fame as a historical painter. Public
Institutions, the wealthy
upper middle-class, the king
of Belgium Leopold II and
the king of France Louis-
Philippe commissioned him
for historical paintings,
genre scenes and portraits.
His art is at the turning
point between the trends of
documentary accuracy and
unobtrusive Romanticism.
A fine example is *Art and
Liberty* (inv. 2567), the
proud character of a young
girl playing the violin in
front of a background that
glorifies the art of writing.

1. *Gustave Courbet*
**Señora Adela
Guerrero,
the Spanish Dancer**,
*1851, oil on canvas,
158 x 158, inv. 6417.*

2. *Gustave Courbet*
**The Sources of
the Loue**,
*1863-1865, oil on canvas,
80 x 100, inv. 5030.*

3. *Louis Dubois*
The Roulette,
*1860, oil on canvas,
153 x 124.5, inv. 6337.*

4. *Louis Dubois*
The Storks,
*1858, oil on canvas,
153 x 277, inv. 2807.*

● GUSTAVE COURBET
(1819-1877)
Gustave Courbet originated
from Ornans (Franche-
Comté). At twenty, he
moved to Paris to receive
further artistic training.
Seven years later, in
Holland, Rembrandt's work
made him aware of the
perspective of an art geared
to reality. He produced two
major works that same year:
The Burial at Ornans (Paris,
Musée d'Orsay) — which
caused upheaval at the
Salon of 1850, because it
pictured middle-class pro-
vincials—and *The Stone
Breakers* (destroyed during
World War II), which initiated the Realist movement in
Belgium when it was shown
at the Brussels Salon in
1851. His contribution to
the history of painting does
not rest exclusively on his
choice of subjects: he simultaneously ventured to resort
to a laboured manner and a
chromatic atmosphere in
which the glossy effect, so
fashionable in academic art,
is willingly neglected.

1

2

Realism
The rejection of Gustave Courbet's paintings by the jury of the
great World Fair of 1855 in Paris caused him to open his
"Pavillon du Réalisme", a nearby barrack in which he could exhibit them. He published a "Manifesto of Realist Art" in the
catalogue, hence becoming the movement's leading figure.
Following the French Realists' example, a group of Belgian painters created the "Société Libre des Beaux-Arts" in 1868: some
fifteen artists such as Louis Artan, Charles De Groux, Constantin
Meunier, Félicien Rops, Alfred Verwée, Alfred and Joseph Stevens
gathered around the personality of Louis Dubois. Some of them
were landscapists, mostly influenced by the School of Barbizon,
and intended to oppose their individualistic, true to life interpretation to the commonplace dictates of historical painting stemming from Romanticism. A form of Naturalist painting developed simultaneously, showing awareness of the social implica-
tions of Industrial Revolution and motivation to render proletarian misery. With kindred concern for minutiae, others became
observers of society's privileged circles.

GUSTAVE COURBET

☐ **Señora Adela Guerrero, the Spanish Dancer**
The haughty dancer—a most unusual theme in Gustave
Courbet's work—was portrayed with the painter's characteristic imposing strength and personality. The sharply
contrasting hues are not representative of his manner but
confirm his concern for an almost documentary rendering.
Spanish exoticism was fashionable in France in the mid-19th century. The influence Goya had on Manet exemplifies its impact on
painting altogether. During his stay in Belgium in 1851, Courbet
is said to have been delighted with the way his canvases had been
welcomed at the Salon, and had painted this portrait to offer it
on the occasion of a party in honour of king Leopold I.

☐ **The Sources of the Loue**
A prolific landscapist, Courbet had often drawn inspiration
from his birthplace Ornans and its surroundings. The river
watering Ornans is the Loue, and its banks, bridges and
source have been recurrent themes of a series of canvases.
The painter depicts the cave from which the river springs
in a faithful restitution of its strange atmosphere, haloed by
a faint, gloomy light. The massive, towering rocks, mossgrown

4

and damp, are treated with a reduced range of greens, ochres and greys, barely enhanced by a few lighter touches.

LOUIS DUBOIS

☐ *The Roulette*

A small number of gamblers gathering around a roulette table offers the painter a variety of postures and mimicry, which his naturalist portraying carefully singles out. The heavy overall surliness of the scene reflects the state of mind of that minority of the middle class that idly entertained itself with specious amusement.

☐ *The Storks*

In his landscapes, Louis Dubois attempted to simultaneously render the climate, the air's density, the various types of vegetation and the emotions that all these elements have stirred up within him. The prevailing image of the foreground, a vast, monotonous moor, includes those storks at rest by a pool. But from there, as if inadvertently, the painter suddenly runs into an almost unreal expanse, an immense area. The big birds, forerunners of Symbolism, stand like guardians on the boundary between two worlds.

CHARLES DE GROUX

☐ *Saying Grace*

A typical family of peasants gathers around the cooking pot. The father stands upright as he recites the prayer, to which his people listen piously before sharing the meal. The scene is filled with humbleness and shows how plain country folks fully accept the modest condition of their toiling fate.

The painter has conveyed a touching simplicity by means of a homogeneous range of subdued shades, highlighted by a few discreet lighter strokes. The painter also succeeded in dividing up the light very astutely, so that the family father's face is singled out and set against the lit up wall, and the other features are accentuated by the play with light and shade.

● LOUIS DUBOIS (1830-1880), was a keen admirer of Gustave Courbet, and he became one of the fieriest propagators of Realism in Belgium. He co-founded the "Société Libre des Beaux-Arts" in Brussels in 1868.

● CHARLES DE GROUX (1825-1870) has devoted himself to Realism—with an outspoken trend of social awareness—since 1849, when he produced his first version of *The Poor People's Pew*. He was a founding member of the "Société Libre des Beaux-Arts" and deeply influenced a number of young Realists, and one of them was his pupil Constantin Meunier.

5. *Charles De Groux*
Saying Grace,
*c. 1860, oil on canvas,
80 x 154, inv. 2260.*

5

● JOSEPH STEVENS (1816-1892) had immediately chosen to specialise in painting dogs. He was from Brussels, but he frequently stayed in Paris, where his brother Alfred pursued an entirely different career. He was well appreciated by Gustave Courbet, and Charles Baudelaire dedicat-ed a poem to him, *Les Bons Chiens*. He had already practised his rigorous Realism for twenty-five years when he participated in the foundation of the "Société Libre des Beaux-Arts" in Brussels in 1868.

● ALFRED STEVENS (1823-1906) he had been a pupil of J. F. Navez in the Brussels Academy before he settled in Paris in 1852. He was an accomplished colourist and a keen admirer of Édouard Manet, and he became a specialist of the lavish realist portraits of the women of high society and courtesans of the *Second Empire*. He was a regular visitor of the court at the Tuileries and at Compiègne until the fall of Napoleon III. But the rise of Impressionism relegated him somewhat in the background.

JOSEPH STEVENS
☐ The Dog with a Fly
Joseph Stevens—dog's best friend—has an amazing intelligence of his models and uses his amazing talent in order to prove this. The expressivity of *The Dog with a Fly* lies in the paws' tension, in the position of the head, in the nose turned upwards and in the pricked up ears, all combining to render the pet's concentration so perfectly that there is no need to look at its eyes.

In *An Episode from the Dog-market in Paris (inv. 1471)*, the painter shares the animals' distress, in such a way that the spectator is moved too. In a way, this can also be considered as social realism.

ADOLPHE FASSIN
☐ Napolitean Acquaiuolo
The water carrier can easily be identified by the implements of his trade. Fassin has captured him in full motion: the swaying of his hips, the breeches sliding off, and the way his eyes concentrate on the container he balances on his left hand come over as narrative elements. The *Acquaiuolo* is by no means the statue of a posing figure, and does not evoke a mythological episode at all. It's a vivacious working-class boy, caught by the artist in the heat of everyday action.

ALFRED STEVENS
☐ Autumn Flowers
This canvas is dated 1867, the peak of the painter's career. He knew how to create a lush atmosphere around his characters by means of a glittering rendering of fabrics and precious props. In *Autumn Flowers*, he succeeded in creating a dazzling effect with a somber overall tonality and rather discreet contrasts. His refined blend of dull hues—greys, blacks, olive-coloured greys—is highlight-ed by a few touches of light, and creates an impression of unaffected wealth, of inconspicuous munificence.

3

1. *Joseph Stevens*
The Dog with a Fly,
*1856, oil on canvas,
73.5 x 93, inv. 7652.*

2. *Adolphe Fassin*
**Napolitean
Acquaiuolo**,
*1865, statue, marble,
155.5 x 51.5 x 71,
inv. 1828.*

3. *Alfred Stevens*
Autumn Flowers,
*1867, oil on canvas,
74.5 x 55, inv. 3526.*

4. *Jean-Baptiste Carpeaux*
**Antoine Watteau,
Painter**,
*c. 1863-1864, statue,
bronze,
122.5 x 48.5 x 47,
inv. 4808.*

JEAN-BAPTISTE CARPEAUX

☐ *Antoine Watteau, Painter*

This portrait is the consequence of a deepgoing empathy between the sculptor and the painter of the "*Fêtes Galantes*", whose outward frivolity does not overshadow his inward profundity. The silhouette is elegant, the hip's curve is determined by the fact that the painter puts his weight on one foot, his concentration is unaffected as he gracefully holds his paintbrush, the costume is quite refined. Like in a rough sketch, the contours are blunt and fragmented, and their unevennesses catch the light.

● ADOLPHE FASSIN (1828-1900?)
His fascination for the *Quattrocento* sculptors led him to spend five years in Rome after his academic training in Belgium. During that stay, he moulded the plaster cast of the *Acquaido*, that was to be exhibited at the Brussels Salon of 1863, together with two marble statues inspired by Italian working-class types. The young sculptor— aged thirty-five at the time—opposed an unprecedented freedom to the dictates determining the facture, the choice of subjects and the postures of the figures. He became a Roman resident in 1882, but thereafter, track of him seems to have been lost.

● JEAN-BAPTISTE CARPEAUX (1827-1875), had resided five years at the French Academy in Rome, and he was already a famous artist in 1860. He made a proposal to the mayor of his birthplace, Valenciennes: he would cast a statue of another famous citizen of Valenciennes, Antoine Watteau, a memorial for which he only demanded the reimbursement of his expenses. He was a painter as well as a sculptor, and felt he had deep affinities with his peer, although there was a quarter of a century between them.

4

1. *Charles Hermans*
At Dawn,
1875, oil on canvas,
248 x 317, inv. 2812.

1

CHARLES HERMANS
☐ *At Dawn*

A number of realist painters—such as Alfred Stevens—were the chroniclers of the wealthier class of society. Others, like Eugène Laermans or Léon Frederic, were the observers of the unprivileged. Charles Hermans has confronted them, clearly indicating where his support goes. At dawn, a group of roisterers leaves the inn where they had obviously gone on a binge all night, and head for the waiting hackney under the eyes of a family of labourers, wearing clogs and setting out for work. The eldest hangs his head, but the others seem intrigued and gaze at this scene from another universe. In the gutter on the foreground, the coarse spilled refuse symbolically lies right next to a delicate posy of flowers, abandoned on the street.

In order to express this great social rift, Charles Hermans (1839-1924) composed a very strict plastic counterpoint. He opposes the verticality of the group of workers to the oblique of the tipsy revellers. He uses the same tonalities on either side, but in a different register: the bluish pink of the woman's apron echoes the rosish ochre of one of the dresses. The ochre-shaded white colour of the child's apron is a dull answer to the bourgeois' shirt front. His suit is of a deeper black than the old labourer's worn out working clothes. This painting, Charles Hermans' opus maius, aroused a variety of sharp reactions when it was exhibited at the Brussels Salon of 1875.

● PAUL DE VIGNE (1843-1901) has resided in Rome on two occasions. He was so passionately engrossed in the *Quattrocento*, that he still held conversations with sculptors of that period at the end of his life, when he had become disconsolate. The work he produced in the 1870's revealed a strong Italian influence, as exemplified by this *Poverella*. In 1879, he was commissioned for one of the sculptural groups that enhance the façade of the Royal Museums: *Art Rewarded*. Paul De Vigne gained enough celebrity to enjoy a career with numerous commissions and honorary distinctions, in his own country as well as in France and Germany.

PAUL DE VIGNE
☐ *Poverella*

This pauper may be an itinerant musician, overcome by exhaustion. This evocation of the people's precarious condition is more closely related to litterary Romanticism than to social commitment. The attractiveness of this statue lies in the graceful expression of the face, the nape of the neck and the body's unrestrained surrender.

3

2. *Paul De Vigne*
Poverella,
1876, seated statue,
marble,
127 x 55.5 x 73.5,
inv. 3394.

3. *Guillaume Charlier*
Prayer,
1886 or a little earlier,
group, marble,
123 x 48.5 x 101,
inv. 3048.

GUILLAUME CHARLIER

☐ Prayer

A young working-class woman is kneeling, and her son huddled against her is part of her prayer. The simplicity of this couple is moving, the artist's manner is lithe and sensitive, attaining academic perfection.

Guillaume Charlier (1854-1925) sculpted this marble statue in 1886, when Constantin Meunier produced his first workers' figures. Charlier has the same concern for the misery of the industrial proletarian, though he is even more interested in his condition of life than in the various aspects of his work. Besides, he has devoted a number of figures to marine work. He was a highly valued artist, and obtained countless commissions for portraits and for monumental sculpture.

LÉON FREDERIC

☐ The Chalk Sellers

This triptych is dedicated to three different moments of the daily life of a family of pedlars. Paradoxically, the expression of their tangible misery' is at its strongest in the central panel, picturing them as they relax during lunch hour. Foreshortenings stress the sloppiness of the postures, the figures are dressed with rags and tatters, they express stupor, the atmosphere is dreary, and these elements combine to create a bitter account of despair.

● LÉON FREDERIC
(1856-1940) After the years of apprenticeship and irresolution, Léon Frederic chose his first orientation when he was twenty-six, in 1882, and stayed in the Ardennes for an extended period of time: the coarse and arduous life of the peasants and labourers inspired the accurate and scrupulous style of this observer of their condition. Less than ten years later, he adopted an altogether different point of view.

4. *Léon Frederic*
The Chalk Sellers,
1882-1883, oil on canvas,
triptych, central panel
200 x 267.5, each wing
200 x 115, inv. 3263.

4

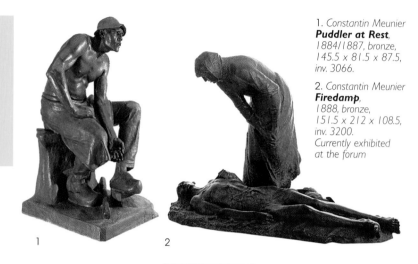

1. *Constantin Meunier*
Puddler at Rest,
*1884/1887, bronze,
145.5 x 81.5 x 87.5,
inv. 3066.*

2. *Constantin Meunier*
Firedamp,
*1888, bronze,
151.5 x 212 x 108.5,
inv. 3200.
Currently exhibited
at the forum*

1   2

● CONSTANTIN MEUNIER (1831-1905) was admitted at the Academy of Fine Arts of Brussels before the age of fifteen. He practised sculpture for eight years, then spent a year in the studio of the painter François-Joseph Navez. Subsequently, he gave up sculpture to exercise painting and draftsmanship for a period of thirty years. Meunier was fifty years old when he became acquainted with iron and steel industry and with the coal mines. From then on, he devoted himself to the celebration of the merit of labourers who toil and suffer hardships and slave away. He believed that sculpture would suit his subject better, so he started moulding and casting again towards 1884. In twenty years, he produced an amazingly powerful and truthful œuvre.

CONSTANTIN MEUNIER

☐ **Puddler at Rest**

The puddler used to churn molten iron up twelve hours a day in front of the blazing mouth of an oven. He is taking a short break here, catching his breath, sagging, a blank look on his face. His clogs, breeches and leather apron have been moulded amply; together with the athletic arms and torso, they tell the efforts this exhausting work implied.

Constantin first exposed the wax model of this statue at the Salon des XX in 1885. The impact on the public as well as the critics was immediate and significant. As one of them put it: "The labourer has barely been shown in sculpture to this day. Due to the restrictive classical traditions, they have treated the nude, the toga or the redingote; never the overalls."

☐ **Firedamp**

Firedamp explosions and other mine disasters were a permanent hazard for coal-miners. On March 4, 1887, over a hundred and twenty men perished in the colliery of La Boule in the Borinage. The rescuers were raising the charred corpses. Constantin Meunier personally witnessed the heartrending scene of a mother who had come to identify the body of her only son. Beyond the tragedy, the posture of the old hag, worn out by existence, bent over the crooked corpse, expresses the miserable fate of an entire population, entrapped in its horizon of slag heaps and plant chimney fumes. The artist summarizes the fateful scene in beams of angled lines and acute angles, conferring eloquence to the slightest detail of this modern pietà.

Meunier's thought process was geared to the end of the century's growing social trend. His first sculptures are contemporaneous with Émile Zola's *Germinal* and with the foundation of the *Parti Ouvrier Belge* (Belgian Labour Party).

4

EUGÈNE LAERMANS

☐ Strike Night

Mobilised around the red banner, the snarling mass of surly workers is about to hurl the labour demands at the factory's boss. The plant's menacing chimneys rise on the canal's opposite bank. Eugène Laermans' report acquires the dimension of a symbolical expression of this type of conflict. He resorts to a layout he is familiar with, structuring the composition around an oblique that vanishes in infinity. Set against the smoky night, the landscape is overrun by tight swarms of dark caps. Only a handful of stooping silhouettes are detailed on the foreground, and some weathered faces of which the expressions are summarized in a very limited amount of rough features, after Bruegel's synthetic manner.

Belgium largely benefited from the fabulous development of iron and steel industry and coal mining in the last quarter of the 19th century. But the underpaid working-class lived in shocking misery, without any form of social protection, and the labourer's terrible working conditions were unregulated altogether. The Belgian Labour Party was founded in 1885 to support the proletarian demands and gradually compel the bosses to humanize working conditions. The strikes proved to be their most effective type of action, although they often deteriorated into violent riots.

☐ The Corpse

Never mind the cause of this young man's death, no-one needs to know whether those who grieve him are his mother and sister and who are those carrying him. This canvas obviously depicts fate itself.

Eugène Laermans has reached the peak of his talent in the first decennium of the 20th century, and The Corpse may well be his masterpiece. The outstretched wall conveys how lengthy the ordeal is. The symmetric rhythm of the composition is given by the stooping figures, bearing the weight of their fate. The corpse is as huge as the sense of despair this canvas conveys. Laermans departed from a Realist concept, but he gradually flowed over into an Expressionist plastic synthesis, foreshadowing Permeke.

3. *Eugène Laermans*
Strike Night,
1893, oil on canvas,
106 x 115, inv. 4681.

4. *Eugène Laermans*
The Corpse,
1904, oil on canvas,
121.5 x 175.5, inv. 3951a.

● EUGÈNE LAERMANS (1864-1940) made his début in the tracks of the Realist Charles De Groux, with whom he shared his compassion for the hardships of peasants and labourers. He was already acclaimed in a number of high-ranking exhibitions, such as the Viennese Secession exhibitions, when he was only twenty-seven. He gradually stepped away from anecdotal aspects and attained a powerful Expressionism. His deeply pessimistic vision probably stems from the calamities that pounded on him: He was aged eleven when a meningitis left him deaf and almost dumb. At the height of his talent, a disease kept him from working for three full years. And blindness eventually put a final stop to his career at the age of sixty.

1. *Henri De Braekeleer*
Man at the Window,
*c. 1874-1876, oil on
canvas, 80.5 x 70,
inv. 3857.*

2. *Henri De Braekeleer*
The Card Game,
*1887, oil on canvas,
52 x 70.5, inv. 4400.*

● HENRI DE BRAEKELEER
(1840-1888) had two men-
tors: his father, a historical
painter, and his uncle Henri
Leys. But he found his own
way upon discovering the
work of Vermeer and the
minor Dutch masters of the
17th century. In his own
meticulous realist style, he
depicted remote places with
a warm prevailing atmos-
phere. He suffered from
anxiety, and had found an
appropriate climate for his
tormented soliloquy. His
mental health prevented him
from working between 1880
and 1884. When he took up
painting again, he stepped
away from the academic
facture he had deemed sufficient to animate his rêverie
until then. He elaborated a
new technique, consisting of
series of slight brushstrokes
that create an effect of optical vibration, transforming
the image in a hovering
mirage.

HENRI DE BRAEKELEER

☐ Man at the Window
De Braekeleer hardly ever left his town of birth: he
regarded Antwerp's setting of antique interiors as silent
sanctuaries. There is nothing to meet the expectations
of the *Man at the Window*, entrapped in an empty room.
On the inside and on the outside, reality consists of a
harsh, distressing universe of straight lines and sharp
angles, save the faded contours of the reflections
between the transoms and mullions of the windows.

☐ The Card Game
Two children play cards; they do not require any particular
attention. They have been handled with the same
technique as the abundant furniture in which they fade
away. A seedbed of fine brushstrokes, side by side,
produce a shimmering light that transforms shapes across
the entire canvas. The sparkling effect is heightened by
the omnipresent ornamental excess, whereas the
vanishing lines of the floor suggest the room's depth.

HENRI EVENEPOEL

☐ The Man in Red
The artist sets the elegant figure of the painter Paul
Baignières against a large wall painting with subdued green
hues, apparently the fresco on which he is currently
working. The silhouette is outlined by means of a flat,
even application of wavering cadmium red, and its dash
is not slackened by the broken contrast of the pink shirt.
When Henri Evenepoel visited a major Manet exhibition in
Paris in 1894, he was stunned by *The Fifer*, and wrote: "There
is such a colourful quality to his use of paste, a subtlety in the
tonalities and a simplicity in the facture that you can hardly
imagine how lively his painting is." That is how the artist wor-
ded his pictorial ideal for the last five years of his short life.
He immediately worked after Manet's simplified manner and
produced this masterful canvas, *The Man in Red*.

3

4

3. *Henri Evenepoel*
The Man in Red,
1894, oil on canvas,
225 x 151, inv. 3753.

4. *Henri Evenepoel*
The Orange Market at Blidah,
1898, oil on canvas,
81 x 125, inv. 6171.

5. *Henri Evenepoel*
Henrietta with the Large Hat,
1899, oil on canvas,
72 x 58, inv. 4939.

☐ The Orange Market at Blidah

Evenepoel spent the 1897-1898 winter in Algeria and painted a series of views of the Orange Market at Blidah. In his pictorial transposition, the scene's picturesque anecdote has faded out: it is not a teeming crowd of market-goers anymore, but an arrangement of coloured volumes and planes, of exquisite tonal harmonies.

The painter has applied broad, flat adjacent patches of colours with a shot effect—off-whites, a whole range of greys, blacks, ochres, carmines, greens—intensified by their closeness. From Manet's lesson, he had drawn the underpinnings of what became Fauvist aesthetics shortly after his death.

☐ Henrietta with the Large Hat

The painting is organised around the cloak's broad dark triangle. The shade of the dress is a toned reply to the threatening sky's bluish grey. The gaze is dark, the face sullen—bright red blotches on fleshy pink. The delightful counterpoint is given by the huge straw hat that haloes the girl's head, her golden locks streaming down and the added violet touch of a feather.

Under Evenepoel's paintbrush, the close arrangement of well-determined colour planes acquires the dimension of a very direct idiom of plastic expression. This is particularly well exemplified by this portrait, one of Evenepoel's very last works.

5

● HENRI EVENEPOEL
(1872-1899)
was born in France to Belgian parents. He received artistic training in Brussels before settling in Paris, where he completed his training in the School of Fine Arts. He was in Gustave Moreau's class and Georges Rouault and Henri Matisse were his fellow pupils. He first discovered the work of Edgar Degas and Henri de Toulouse-Lautrec, then Edouard Manet's work at the age of twenty-two, a genuine revelation to him. Later, in October 1899, he was invited to exhibit his work at "La Libre Esthétique", and he wrote to secretary Octave Maus that he intended to settle in Brussels permanently.
But he was stricken by a disease and passed away two months later.

1. Jakob Smits
Symbol of the Kempen,
1901, oil on canvas,
115 x 140, inv. 3800.

2. Jakob Smits
Mater Amabilis,
1901, oil on canvas,
146 x 115, inv. 4762.

JAKOB SMITS

☐ Symbol of the Kempen

Jakob Smits was thirty-three when he became a resident of the Kempen, an untamed countryside where Christ is said to have halted. This canvas, painted in 1901, is the eventual result of twelve years of intensive research—drawings, sketches, paintings—around Rembrandt's *The Emmaus' Meal*. It was a milestone in Smits' œuvre, after which he gradually emancipated from Rembrandt's magical chiaroscuro and tended towards pure light, as hinted at by its reflection in the clouds, clustered like gawpers beyond the window.

☐ Mater Amabilis

The originality of the research comes to light even better in this painting, contemporaneous to the previous one. Although the painter has not yet neglected the contrasts between light and shade that indicate the origin and direction of light, the chalky-white background is intended to actually reject the light. Later on he thickened the curdled pictorial matter more and more, in an almost mystical attempt to reveal the immanent quality of light within matter. As Smits later wrote: "[...] a luminous painting must reject light, one should be able to see and judge it even when it is dark."

● JAKOB SMITS
(1855-1928)
Jakob Smits was born in Rotterdam, and has studied in Amsterdam and Munich. He launched his painter's career in the Netherlands, where he was commissioned for significant decoration works of public edifices and became the director of the Haarlem school of decorative arts. He left his country and abandoned his position to settle in the Kempen in 1888, and acquired the Belgian nationality in 1902. He was faced with a severe lack of material comfort during his quest of light-matter. He had set up a sort of enclosure made of light-refracting panels, so that he could work in concealed lighting in his studio at Achterbos, close to Mol in Antwerp's Kempen.

VINCENT VAN GOGH

☐ Portrait of a Peasant

Vincent Van Gogh (1853-1890) had attempted to be a lay preacher in 1879 in a Belgian mining area, but gave up after six months. He decided to dedicate his life to drawing and painting and returned to Holland, where he first practised draftsmanship. His first oil paintings date from 1882. In 1883, he settled in Nuenen, where his parents lived, and remained there for two years during which he painted both versions of the *Potato Eaters*. This *Portrait of a Peasant* stems from the same period. The face, engulfed in semi-darkness, is modelled by both the strong graphical treatment and the play with light and shade. Compassion had driven Van Gogh to preach the Gospel to the toiling coal-miners of the Borinage. Compassion with the overworked peasants and labourers underlies his painting. This hallucinated face expresses an unbelieving resignation towards the hardships of life.

THÉO VAN RYSSELBERGHE

☐ Arabian Fantasia

The crowd, rendered by a range of ochre, black and off-white tonalities, is swarming on either side of an expanse of orange-shaded sand. A few colourful highlights achieve to set the horseman out against the painting's overall tone.

When Théo Van Rysselberghe (cfr. p. 136) was in Belgium in 1883, he participated in writing up the articles of the group of XX. He then spent the winter in Tangiers, from where he brought this canvas back. He was aged twenty-two. Outdoor painting had confronted Belgian and French artists with a number of new problems concerning light in the second half of the century. Faced with these questions and with the luminosity of the African scenery, young Van Rysselberghe succeeds in producing a brilliant composition. This canvas is still related to Realism, from which he stepped away completely to devote his entire work to chromatic research.

3

3. *Vincent Van Gogh*
Portrait of a Peasant,
1885, oil on canvas,
39 x 30.5, inv. 4910.

4. *Théo Van Rysselberghe*
Arabian Fantasia,
1884, oil on canvas,
170 x 300, inv. 4139.

4

1. *Fernand Khnopff*
**Portrait of
Marguerite Khnopff**
*1887, oil on wood (maho-
gany), 97.5 x 75.5
Loan of the Fondation Roi
Baudouin*

● FERNAND KHNOPFF
(1858-1921) Fernand
Khnopff was born in 1858
on the family estate of
Grembergen-lez-Termonde.
His father was a magistrate
in Bruges, where he spent
his six youngest years. Then
his family moved to
Brussels and a little sister
was born to him:
Marguerite. In 1876, after
an attempt to study law, he
registered with the
Academy of Fine Arts. He
encountered his first significant revelations in Paris in
1878: the work of Gustave
Moreau and of Burne-Jones.
The English Pre-Raphaelites
gave his work a decisive
impulse. He was already
acknowledged as an artist
by 1883, when he participated in founding the group of
XX and designed its acro-
nym. Khnopff was a keen
reader, and Symbolist literature proved to be a vivid
source of his inspiration.
Stéphane Mallarmé had a
far-reaching influence on
him, and he had essential
affinities with Georges
Rodenbach, who loved
Bruges as passionately as he
did. Like many others, he
became fascinated by the
writing of Joseph Péladan

Symbolism

*The poets were the first to try to determine the concept of
Symbolism. As Jean Moréas put it in his* Manifesto of Symbolism
*in 1886: "Symbolist poetry seeks to endow the idea with a
perceptible shape that would not be an aim in itself, but would
remain subservient while being used to express the Idea." In 1891,
Stéphane Mallarmé declared: "To name an object is to suppress
three quarters of the poem's delight, made of the joy of guessing
bit by bit. To suggest it, that is the dream. The symbol consists of the
perfect implementation of that mystery: to hint at an object gradually
to show a state of mind, or the other way, to select an object and
have a state of mind emanating from it by means of successive
deciphering." Applied to painting, this may be understood as plastic
transposition of thought, an allusive image, hermetic in itself, of an
intuition that could not be entrapped in any definition. Symbolism
was an international development: since the middle of the century,
the Preraphaelites in England—like Dante Gabriel Rossetti and
Edward Coley Burne-Jones—then later in France, from Pierre Puvis
de Chavannes to Paul Gauguin, and in Belgium, from Félicien Rops
to Léon Spilliaert, very different artists were linked with the
movement. Their common trend was to show very little interest for
the evolution of contemporary representational techniques and to
focus on materializing a hidden meaning in objects.*

FERNAND KHNOPFF

☐ *Portrait of Marguerite Khnopff*
A graceful artist and a mundane dandy, Khnopff had quickly
asserted himself as the leading portrayer of the cultivated
upper middle-class of Brussels. The *Portrait of Miss Van der*

2

2. *Fernand Khnopff* **Memories / of Lawn Tennis**, *1889, pastel on paper glued to cardboard, 127 x 200, inv. 3528.*

Hecht (inv. 3980), the three-year old daughter of one of his peers, already exemplifies his refined talent. Four years later, with the *Portrait of Marguerite Khnopff*, he revealed the full extent of his aims and capacities. This is not a commissioned work anymore, but the likeness of his sister, the ideal figure of the immaculate woman. From the waist, she is draped in a dress cut by the bottom of the frame, so that her feet cannot be seen; her bust is entrapped in a tightly-laced bodice right up to her chin, her gloves' cuffs rise above her sleeves, her entire silhouette appears to be defended as by an armour. Her head is the only unveiled element, but she turns her gaze away in unconditional refusal. This distance determines the angelic type of the inaccessible, asexual woman who will be the recurrent model in Khnopff's work until the turn of the century.

☐ *Memories / of Lawn Tennis*

Seven young women wearing sporting clothes stand in a group, in the manner of fashion plates. And five of them hold a racket. Nothing happens. The stilted postures of the figures suspend the course of time. The absence of action or of a plot in this imaginary scene—by no means a representation of a real event—is explained by the fact that every character is a likeness of the same person: the painter's sister. This multiplied image of Marguerite Khnopff as an elegant Victorian lady may have been an instrument of invocation for her brother, as the title suggests: Memories. But it can also lead the spectator into a rêverie that ravishes him far away from reality.

The preliminary studies for Fernand Khnopff's works were mostly drawn after a photograph of the model. He took the picture and developed it himself, fixing the model's image in a frame that isolated it from a reality to which the painter did not have to refer to anymore. Six photographs of Marguerite have been kept, and in each of these she wears the outfit and takes the pose we find in *Memories*. Khnopff has organised the figures in the painting's space without changing anything at all. There is neither a sketch of the overall composition nor a photograph of the first dreamy figure on the left, quite close to the *Portrait of Marguerite Khnopff* of 1887.

and took part in the Salons of the Rosicrucians. His work was soon acknowledged throughout Europe. He was invited to the Salon de l'Art Nouveau, organised by the Bing Gallery of Paris in 1895. His works occupy an entire room in the Viennese Secession of 1898. From 1900 to 1902, he focused on the house he had asked the architect Edmond Pelseneer to design for him. It was the earliest example of Viennese influence on architecture in Belgium, even before Josef Hoffmann's 'Stoclet House'. More than a residence, it resembled a temple devoted to his work, emphatically structured around the sanctuary of his studio. Rooted as he was to the idealised image of his sister and favourite model Marguerite, he had remained a bachelor until he was fifty: he married Marguerite Worms in 1908, who was twelve years younger than him, but their marriage failed after only three years. Fernand Khnopff eventually passed away in Brussels in 1921.

1. Fernand Khnopff
Caresses / Art,
1896, oil on canvas,
50.5 x 151, inv. 6768.

2. Fernand Khnopff
An Abandoned City,
1904, charcoal, black pencil and pastel on paper
pasted to canvas (marou-
flage), 76 x 69, inv. 7030.

● EDWARD COLEY
BURNE-JONES (1833-1898)
was the assistant of Dante
Gabriel Rossetti, one of the
founding members of the
Pre-Raphaelite
Brotherhood, and a friend of
William Morris, the leading
figure of the "Arts and
Crafts" movement. With the
latter, he took part in the
stylistic evolution that foreshadowed Art Nouveau in
England. The better part of
his work draws inspiration
from literary themes, and
Burne-Jones can be reckoned as a remote artist, withdrawn in the ivory tower of
an exclusively Symbolist
creativity.

☐ **Caresses / Art**
By placing a lewd female sphinx, hybrid of a woman and
a cheetah, cheek to cheek with an androgynous youth,
Fernand Khnopff has deviated Oedipus' dialogue with the
sphinx to celebrate ambivalence. It can be regarded as a
reflection of the esoteric tenets in which the Symbolists
found nourishment for their ideologies: some claimed
that the human being had initially been created an andro-
gyn and that he should seek to reconquer this primitive
state of being.
The symbols in this canvas allow many interpretations. Besides
the meaning the painter intended to convey, it is quite significant as a turning point of his vision of women. He frees her
from the constraints of ideal virtues and allows her to discover the disturbing agitation of sensuality.

☐ **An Abandoned City**
It is known that the port of Bruges had lost its access to
the sea as far back as the 15th century, due to the silting
up of the Zwyn: one of the wealthiest cities of Europe
had irrevocably been isolated and ruined. Khnopff has
represented this slow process of choking by a gradual
swamping with water. He departed from an existing
place, Memlinc square, cut out some of its buildings and
debunked the statue in its centre; and he created a place
where memory and fantasy could meet.
Fernand Khnopff was six years old when he had to leave
Bruges, the setting of his early childhood. During his entire life,
he refused to visit the town out of fear that the magic of the
memories would be broken. When he had to be there by
chance, he would just attend the business he had come for
without ever staying any longer than he had to. Indeed, he did
not draw An Abandoned City from life, but based himself on a
photograph, as he usually did: this one was an illustration from
Georges Rodenbach's book Bruges-la-Morte (Bruges-the-dead).

EDWARD COLEY BURNE-JONES
☐ **Psyche's Wedding**
Psyche, a heroine from Greek mythology, was the prettiest
among a king's daughters. He sought to marry her and
consulted the oracle of Milete. The prediction promised
Psyche to a gruesome monster. But Eros, the god of love,
denied the prediction by taking her away. From the many
changes of fortune of this ancient legend, Burne-Jones

3

4

3. *Edward Coley
Burne-Jones*
Psyche's Wedding,
*1895, oil on canvas,
119.5 x 215.5, inv. 7350.*

4. *William Degouve
de Nuncques*
The Peacocks,
*1896, pastel on paper,
glued to canvas,
59.5 x 99, inv. 9397.*

has chosen the episode of the bridal procession, supposedly leading her to the monster. Hence the gloomy atmosphere of the scene. In the semi-darkness of dusk, Psyche is tight with anguish as she walks behind five virgins: one carries a torch and the four others throw rose petals before her feet. Musicians follow her, and her father's stooping, fateful figure closes the march.

This procession of virgins' immaterial lightness is conveyed by the fine texture of the materials, the chromatic subtlety and the graceful mannerism of the gestures. Burne-Jones enigmatically loads this mythological theme that often recurred in his work over a period of thirty years. Has he drawn inspiration from Khnopff's *Memories*, which he is very likely to have seen? The kindred overall tonality of the two paintings and their very similar framing could hint at that; all these virgins are sisters and resemble his own daughter.

WILLIAM DEGOUVE DE NUNCQUES

☐ *The Peacocks*

Reflected by the little flowers scattered in the grass, a strange light emanates from the peacocks in the gloom of the undergrowth. It is the image of an expectation, a suspense, a timeless place to dream about some obscure symbols at dusk.

● WILLIAM DEGOUVE DE NUNCQUES (1867-1935) received his training from Jan Toorop, whom he had known while still a teenager. At twenty-seven, he married Emile Verhaeren's sister-in-law; Maurice Maeterlinck entrusted the stage-sets of most of his plays to him. He was very much involved with Symbolist literary and artistic circles indeed. He drew these fascinating pastel *Peacocks* in 1896; and *Storm at Mallorca, North Coast* (inv. 10262) is much more than a memory of his stay in Mallorca from 1900 to 1902, it is the vision of a seer. His orientation deviated after the turn of the century, but he had already produced a number of works laden with such an intense sense of poetry.

2

1. *Jean Delville*
**The Treasures
of Satan**,
*1895, oil on canvas,
258 x 268, inv. 4575.*

2. *Jean Delville*
**Portrait of Mrs Stuart
Merrill**,
*1892, pastel, crayon, black
lead, 400 mm x 321 mm,
inv. 12, 029.*

● XAVIER MELLERY
(1845-1921)
From 1860 to 1868, Xavier
Mellery attended the Royal
Academy of Fine Arts in
Brussels. He carried off the
Prix de Rome in 1870. He
presented his work repea-
tedly at Les XX and La
Libre Esthétique between
1885 and 1894. Incidentally,
his drawings inspired 48
figurines, representing different trades, which adorn the
balustrade of the "Petit
Sablon" square in Brussels.
In his quality as a Symbolist
draughtsman and painter,
Mellery translates his reverie on the hidden life of
things into sensitive images.

JEAN DELVILLE

☐ **The Treasures of Satan**
The archangel of the nether world rules over an ambiguous
world, where fire and water unite. His wings have become
writhing reptilian tentacles, wrapping up his own dance. He
leaps across the surrendered bodies of his intertwined
victims, still clasping their gold and jewels. In the gleaming
reflections of the flames, serene fish can be seen threading
their way through coral and seaweed. These captivating
depths have little in common with Hieronymus Bosch's
terrifying evocations of hell: the lecherous beauty of the
devil is extolled with jubilation here.

☐ **Portrait of Mrs Stuart Merrill**
The eyes roll upwards in a flaring mask, haloed by a
shock of frizzling hair: the face is that of a medium,

● JEAN DELVILLE
(1867-1953) has asserted
himself mainly through the
ideology conveyed by his
work and spread by his writing. He had an overall academic and outspokenly reac-
tionary attitude towards aesthetics. He absolutely dispa-
raged the "the disgraceful
spectacle of canvases by
Ensor, Monet, Seurat and
Gauguin, who pretext aes-
thetic freedom to put a frame
around their studio's most

loathsome refuse, under the
applause of the fools and the
snobs". However, Satan's silhouette in *The Treasures of
Satan* radiates with these
whiplash lines that typify Art
Nouveau. Before these lines
broke all over Europe, they
had appeared in Brussels
two years earlier in Victor
Horta's architecture. Delville
has proven to be more of a
modernist in the field of
decorative painting, in which
he excelled.

transfixed with the experience of cosmic marvels. She is leaning on a book in which she found the keys to that knowledge. It is the *Book of the Holy Triangle*, which, according to Delville's own words "harmonises the three great Verbs of Life: the Natural, the Human and the Divine."

The Belgian wife of American writer Stuart Merrill inspired this portrait. She and her husband lived near the artist's studio, and her strange beauty captivated him. However, beyond his model's personality, Delville endeavoured to set an icon of the inexpressible down on paper. He first presented it at the second Parisian Salon de la Rose-Croix, in 1893, under its original name: *Mysteriosa.*

XAVIER MELLERY

☐ *Immortality*
Childhood, maturity and death: three metamorphoses of life. Three phases of immortality. A man of mature years faces the mirror and perceives yet an ominous skeleton waiting at the gate of his estate. As he envisages the oncoming pointlessness with distrust, he addresses it sharply:

Tell me, skeleton: Where did you take my soul?
Why has the torch lost its flame?
The cage is deserted:
What became of the songbird?
Volcano, did your lava vanish?
If you were a slave—Where is your master?
The diatribe is a loan from a poem by Victor Hugo.

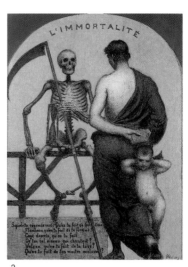

3

3. *Xavier Mellery*
Immortality,
1907, watercolour, ink and pencil on paper, pasted on cardboard; gilded background.
80 x 58, inv. 3, 914.

● THE IDEALISTS' GROUP. Jean Delville was aged twenty-three in 1890. He felt attracted by Symbolism and its inherent esoteric tenet and became the most active of the French writer Joséphin Péladan's Belgian disciples. Léon Frederic was thirty-four then, and he had already been a prolific painter involved with social Realism (cfr. p. 115). But he also boarded the Symbolist ship with his large triptych, *The Stream*. Péladan organised the first Rosicrucian salon in Paris, and Delville supervised the salon "Pour l'Art" in

Brussels, and both opened in 1892. A nominee for the Prix de Rome, Constant Montald, left for Italy at the age of thirty and became fascinated by Giotto. Jean Delville painted *The Treasures of Satan* in 1895 and founded the "Salon d'Art Idéaliste" in Brussels the next year, together with Léon Frederic, Constant Montald and others. The doctrine they professed, as explained in Delville's numerous writings, militated against all forms of art— including Impressionism— dedicated to the representation of reality, and against the

egotism Fernand Khnopff haughtily supported. They intended to share their ideal of beauty to a large public, convinced that this would become the underpinning of a harmonious society. Delville reckoned that a work of art was an esoteric way to reveal "the living prisms of divine beauty, in which the Universal Soul's splendour is refracted" to the initiate. In 1907, Montald—who had a true vocation for large-scale decorative painting—produced *The Boat of Ideal* and *The Fountain of Inspiration* (cfr. p. 18).

1. *Charles Van der Stappen*
Man with Sword,
1876-1879, marble and bronze, 186.5 x 101.5 x 89.5, inv. 2805.

2. *Valerius de Saedeleer*
Winter in Flanders,
1927, oil on canvas, 84 x 96, inv. 4688.

● CHARLES VAN DER STAPPEN (1843-1910), was already a plasterer as a teenager, who had attended evening courses at the Brussels Academy and chosen sculpture from the start. He dedicated his entire life to experimenting what its various possibilities were. He defined himself as "a worrier who is always on the lookout for a new formula, [...] willing to search everything, to try anything as long as it is somehow related to sculpture." His vast culture has largely contributed to the amazing variety of his œuvre, as confirmed by the number of his subjects that stemmed from remote literary work, and by his frequent study journeys to French and Italian museums for his own cultural nourishment. His career began when he sent a sculpture to the Salon de Bruxelles at the age of twenty, and only death interrupted it when he was sixty-seven. He had tackled all genres and had drawn inspiration from the largest variety of styles. One can easily appreciate his manifold scopes of interest and his perfect technique mastery by comparing the *Man with Sword* (1876) with *Death of Ompdrailles* (1886, inv. 3981) perpetuating Rodin, and with the *Sphinx* (1898, inv. 3465), an outspoken Symbolist work.

1

2

CHARLES VAN DER STAPPEN
☐ *Man with Sword*
This hymn to the graceful pride of youth has no other purpose than aesthetic delight: the *Man with Sword* is reminiscent of Renaissance sculpture, which Van der Stappen had studied in Florence and Rome. It is also likely that he drew inspiration from the bronze *David* (Paris, Musée d'Orsay) by the French sculptor Antonin Mercié, whom he is likely to have known. The artist used bronze for the sword because marble did not enable him to give it such a bearing and slenderness, but this also hints at his interest for applied arts and later for Art Nouveau: Van der Stappen resorted to mixed materials several times later on, as e. g. ivory and gilded silver in *The Mysterious Sphinx* (Brussels, Royal Museums of Art and History).

Two artists prevail in Belgian Symbolist sculpture: George Minne and Joseph Rulot. They are both well represented in the Gallery of Sculptures (cfr. p. 150-151).

VALERIUS DE SAEDELEER
☐ *Winter in Flanders*
This is an essentially graphic painting: the bare and slender trunks mark the landscape's rhythm, the incisive line of the houses and trees set them out sharply against the snow. From the black sky to the yellowish white ground, the abstraction of the colours and the absence of life in this disembodied composition produce a Symbolist representation, miles away from the Bruegelian model it evokes.

GUSTAVE VAN DE WOESTYNE
☐ *Jesus Christ Offering his Blood*
Like an exegesis, the painting's title accurately defines the message it conveys: Jesus died on the cross for the sake of mankind. Mary and John cup their hands to collect the sacrifice's blood. Realism has deliberately been excluded from this image to stress its symbolic function. The fine gold of the halo's—taken over from millenary tradition—the abstract dark brown shade of the background, the fleecy

3. *Gustave van de Woestyne*
Jesus Christ Offering his Blood,
1925, oil on canvas, 208 x 178, inv. 4618.

4. *Albert Servaes*
Lamentation,
1920, oil on canvas, 88 x 96, inv. 4183.

white blanket of clouds, the brown ochre of Jesus' body: all hues are arbitrary. Van de Woestyne had probably been influenced by the Florentine fresco's of the Quattrocento he had just seen, and he favoured their predominant draftsmanship with the polished effect of the colours and dull tonalities. He is likely to have drawn inspiration from the 16th century Flemish Mannerists for the crucified Christ and the hallucinated exaltation in the bloodshot eyes.

ALBERT SERVAES

☐ **Lamentation**
United by the grievance around the Christ's body, the dark group is set out against the background luminosity. The brown soil, symbolizing the suffering of mankind Jesus has just left, contrasts with the gleaming yellow colour of Redemption achieved by sacrifice. The scarcity of chromatic means to which Servaes has resorted in this *Lamentation* attests his belonging to Symbolism and link him to Expressionism.

● At the age of thirty-one, VALERIUS DE SAEDELEER (1867-1941) was—together with George Minne—the first artist to settle in Laethem-Saint-Martin. This little village, huddled in a bend of the Leie river, seven miles away from Ghent, was to become the refuge of two generations of artists. De Saedeleer remained there for ten years and converted to catholicism. In his art, he then stepped away from every picturesque element, tuning his art to his religion: "The true vocation of the artist", he said in his later days, "is to glorify, to glorify in thankfulness". In order to do this, he rendered the motif's essence by means of a synthesis in which composition, light, colour and technique blend to express the work's dramatic sense. This was De Saedeleer's only aim until his demise.

● GUSTAVE VAN DE WOESTYNE (1881-1947) found his way in Laethem-Saint-Martin when he settled there for nine years in 1900. Henceforth, he identified the artist's function with a spiritual task to which he dedicated his entire life. He gradually ran over from typified Symbolism into religious Expressionism, of which his *Kiss of Judas* (1937, inv. 6083) is an intense example.

● ALBERT SERVAES (1883-1966), was a tradesman's son and almost a completely self-taught painter. He settled in Laethem-Saint-Martin in 1904, when Frits Van den Berghe came to spend the summer there, but still painted after the manner of Émile Claus. Servaes had more affinities with Gustave van de Woestyne and George Minne. His approach was decidedly spiritualistic when he became a catholic. However, he stood out very early by his deliberately less finished technique and by his dark tonalities, foreshadowing expressionism.

1. *Alfred Verwée*
The River Mouth of the Scheldt,
1880, oil on canvas, 126.5 x 176.5, inv. 3529.

2. *Louis Artan de Saint-Martin*
The Wreck,
1871, oil on canvas, pasted on wood (marouflage), 142 x 248, inv. 2971.

1

2

● ALFRED VERWÉE (1838-1895) stayed in Paris around 1860. His style there was branded by the teachings of Constant Troyon—who painted animals in the countryside due to acquaintances with Dutch painting—and Antoine Barye, the sculptor of animals. He eventually settled in Knokke, on the Belgian coast. In 1868, he was a co-founder of the "Société Libre des Beaux-Arts". Ten years later, his love for light gradually led him to a more Impressionist manner.

ALFRED VERWÉE
☐ **The River Mouth of the Scheldt**
This accomplished canvas is quite representative of Verwée's manner and of his favourite subject: West Flemish landscapes and farm animals. He has truly captured the atmosphere of the pastures blending with the river. Cows peacefully graze in the vicinity of the barges, under a lyrical skyscape of towering clouds.

LOUIS ARTAN DE SAINT-MARTIN
☐ **The Wreck**
The wreck seems to be engulfed in the swirl, and can only be guessed at in this spectacular motion from which the narrative has been excluded. Only the alliance of the sky and the water remains, battling with the wind in a pale, leaden light. The eminently subjective orientation of Artan can already be perceived here, ten years before he became a forerunner of impressionism and beyond, of an Expressionist vision of the landscape.

3. *Hippolyte Boulenger*
The Old Hornbeam Alley. Tervueren,
1871-1872, oil on canvas, 130.5 x 93, inv. 2632.

4. *Hippolyte Boulenger*
The Flood,
1871, oil on canvas, 102 x 144, inv. 3634.

● Louis Artan de Saint-Martin (1837-1890) had met Jean-Baptiste Corot and Gustave Courbet in Paris around 1860. He discovered Brittany's coast in 1867, a decisive revelation. As a convinced Realist, he took part in the creation of the "Société Libre des Beaux-Arts" in Brussels in 1868. His preference for coastal landscapes gradually became an exclusive passion. In 1882, he settled in La Panne and had a studio-shed built on the beach, from where he was free to observe the sea at will.

HIPPOLYTE BOULENGER

☐ The Old Hornbeam Alley. Tervueren
This superb perspective is hallowed by the autumn's gold. The painter did not resort to draftsmanship at all to render the magnificent foliage surrounding the painting: he merely applied contrasting hues with tiny, vivid brushstrokes.

☐ The Flood
The strokes are broader than on the previous canvas, in accordance with the dramatic motion of wind and water. The drawing of the house is drastically reduced to a mass, the trees and fences are outlined by elementary lines. In this overwhelmed world, the picture's dimensions are given by the oblique beam shining through a thick blanket of clouds and reflecting on the wavelets' crests.

● Hippolyte Boulenger (1837-1874), stayed in Tervueren (just outside Brussels) from 1864 and practised outdoor painting. The nearby forest of Soignes offered a variety of ever changing aspects, and the site attracted a small group of artists who were all concerned with a most accurate and faithful rendering of nature. This ideal of Realism led the painter to paint from nature and opened the way for Impressionism. In 1866, when he presented one of his works at the Salon of Brussels, Boulenger registered as an artist from the "School of Tervueren", obviously alluding to the School of Barbizon.

1. *Claude Monet*
**Étretat, Cliff
and Arval Passage.
Sunset**,
*1885, oil on canvas,
60 x 73.5, inv. 9025.*

1

● CLAUDE MONET
(1840-1926) was forty years
old at the time of this stay at
Étretat, during which he
painted several seascapes.
Guy de Maupassant reports
having accompanied him:
"he went out, followed by
children who carried his
canvases, five or six canvases depicting the same
subject, at various hours and
with different effects. He
worked on them then left
them aside, depending on
the sky's fleeting changes.
And the painter, facing his
subject, would wait and
watch the sun and the shadows, then suddenly seize a
gleaming sunray or a pas-
sing cloud in few brushs-
trokes...". The shapes are
generated by mere patches
of colour, thick and oily, but
also broad and dynamic,
sometimes like impasto's.
There is no drawing, no line
at all. Monet soon began to
paint in Giverny, where he
made his garden a genuine
sanctuary of Impressionism.
He started painting his
series of *Waterlilies* in his
specially created garden in
1904, pursuing
Impressionism to its almost
abstract conclusions. Ten
years later, he had a huge
studio built in his garden, so
as to be able to paint from
nature on monumental can-
vases. He died in the work
at the age of eighty-six.

Impressionism

*It seems that Claude Monet initiated the idea of a group of
painters—who were at odds with official art—to incorporate
a society in order to organise collective exhibitions. The first of
these was held in April 1874, in rooms on the boulevard des
Capucines in Paris, made available by Nadar, the photographer.
The event rallied some thirty artists such as Edgar Degas,
Camille Pissarro, Paul Cézanne, Claude Monet, Pierre Auguste
Renoir, Alfred Sisley. There were many derisive visitors. One of
Monet's exhibits depicted the port of Le Havre under a rising
sun. This canvas was named* Impression, rising sun
*(Marmottan Museum, Paris), and the critic who chose "The
Impressionists' Exhibition" as a title for his press review intended
it as mockery. But the artists exploited that name, although
without suspecting how famous it would become. Their main
characteristic was the concern they showed for the effects of
light and for the nuances of atmosphere. Their technique consisted of distinct, rapid brushstrokes creating a coloured vibration
and blurring the outlines of objects, blending with the overall picture. The multiplicity of strokes also enabled the painters to capture sudden changes of light.*

*In 1978, Mrs Blanche Hess-Vandenbroeck left a series of small
paintings to the Royal Museums, most of which were
Impressionist works. The Monet and the Sisley described
hereafter are the two masterpieces of this bequest.*

CLAUDE MONET

☐ *Étretat, Cliff and Arval Passage. Sunset*
This dazzling sunset behind one of the arcades of the cliff
of Étretat confirms that Monet had attained the highest
peaks of inspiration. The anecdote has been banished;
only the rocky sentinel remains, boldly jutting out into the
subdued sea, right to the centre of the painting. The sea
gently rolls over the shingles, and reflects the promonto-
ry's dense shadow with its gold brocade hemming the
wavelets, outlined by the beam of light defined by Arval
passage. The rest of the canvas is but a shimmering of gold
and rose upon the skies' and waters' infinity.

2. *Alfred Sisley*
**Bank of the Canal of
the Loing**,
*1885, oil on canvas,
54.5 x 74, inv. 9030*

3. *Félicien Rops*
The Beach,
*oil on canvas, 41 x 58.5,
inv. 3568.*

● ALFRED SISLEY
(1839-1899) and Claude
Monet were peers at the
Paris School of Fine Arts.
For a long time, he worked
after Jean-Baptiste Camille
Corot's manner. He started
following Monet's example
in 1873, observing an identical subject under changing
light, depending on the time
and on the seasons. The following year, he participated
in the Impressionists' first
exhibition. He settled in
Moret-sur-Loing (Seine-et-
Marne, France) after 1880,
and produced landscape
series for seventeen years.
He was an outspoken follower of the aesthetic tenet of
Impressionism, and is still to
be reckoned as one of its
key references.

ALFRED SISLEY
☐ *Bank of the Canal of the Loing*
The painting's title appears particularly meaningful here, as
the painter has essentially treated the canal's bank: the align-
ment of the houses and thickets on the opposite bank
becomes a vanishing line, after having enlivened the chop-
py waters with playful reflections. Clusters of clouds tower
in the sky. Sisley has resorted to the entire variety of
Impressionist means—contrasted areas of saturated
shades and expressive strokes—to animate the charming
image of a most common site with the purest colours.

FÉLICIEN ROPS
☐ *The Beach*
The sky is alive with heavy clouds of thick paint. The sea
unfurls beneath them, treated with somewhat slighter
strokes, and becoming even lighter towards the beach and
the dyke. The beach cabins are dashed off delicately. The
figures have been captured with swift, spontaneous strokes,
their shadows barely sketched. Due to a number of com-
parable achievements, Félicien Rops has largely contributed
to the introduction of Impressionism into Belgium.

● FÉLICIEN ROPS
(1833-1898)
was born in Namur
(Belgium), but often stayed
in Paris as soon as 1862. He
is particularly renowned as
an illustrator of the
Symbolist poets who deve-
loped an unusual creative
blend of eroticism and sata-
nism. He became a full resident of Paris in 1874, the
year of the first exhibition of
the Impresionist group, but
travelled to Belgium in the
following year. That is when
he wandered alongside the
North Sea shore with his
friend Louis Artan de Saint-
Martin and painted *The
Beach*.

ÉMILE CLAUS
☐ *Cows Crossing the Leie*
This lively scene of rural life is first of all a celebration of
light. On the foreground, in this eddying area where
reflections are multiplied, a dialogue between deep green
and purple hues echoes the effect of the sun's play in the
trees that shade the river. Further back, at the height of
the copse, the stream is pacified by light, gleaming yellow
strokes. By treating the river's opposite bank of that arm
like a slide, the painter has succeeded in gradually stageing

● ÉMILE CLAUS
(1849-1924)
After his training at the
Antwerp academy, Émile
Claus first painted in a
conventional Realist style
with a social trend in it. At
the age of thirty-four, he installed his studio, then his
house, in the village of
Astene, watered by the Leie,
in the vicinity of Ghent. He
was influenced by Claude
Monet and his peers, whose
work he saw in Paris, and
adopted the discipline of
outdoor painting. These two
factors led him towards a
style in which Realism and
Impressionism combine,
around 1890. He founded
the "Vie et Lumière" circle
with a few fellow painters in
1904: they were mainly
engrossed in the expression
of luminous effects, and
hence were called
"Luminists" by the critics.
They were the last significant milestone of
Impressionism in Belgium.
Émile Claus fled into exile
in London during the First
World War, and he painted
many views of the Thames.
He followed William
Turner's and Claude
Monet's example in his play
with the refraction of light in
the moist atmosphere and
fog of London, but never
went as far as they did in
blurring the shapes, never
became quite as refined.

more and more luminous planes. Both the herd and the
children are rendered with almost photographic realism,
although with an Impressionist manner that Claus has
outstandingly adapted to his personal vision.

☐ *Portrait of Jenny Montigny*
In this painting, Émile Claus uses light with sovereign dis-
cretion. The light is splashed on a grassy background and
surrounds the model's silhouette. Shaded off by the hat,
it brushes past her hair and delights in the daydreaming
eyes. It is reflected by the young painter's portfolio in her
lap, thrust upon the back of her chair, then slides down
subdued on her right hand. The fragmentation of the pictorial matter on the background by means of vivid strokes
allows for occasional impasto's. But the layers become
thinner to render the fine grain of her skin, almost transparent to veil the right arm with flowery tulle, light and
frothing for the collar and bodice.
This portrait is dated 1902 and demonstrates the painter's
unconstrained mastery and the efficiency of his technical
options. In his fifties, he was surrounded by friends, admirers and
a handful of carefully selected pupils such as Jenny Montigny. Two
years later, with the "Vie et Lumière" movement (*"Life and
Light"*), he asserted himself as the leading figure of a trend that
was to be followed by a great many disciples and epigones.

Divisionism
*The infinite range of shades is a consequence of the countless
possible combinations of seven colours of the light spectrum. In
the course of art history, painters have generally mixed pigments to obtain the desired tonality. By applying adjacent,
equal-sized dots of pure colour on the canvas, Georges Pierre
Seurat (1859-1891) forced the spectator's eye to go through
that mixing process by itself. Those dots would blend to complex
tonalities when observed from an appropriate distance.
Impressionists had often used brushstrokes of pure colour, but
in an entirely empirical way. Seurat developed a real method,
based on the progress of optical research at the time. At the
last Paris exhibition of the Impressionist group, in 1886, he
exhibited* Sunday at the Island of La Grande Jatte *(Art
Institute of Chicago), a painting intended as a manifest of his
principles. It aroused the public's stunned reproof, although*

3

4

some of the visitors, and one of them was Théo Van Rysselberghe, were delighted. Paul Signac, who had become acquainted with Seurat two years earlier, immediately joined his aesthetic views and actually codified them in his essay From Eugène Delacroix to Neo-Impressionism, published in 1899, long after Seurat's demise. The French art critic Félix Fénéon had created the word "Neo-Impressionism" as soon as 1886 to refer to Divisionist technique. Seurat did not appreciate the term "Pointillism" at all, although it soon occurred in common speech. If he regarded the tip-of-the-paintbrush dots as the most efficient instrument of optical mixing, by no means did he restrict himself to that technique. A number of his works combine points, cross-hatching and comma-shaped strokes.

Georges Pierre Seurat

☐ The Seine at La Grande-Jatte

The island of La Grande-Jatte, in the Seine, near Asnières, has become an almost mythical place: the place of the Pointillist revelation. For this small canvas, Seurat chose a different viewpoint to treat a detail of the background of A Sunday at the Island of La Grande-Jatte, painted two years before. If one ever was needed, this would be the perfect confirmation that the intellectualism of Seurat's concept has by no means stifled the painter's sensitivity. The vibration brought about by pointillism gracefully conveys the moist quality of the atmosphere of that part of the scenery, the rustle of the leaves, and it brings life into the long, shimmering oblique reflections on the river's surface.

Seurat began to study his aesthetic system more thoroughly in 1886, at the age of twenty-seven. It attracted several painters who were at odds with Impressionism; some, like Paul Signac, persevered, but most gave it up after some years. None of his epigones ever attained the aerial poetry irradiated by his canvases. He was struck by a fatal disease at thirty-two, and the magnificent pointillist universe he invented will always be linked to his person.

Paul Signac

☐ La Calanque (The Creek)

The contrasts between the orange-tinted yellow and the blue suggest the Mediterranean atmosphere and its sunshine on the almost bare rocks, shaded by a scarce growth. Twenty years after the apparition of pointillism, Signac still divided his tonalities up, but his strokes had gradually become broader, till they ended up creating the effect of a mosaic.

1. Émile Claus
Cows Crossing the Leie,
1899, oil on canvas, 200 x 305, inv. 3584.

2. Émile Claus
Portrait of Jenny Montigny,
1902, oil on canvas, 106.5 x 89, inv. 6234.

3. Georges Pierre Seurat
The Seine at La Grande-Jatte,
1888, oil on canvas, 65 x 82, inv. 5091.

4. Paul Signac
La Calanque (The Creek),
1906, oil on canvas, 73 x 93, inv. 5090.

● PAUL SIGNAC (1863-1935) was only four years younger than Georges Pierre Seurat but lived forty-four years longer than he did. They had discovered their affinities from their first meeting in 1884, and Signac had been a supporter and follower of Divisionism from the beginning. He remained faithful to it and proved to be its most fiery disseminator.

The XX and 'La Libre Esthétique'

In Autumn 1883, dissident members of the artistic circle L'Essor founded the group of XX. The intent behind the creation of artistic groups—widespread at the time—was to provide access to exhibitions for their members, without having to submit to the decisions of the selection juries that ruled official salons. The group of XX fixed the amount of its members—twenty—from the start; they were to be co-opted. Every idea of a program or jury was ruled out, and the movement was geared to a perspective of independence and innovation. They contributed freely to the salons they organised, and also invited twenty artists who were not members of the group. Their activities were coordinated by a secretary, a task entrusted to barrister Octave Maus. He was also an art lover and a musician who had been co-managing l'Art Moderne, a controversial magazine. He brought his combativeness over to the new group. "We want to produce proud and independent art, and if the issue implies shoving and struggling, then I'm with you... We intend to break down everything in order to restore our little middle-class country's position and put it back where it belongs." Théo Van Rysselberghe, who often travelled to Paris, assisted him in his choices. For ten consecutive years, starting from 1884, the yearly salon of the XX welcomed, besides the nucleus of the XX that included James Ensor, such prestigious artists as James Abbott Mac Neill Whistler, Georges Seurat, Paul Gauguin, Vincent Van Gogh, Henri de Toulouse-Lautrec, Auguste Rodin and many others. In this process, Brussels became a European capital of art. The exhibitions were linked to concerts and literary conferences. At the end of 1893, Octave Maus broke up the group of XX and replaced it by "La Libre Esthétique" ('The Free Aesthetic'), which he managed to keep active until 1914.

THÉO VAN RYSSELBERGHE

□ *Portrait of Octave Maus*

Théo Van Rysselberghe's elegant stageing of the secretary of the group of XX at his piano's side, his back to a mirror, enables him to develop a subtle play with reflections, in rare, almost affected tonalities. Inspired by fashionable Japanese prints, the broad, flat, dull plane of the silhouette contrasts with the piano's glossy lacquer and determines the composition's vertical axis. The drawing is blurr-

● THÉO VAN RYSSELBERGHE (1862-1926) was a gifted pupil of Jean-François Portaels at the Brussels Academy. He held his first exhibition in Ghent at the age of nineteen. In 1883, he took part in the foundation of the group of XX, and his role at the side of Octave Maus was decisive. His huge *Arabian Fantasia* is a painting he brought back from a stay in Tanger during the winter of 1883-1884. In 1884, at the first salon of the XX, he became acquainted with Whistler. The *Portrait of Octave Maus* reveals the influence that meeting had upon him and how easily he could adapt. He saw Seurat's revolutionary canvas, *Sunday at the Island of La Grande-Jatte*, in Paris in 1886, and joined the Neo-Impressionists two years later. He painted in that style for the following sixteen years. After 1904, he adopted a rather academic Fauvist manner. He had settled in Paris in 1898, then in the Var in 1910. That is where he eventually passed away in 1926.

1. *Théo Van Rysselberghe*
**Portrait
of Octave Maus**,
*1885, oil on canvas,
90.5 x 75.5, inv. 6383.*

2. *Théo Van Rysselberghe*
**Portrait of Mrs
Charles Maus**,
*1890, oil on canvas,
56 x 47, inv. 6384.*

3. *Henry Van de Velde*
**The Village's
Events. VII.
The Mender**,
*1890, oil on canvas,
78 x 101.5, inv. 7797.*

ed into fine luminous vibration, the features are summa-rized in a few shades, slightly accentuated by a combina-tion of barely contrasting ochres and roses.

In 1884, Octave Maus had invited James Abbott Mac Neill Whistler to the first salon of the XX. The American was aged fifty at the time, he was highly praised for his extreme refine-ment and particularly valued for his portrayals. He created delicate relationships between very similar shades and dissol-ved the outline of his figures in an atmospheric vibration, endo-wing them with an uncertain sense of very poetic reality. Together with other members of the XX, Van Rysselberghe was subdued. With the self-assurance of a talent crowned with success in all its ventures, Van Rysselberghe immediately took over this precious manner.

☐ Portrait of Mrs Charles Maus

The severity of the huge dark dress prevails in the ambient tremor, well rendered by pointillist shimmering. The reflection of light, falling in from the right, models the head, delicately separated from the background by subtle luminescence. But the force of this portrait lies in its psy-chological insight: the gravity of the face, its inward gaze, the constrained bitterness of the tightly sealed lips, the self-control expressed by the hands. Van Rysselberghe was above all a portrait artist; he has painted characters that seem more attractive at first, but in this likeness of the mother of his friend Octave Maus, he reaches such an emotional depth that this may well be his masterpiece.

Van Rysselberghe adopted Divisionism as soon as 1888, and he was almost the only one to apply it to portraits. He succeeded with his natural bravura, as exemplified by his daring treatment of Mrs Maus' black dress with a technique essentially based on colour. However, Van Rysselberghe's pointillism seems to have been applied to the shape afterwards, more than it actually determines the shape. He did not follow Signac's theory too closely, who had insisted that all dots should be of the same size: it is obvious here that the background's dots are broader than those on the face and hands. He gradually freed himself from overly rigorous pointillism and began painting in longer strokes. *Promenade*, from 1901 (inv. 3745), stems from the end of his Neo-Impressionist period.

HENRY VAN DE VELDE

☐ The Village's Events. VII. The Mender

By dividing the canvas up into two equivalent, distinct areas, the painter conveys both a certain harshness and an overall decorative effect. On the lawn on the fore-

● HENRY VAN DE VELDE (1863-1957), had been very impressed by Georges Pierre Seurat's *Sunday at the Island of La Grande-Jatte*, exhibited at the 1887 salon of the XX, and he used the Divisionist technique for the next three years. As a conse-quence, he was admitted as one of the XX. At the 1890 salon of the XX, he was completely overwhelmed by Van Gogh's work, particu-larly the *Sunflowers*. He developed a manner based on sensitive beams of undu-lating lines, stepping away from the dots, "a despair-ingly slow and passive tech-nique", as he himself put it. But other influences led him towards a trend of social ideology. He was an unyield-ing man, and he gave up painting completely in 1892: he devoted the rest of his life to architecture and became one of the pioneers of Art Nouveau.

1. Anna Boch
The shores of Brittany,
c. 1901, oil on canvas,
108 x 146.5, inv. 3625.

2. Paul Du Bois
Seated Lady,
1893 or shortly before
1894, marble,
154 x 101 x 92,
inv. 3342.

3. Thomas Vinçotte
King Léopold II,
1880, marble,
77.5 x 62.5 x 43,
inv. 2804.

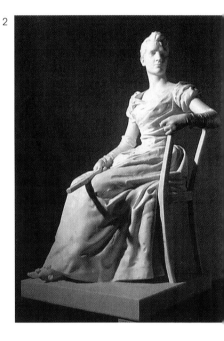

● ANNA BOCH (1848-1936), came from a family of industrials from Hainaut. She first received conventional artistic training. Her cousin Octave Maus introduced her to the group of XX, where she met and was influenced by the greatest Impressionist painters. After Divisionist experiments, her painting became more structured. Her fortune had enabled her to be a patron of the arts and to become quite influential in Brussels' artistic circles. She purchased Van Gogh's *Red Vine*—the only painting he sold during his lifetime— now to be seen in Moscow, at the Pushkin Museum. The Royal Museums owe four major works to Anna Boch: James Ensor's *Russian Music*, Paul Gauguin's *Conversation in the Fields*, Georges-Pierre Seurat's *Seine at La Grande-Jatte* and Paul Signac's *La Calanque*.

ground, the subtle play of shadows on the leaves creates a sense of ambient intimacy around the seated figure. Behind the mender, beyond the path that litterally bathes in light, the village's buildings are linked together in one compact horizontal strip that keeps the sky out of bounds. The verticality of the of the trees determines the perspective. The tight pointillism makes the entire scene shimmer and confers unity to the painting.

ANNA BOCH

☐ **The shores of Brittany**
This cleverly framed, sensitive interpretation of a corner of the cliffs in Brittany does not tally with any strict aesthetic theory. Anna Boch departed from a manner of Realism, kindred with the School of Tervueren, but she incorporated the influence of Impressionism in the eclectic style attributed to the prevailing trends of that period. In a slight evening light, the short, lively strokes of the water surround the Realist rendering of the rocks.

PAUL DU BOIS

☐ **Seated Lady**
In this likeness of his twenty-four year old wife, Paul Du Bois seems more dazzled than tender. The marble's natural coldness has frozen the proud bearing and the expression of the young woman's beautiful face.

3

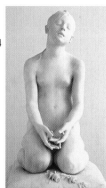

4

4. *Julien Dillens*
Funerary Statue,
*1885 or shortly before,
marble, 98 x 55.5 x 81,
inv. 6783.*

THOMAS VINÇOTTE

☐ *King Léopold II*

The Belgian sovereign was aged forty-five when this remarkably well-studied likeness was sculpted. He appears young yet, his face unwrinkled, but he is draped in somewhat haughty majesty. The mask's draftsmanship is impressive, the continuous line of the arch of the eyebrows under the forehead's bumps is echoed by the curved line of the mouth. Between these two lines, the firm, determined vertical of the nose and the sharp strokes of the searching eyes.

JULIEN DILLENS

☐ *Funerary Statue*

A teenage girl surrenders to despair, destroying her life, clipped in early springtime like the roses in her lap. The adolescent symbolizes both the absent, robbed away from existence, and the abandoned, who has nothing left but tears.

The fineness of this marble's grain, the satin-like smoothness the sculptor has obtained and a slight transluscence tally with the cold chisel work, producing delicate curvaceous lines. The lowered eyelids, the half-open mouth seeming to utter a soft cry, the helpless hands on the legs combine with other details to express her resignation before the irretrievable.

● JULIEN DILLENS (1849-1904) attended Eugène Simonis' workshop together with Thomas Vinçotte. At twenty-one, he participated in his first salon. He was a nominee for the Prix de Rome in 1877 and undertook a four-year journey to Italy, studying Renaissance sculpture. His career started upon his return in 1881. Four years later, he exhibited this *Funerary Statue*. Dillens sculpted countless other funerary monuments and busts, was commissioned for official works, scattered throughout and around Brussels. One of his famous works is the *Everard 't Serclaes Memorial*, just next to the Brussels Town Hall, an altorelievo combining natural and gilded bronze. Tourists traditionally stroke the recumbent figure's arm for good luck.

● PAUL DU BOIS (1859-1938) was one of the founders of the group of XX in 1883. Three sisters were often seen within this artistic circle: Alice, Irma and Marie Sèthe. He married Alice and Marie became the painter Henry van de Velde's wife. Both sisters were portrayed by Théo Van Rysselberghe portrayed Alice Du Bois. The impression Alice makes in the likeness her husband has sculpted is entirely different from the way she comes over in Théo Van Rysselberghe's portrait: she appears smiling through the coloured haze of his tiny dots. One of the original qualities of the XX was that their members were co-opted without regard to their artistic conceptions. It is interesting to notice that Van Rysselberghe's feverish modernism stood alongside Du Bois' academic perfection.

● THOMAS VINÇOTTE (1850-1925) made a name at the age of twenty-four, due to a graceful *Giotto (inv. 2650)* that won him a medal at the Salon de Paris. He was a well-educated man, close to the royal court and to the high society, and was commissioned for most prestigious works. His very prolific œuvre shows flawless craftsmanship and perfect elegance. Besides an impressive number of monumental statues and decorative works, he also sculpted many busts of influential personalities, portraits that confirm his fine psychological insight.

1

2

● PAUL GAUGUIN (1848-1903) entered the merchant navy as a candidate officer when he was seventeen and sailed across the world's seas and oceans for six years. He began a stock-exchange dealer's career at the age of twenty-three, working for a Parisian stockbroker. In 1873, he married an upper middle-class Danish girl who gave him five children. His comfortable financial situation enabled him to acquire quite a collection of Impressionist paintings, and he started to paint as an amateur. He was gradually acknowledged by his peers, so he took part in exhibitions of the Impressionist group from 1879 on. A financial crash in 1882 convinced him to dedicate his life to painting, as a consequence of which he went bust and his marriage broke up. Two years later, his wife returned to Copenhagen, taking the children with her, an irremediable separation, without return, whatever Gauguin's hopes may have been. Between 1886 and 1890, he travelled to Martinique, spent two months in Arles with Vincent Van Gogh and three stays in Brittany that were decisive for his art. He then spent two years in Tahiti, two in Paris again, and eventually returned to Tahiti, where he passed away in May, 1903.

PAUL GAUGUIN

☐ *Conversation in the Fields. Pont-Aven*

Impetus and verticality are the key elements of this piece of landscape: staged perspective, inspired by the Japanese, two slender birches that determine the scale by comparison with the two figures, lengthy strokes through which the ambient vibration is achieved. Gauguin has borrowed the latter from Impressionism, but in order to serve a range of deliberately unreal tonalities, such as the odd blues and oranges of the leaves. Even the colour of the cattle proclaim the painter's discretionary freedom. Gauguin's art can be summarized in this trend to recreate what he perceives within a well-thought aesthetic order, a form of arbitrary synthesis of sensations.

☐ *Calvary in Brittany*

Gauguin has condensed the main emblematic figures of primitive Brittany in this painting, he was in search of this Brittany and let it impregnate him. The peasant woman's dress matches with dark sky. She has the coarse appearance stemming from immemorial contact with the harsh, wild nature and the omnipresent, threatening sea. She is at rest at the foot of the Calvary that dominates the canvas, and her posture echoes the curve of Christ's body.

During his third stay in Brittany, Gauguin fully mastered an aesthetic conception to which he lent extreme power. He entrapped coloured masses of a monumental force within a closed line, reminiscent of the medieval techniques of stained glass and cell enamelling. This is a masterful application of the "lesson" he had taught young Paul Sérusier (cfr. p. 142) one year earlier. For this descent from the cross, he drew inspiration from the calvary of the church of Nizon, near Pont-Aven. Maybe the moss encrusted in the stone produced this greenish tonality? He used a dull, unreal green hue that endowed the group with its symbolic dimension.

☐ **Portrait of Suzanne Bambridge**

Gauguin disembarked at Papeete in June, 1891. He did not encounter the wildlife he had been expecting, but discovered a small colonial harbour where he found it difficult to integrate. His hope to make a little money by painting portraits of militaries and officials of this society was not fulfilled either, but this tentative *Portrait of Suzanne Bambridge* has neverthless reached us. She was an eccentric English lady who had married a Maori chief. This work foreshadows his later representations of the natives—so filled with poetry—the painter produced after settling in a village just off the lagoon's shore.

1. *Paul Gauguin*
Conversation in the Fields. Pont-Aven,
*1888, oil on canvas,
92.5 x 73, inv. 5092.*

2. *Paul Gauguin*
Calvary in Brittany,
*1889, oil on canvas,
92 x 73.5, inv. 4416.*

3. *Paul Gauguin*
Portrait of Suzanne Bambridge, *1891, oil on
canvas, 70 x 50, inv. 4491.*

1. *Pierre Bonnard*
Nude against the light,
*1907, oil on canvas,
124.5 x 109, inv. 6519.*

● PIERRE BONNARD
(1867-1947) had been a
member of the group of the
Nabis in 1889. Paul
Gauguin had deeply
influenced him at the time.
At the turn of the century,
like Degas, he started painting the female nude and
never stepped away from
that theme anymore. It led
him to adopt an
Impressonist technique
which he was one of the last
major painters to resort to.
Nude against the Light
exemplifies his manner
remarkably well. That canvas stems from 1907, the
year in which Pablo Picasso
produced *'Les Demoiselles
d'Avignon'* as a prelude to
Cubism.

The Nabis

*In the course of his second stay in Pont-Aven, Paul Gauguin
had asserted himself as a leading figure among the artists
on the lookout for innovative ways. Paul Sérusier showed him
one of his canvases. Gauguin made the proposal to teach
him "a lesson". Maurice Denis has reported Gauguin's words
to his pupil as they had painted outdoors together. "How do
you see those trees?" asked Gauguin. "They are yellow. Well!
Use yellow paint; that shadow there is rather bluish: use pure
ultramarine. Those red leaves? Use vermillion." The result was
The Talisman, a small non-figurative painting owned today
by the Musée d'Orsay in Paris. When Sérusier returned to
Paris, he showed it to a group of friends: Maurice Denis, Pierre
Bonnard, Édouard Vuillard. They were subdued by Gauguin's
concept, who advocated giving up tentative restitutions of
nature and favouring a conversion of nature into series of
simplified colours and expressive lines. These young painters
gathered under the name of "Nabis" (Hebrew word for
prophets), thus revealing the symbolism their ideals implied.*

PIERRE BONNARD
☐ **Nude against the light**
The scene of a naked woman washing and dressing is the
painter's pretext to play with sunlight on the fleshy modelling of a radiant body. The warm shades of grey, blended
with ochres, are adjacent to the bright tonalities, applied
with vivid brushstrokes and lighting the room with a
delightful intimist atmosphere. The contrast between the
woman's black sandals and the gown dropped at her feet
accentuates the luminosity of the entire painting.

2

2. Édouard Vuillard
Two Schoolchildren, *1894, size paint on canvas, 214 x 98, inv. 6681.*

● VICTOR ROUSSEAU (1865-1954)
already worked with his father and uncle at the age of eleven: they carved the stone on the yards of the Palais de Justice in Brussels. He started attending courses at the Academy of Fine Arts at the age of fourteen. He was twenty-four when he was admitted in Charles Van der Stappen's class. He competed for the Prix de Rome at the age of twenty-nine. His precocious activity never slowed down, and his production was even more prolific due to the fact that he lived to be almost ninety and only stopped working a couple of years before his demise. Amongst the countless sculptures he has left—ranging from monuments to a small ivory mask—*The Secret*, so full of graceful poetry, typifies this most cultured, refined artist who was fond of idealism.

ÉDOUARD VUILLARD

☐ Two Schoolchildren

Public Gardens was a generic title for a series of nine paintings of the same height with linked motifs. *Two Schoolchildren* belongs to that series, produced by Vuillard in 1894 for Alexander Natanson's town residence. Nowadays, three of these panels are in the United States and five are in the Musée d'Orsay, Paris.

Vuillard had joined the Nabis from 1890 to 1900 and had put Gauguin's lesson to practice. He had transposed the colours of reality to their deliberately unreal equivalents. Neither the green of the trees in the middle ground nor the beige shade of the dead leaves belong to nature. He combined a broad, flat application of matching, adjacent patches of colour with a treatment of depth inspired by Japanese prints.

VICTOR ROUSSEAU

☐ The Secret

This couple of young girls appear from the marble as if from the original tide, extolling the tenderness of the act of sharing. Between the two bodies that respond to each other without even touching, a narrow space is created by the echoed curves, a hardly perceptible space allowing for a play with light and shade, generating a subtle vibration. The hairline and the ample draperies discreetly hint at Art Nouveau.

3

3. Victor Rousseau
The Secret, *1916-1917, marble, 49 x 31.5 x 20.5, inv. 4335.*

● JAMES ENSOR (1860-1949) James Ensor was born in Ostend in 1860, to an English father and a Flemish mother. He attended courses at the the local academy, then at the Brussels Academy of Fine Arts, where Fernand Khnopff was a fellow student of his. He returned to Ostend at the age of twenty, when he had completed his training, and practically never left his native town anymore. He took part in an exhibition for the first time in 1881: he showed *The Lamplighter* and *A Colourist* at the Salon de la Chrysalide in Brussels. That was the first turning point in his career. He stepped away from the initial Realism of his manner in order to let the light dwell in his world of strange intimacy. Over a period of two years, he produced the impressive series of "Bourgeois interiors", where an Impressionist technique opens up on a Symbolist sense of poetry. James Ensor participated in the creation of the dynamic group of XX in 1883, who reinvigorated the Belgian art world. That same year, masks began to appear in his work. It his known that his mother ran an Ostend souvenir and shell shop, and how popular carnival used to be in Ostend. An invaluable treasure of forms and faces had accumulated in the painter's memory since his childhood years, and he started bringing them to life in his odd way. The monumental canvas (257 x 378.5 cm) about the *Entry of Christ in Brussels* (Malibu, California, Paul J. Getty

1. *James Ensor*
The lamplighter,
*1880, oil on canvas,
151.5 x 91, inv. 3294.*

2. *James Ensor*
A Colourist,
*1880, oil on canvas,
102 x 82, inv. 10288.*

JAMES ENSOR

With its indomitable peculiarity, James Ensor's work has deeply marked Belgian painting of the beginning of the 20th century, both in the fields of chromatic research and of poetic invention. The Royal Museums present a comprehensive series of milestones of his itinerary.

☐ The lamplighter
James Ensor had barely completed his academic training when he produced this first large canvas, in 1880, an already powerful painting that exemplifies the painter's Realist facet, from which he stepped away quite early. The youth's face is roughly modelled by the blue shadows. The dark mass of the figure is set out forcefully against the gleaming background. The fine rendering of the transparency of the lamp's glass only relies on a few strokes of white and ochre. This young painter's initial manner shows concern for the restitution of reality, and sharply contrasts with the increasingly subtle handling found in his "bourgeois" period.

☐ A Colourist
A Colourist stems from the same period as *The Lamplighter*. It probably is Ensor's first paler, lighter painting, and therefore represents a significant step in his œuvre. His concern for the glistening sheen of colours and reflections already comes to the fore, hinting at his kinship with the Impressionists. This canvas blazes the trail of an impetuous career that would be marked out with a series of stunning upheavals.

3. James Ensor
The Russian Music,
1881, oil on canvas,
133 x 110, inv. 4679.

4. James Ensor
The Lady in Blue,
1881, oil on canvas,
68.5 x 58.5, inv. 6525.

☐ **The Russian Music**

In 1881, Ensor entered the period dedicated to bourgeois interiors. This is a typical representation of the mores of the provincial middle-class of that period: the landlady plays the piano to her attentive visitor. However, time seems suspended. The sound is muffled in the snug space of the draught-roof lounge, but paradoxically, an impression of inner music and of silent collusion emanates from the scene. The painter moves away from the reassuring shores of Realism to drift away in waking dreams.

On the large patches of generally dull shades, applied with generous strokes, pale highlights and slight shimmering glaze bring about the play of light. The background and the characters are like wrapped in a vibration that blur their outline. The carpet has been treated with short brushstrokes and reminds us of the lapping of an unstable element upon which the scene seems to hover. The slight tremor of the lounge's confined atmosphere is an original new complement to the Impressionists' outdoor research. But Ensor, as if responding to an inner vocation, extracts the ferment of uncertainty and strangeness from it.

☐ **The Lady in Blue**

The Lady in Blue first appears to be an elegant woman devoid of mystery, engrossed in her needlework. It is the lightest of the paintings stemming from the "bourgeois" period, the closest one to French Impressionism, judging by the facture. But a closer look reveals that the colours of her dress are echoed in the carpet on the foreground. And a reminder of red—that of the knitting—confirms a puzzling impression of reflection, as if by a mirror. The virtual element has stealthily been introduced in the ordinary to subvert it by the mere play with colours.

Museum) dates from 1888. In this teeming vision of caricature-like figures, a paroxysm of Ensorian Expressionism, the artist gives the measure of his anarchist leanings. After the turn of the century, the amazing creative energy of this tormented genius gradually ran out of breath. He still achieved a few highlights but the better part of his work has already been produced. Acknowledgement and honours came later. The Palais des Beaux-Arts in Brussels organised a huge Ensor retrospective in 1929 and king Albert 1st made him a baron. In 1934, James Ensor was proclaimed "Prince of the painters". He passed away in Ostend in 1949, at the age of eighty-nine.

1. James Ensor
Scandalized Masks,
1883, oil on canvas,
135 x 112, inv. 4190.

2. James Ensor
Odd Masks,
1892, oil on canvas,
100 x 80, inv. 4194.

3. James Ensor
Skeletons quarreling for
a 'Hareng Saur'(Kipper),
1891, oil on wood,
16 x 21.5, inv. 11156.

4. James Ensor
People before the
poster of 'La Gamme
d'Amour',
1914, oil on canvas,
86.5 x 71, inv. 11167.

5. Auguste Rodin
Jean d'Aire,
1886/1890?, bronze,
204.5 x 71.5 x 66.5,
inv. 4905.

☐ Scandalized Masks

With this work, in 1883, Ensor stepped away from the upper middle class' lavish interiors. These two sinister characters are staged in an almost squalid room. Masks have made their first appearance in the painter's idiom. But they are only masked individuals, like he encountered in the streets of Ostend at the infamous yearly 'Rat Mort' carnival ('Dead Rat' carnival).

The artists depicts the scene with a recurring concern for Realism: the lamp's reflection splashes a superb chrome yellow on the wall, and neither the room nor the characters, however worrying, seem to belong to an alien world.

☐ Odd Masks

This canvas was painted nine years after the *Scandalized Masks* and illustrates the evolution of the mask theme Ensor has followed to the verge of obsession. These are not human figures wearing masks anymore, but puppets without any consistent anatomy, fantastic beings created by the artist's hallucinated mind. Although the symbolic values they convey may refer to the painter's psychism, in essence they are also a part of the end-of-the-century Symbolist mainstream, so fond of weirdness, of ambiguity and perversion with a touch of morbid fascination for death. And it is death indeed, disguised as Pierrot, who lends the pale light of her smoky candle to the returning herd of beings, dishevelled by a peculiar orgy. Ensor has reached the full extent of his capacities. He expresses his unbridled fantasy with the clear, dazzling manner he has invented. The texture of the pictorial matter dramatically dominates draftsmanship. The powerful brushstrokes immortalize the trace of the gesture that modelled these stupefying characters.

☐ Skeletons quarreling for a 'Hareng Saur' (Kipper)
(GOLDSCHMIDT BEQUEST)

In fact, a pun underlies this painting, whereby the painter gives the full measure of his satirical spirit. The French word for 'kipper' is *'Hareng saur'*, pronounced exactly the same way as *Art-Ensor*. As the painter himself once wrote: "You believed that I wished to entertain you. There is my real trick. My trick lies in the revelation of the unexpected, often cruel use of harmless daily objects. It lies in the torture that my tortured mind forces upon whatever it takes hold of." Ensor actually produces a ferocious caricature of his peers and the art critics, who tore his work to shreds with sharp teeth at the time. But beyond the satirical level, the painter depicts his anguished relationship to death, constantly bothering him.

☐ People before the poster of 'La Gamme d'Amour'
(GOLDSCHMIDT BEQUEST)

This painting belongs to a cycle that kept Ensor busy for a long time. In 1906, his friends had offered him a harmonium. "[...] you have guessed," he wrote to them, "what I really missed, and indeed music is—even more than painting—a companion for the lonely man." It can already be perceived that he is beyond the peak of his genius. The harmonium became to Ensor what the violin had been to Ingres: during forty years, he never tired of playing it. Notwithstanding his restricted musical knowledge, he undertook to compose a dramatic pantomime ballet the following year: "La Gamme d'Amour" for two lovers, children, puppets and toys. He wrote the scenario, designed the stage-set and the costumes. He also used this theme in a number of paintings and a series of plates.

James Ensor painted *People before the Poster of "La Gamme d'Amour"* in 1914. It is a faithful reproduction of a fragment of his 1888 canvas, the *Entry of Christ in Brussels* (Malibu, California, Paul J. Getty Museum). In this gigantic work teeming with radically Expressionist caricatural inventions, the three same characters are perched on a platform next to an identical three-coloured panel, although it does not picture a poster here, and assist to Christ's entry in Brussels. A quarter of a century later, the artist has literally copied that part of his major work for an entirely different purpose.

AUGUSTE RODIN

☐ One of the Burghers of Calais: Jean d'Aire

During the Hundred Years' War, the corsairs from Calais had harassed the English fleet. King Edward III of England eventually broke down their stubborn resistance and took in Calais in 1347. He promised to spare the inhabitants provided that six worthy burghers would come bare-footed and bare-headed to surrender and hand the city's keys over to him, wearing but a shirt and a hangman's rope around the neck. Rodin has depicted this episode in the Monument of The Burghers of Calais, a group of six characters; Jean d'Aire is the one responsible for the key.

Closed like a clenched fist to convey the arrogant obstination of a man who will not surrender his dignity, his head emerges from the starched drapery of the long shirt. The harsh features are modelled deeply; the hands eloquently clutch both of the key's extremities in constrained hatred. Expression literally juts out of this statue, its character emanates from the inside.

● AUGUSTE RODIN (1840-1917) was a Parisian. He stayed in Brussels from 1871 to 1877, where he had preferential relationships with a few Belgian artists and worked on decorative sculptures for public sites. After his return in France, he produced an œuvre that carried him to the pinnacle, where its astonishing power of expression consecrated him as a major genius of sculpture. From 1880 to 1889, he gave the *Gates of Hell, The Burghers of Calais* and the famed *Balzac* monument that remain key landmarks of art history.

The gallery of sculptures

Located in the Museum's basement, this vaulted gallery is ideally suitable for smaller and middle-sized sculptures. The intimacy of the place brings the public closer to works of which many are original sketches that conjure up the actual creative gesture.

1

1. Gilles-Lambert
Godecharle
**Minerva Protecting
the Children of the
House of Nassau**,
*1796, terracotta,
26.5 x 14 x 12.5,
inv. 2689 A.*

2. Guillaume Geefs
**Frédéric Count of
Merode, Fallen for
Belgium in 1830**,
*1833 or a little earlier,
plaster, 108 x 192.5 x 73,
inv. 3077.*

GILLES-LAMBERT GODECHARLE

☐ *Minerva Protecting the Children of the House of Nassau*

Minerva was the goddess of knowledge and wisdom, celebrated by Roman scholars. Here she gracefully lays her arm on the shoulders of the eldest son of the King of Holland, the crown prince William. His younger brother Frederick sits at the godess's feet and plays with the weapons. Thirty-four years later, in 1830, those two princes led the Dutch troops who were defeated by the Belgian patriots.

Godecharle's talent can be observed at its best in his countless, remarkably faithful portraits, but also in his terracotta sketches. The refinement and the ease of his modelling confer liveliness and sensitivity to these works seen as they were shaped by his fingers.

GUILLAUME GEEFS

☐ *Frédéric Count of Merode, Fallen for Belgium in 1830*

Count Frédéric was the commander of the militia of volunteers who freed the Belgian territory from Holland's rule in the month of September, 1830. He received a fatal injury in Berchem, near Antwerp, in the heart of a fight. A witness reports: "Around four o'clock in the evening, a bullet broke and went right through his right thigh, very high; he fell, shot twice with his gun and seized his pistol..."

The sculptor has captured an instant and renders it with restrained realism, without surrendering to the period's fashion: he does not dress up the hero in an ancient costume, but pictures him with the ample blouse the volunteers had chosen as a uniform. The treatment of the features, tense with willpower, and the vivid shaping of the drapery contribute to convey the moment's dramatic intensity.

2

ANTOINE WIERTZ

☐ **The Four Ages of Mankind.
Third Epoch. The Light**

This figure represents the third epoch of an emblematic series of *The Four Ages of Mankind*, the three others of which are kept in the Wiertz Museum in Brussels. The Light, draped in her triumph, prevails over the powers of gloom, symbolized by an athlete with the clawed wings of a demon.

Twenty-four years later, Frédéric Auguste Bartholdi sculpted *Liberty Enlightening The World*, standing at the entrance of the port of New York. It seems likely that the sculptor was familiar with Wiertz's work, although there is no hard evidence to prove it; this apparent kinship could be a mere coincidence.

● ANTOINE WIERTZ (1806-1865), was born in Dinant. The director of the Antwerp Academy noticed him as he attended painting courses there from his fourteenth year. He was awarded the Prix de Rome in 1832 and impregnated himself with the examples of Ancient sculpture. When he returned to Belgium, he painted and sculpted with an obvious concern for monumentality. As an exalted Romanticist, he found his spiritual family in the pictorial School of Antwerp, although somewhat stilted in their veneration of Rubens. This explains why he stayed aside from the overwhelming progress of his time, in spite of an undeniable talent. However, particularly in his later days, he contributed to Belgian sculpture by offering it a lyrical drift it had missed until then.

3

3. *Antoine Wiertz*
**The Four Ages of Mankind.
Third Epoch. The Light**,
*1862, marble,
120 x 90 x 49, inv. 2352.*

1. *Léopold Harzé*
The Drunkard's Family,
1875, terracotta,
23 x 39.5 x 21, inv. 3040.

2. *George Minne*
Mother Weeping her Dead Child,
1886, bronze,
45.5 x 16.5 x 27,
inv. 6183.

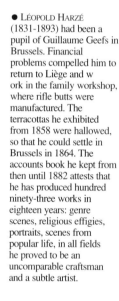

● LÉOPOLD HARZÉ (1831-1893) had been a pupil of Guillaume Geefs in Brussels. Financial problems compelled him to return to Liège and w ork in the family workshop, where rifle butts were manufactured. The terracottas he exhibited from 1858 were hallowed, so that he could settle in Brussels in 1864. The accounts book he kept from then until 1882 attests that he has produced hundred ninety-three works in eighteen years: genre scenes, religious effigies, portraits, scenes from popular life, in all fields he proved to be an uncomparable craftsman and a subtle artist.

LÉOPOLD HARZÉ

☐ The Drunkard's Family

Léopold Harzé was inspired by the daily life of the common people, describing it with an objectivity that includes its sordid aspects, as exemplified by this scene of the return home of a drunken family father. But he is not pathetic and does not intend his work to be a plea. He renders the resignation of the faces with extreme delicacy and details the hair, the materials up to the finest thread, every object, even the hair of the brush, with stunning minutiae. This pious accuracy conveys restrained emotion, bitter-sweet poetry.

GEORGE MINNE

☐ Mother Weeping her Dead Child

The mother's head, tilted backwards in silent lament, replies to the surrendered head of the dead child. From the neck, swollen with sobs, to her feet, the motherly figure is one cry of pain. Part of her has been torn away: the corpse in her lap, shaped from the same clay, remains welded to her own body.

This work is one of George Minne's (1866-1941) earliest sculptures; he was twenty years old at the time. From the start, he created and perfected the purely expressive style—disregarding every form of realism—the Symbolist writers would identify with, starting with Maurice Maeterlinck. George Minne continued this inspired formal simplification for thirteen years, eventually producing the *Fontaine des Agenouillés* (*Fountain of the Kneeling*), an ensemble of five identical figures kneeling around a curb. This major work of sculptural Symbolism asserted Minne's international fame. He settled in Laethem-Saint-Martin the same year.

JOSEPH RULOT

☐ *The Legend*

The city of Liège organized a contest for a memorial to the glory of one of its regional poets, Nicolas Defrecheux, whose song *"Leyiz'm plorer"* perpetuated the name. Joseph Rulot's project was selected. It included a poet's likeness, an evocation of three of his songs and several allegoric statues extolling the Walloon virtue and spirit.

The monument never saw the light. The suggestive power the whole would have had can be guessed by the standards of this sketch, where technical simplification strengthens the symbolic expression. *The Legend* is embodied in this pondering figure, immobile in the stream of a material woven with memories from beyond all memories.

● JOSEPH RULOT (1853-1919), was a native inhabitant of Liège who was trained at the Liège Academy where he became a professor. He devoted his entire life to defend and illustrate his home town he never abandoned. He never managed to have his sketches executed, in spite of their number and originality, resting on idealism and Romantic poetry.

JULIEN DILLENS

☐ *Genie with Lily*

Initially designed for a child's grave, erected in the Laeken cemetery in 1893, this gracious angel's figure setting foot on Earth delicately expresses that intimate melancholy, which earned Julien Dillens the nickname of the "poet of the sad".

In 1897, the sculptor transposed the subject to ivory. The opportunity had come from King Leopold II, who had ordered elephant tusks from his estate in Congo to be distributed to Belgian sculptors who were interested (cf. p. 139).

3

4

3. *Joseph Rulot*
The Legend,
1895, bronzed plaster,
58 x 21 x 22, inv. 11384.

4. *Julien Dillens*
Genie with Lily,
1897, ivory
61 x 17 x 18. 5,
inv. 11, 983.

20th century

Pablo Picasso, based in Paris, invented Cubism in 1907.
Wassily Kandinsky painted his first abstract gouache in
Germany in 1910.
The representational principle had already been called into
question; from then on, it was openly challenged.
Marcel Duchamp installed a bicycle wheel on a stool in 1913, thus
producing a first *ready-made* without preconceived ideas. He
defined it as an action enabling him "to boil down the idea of an
aesthetic concern to a mental choice".
The same year, the International Exhibition of Modern Art, better
known as the "*Armory Show*", was held in New York. One third of
the some one thousand six hundred exhibits stemmed from
Europe, mainly from France.
This monumental confrontation between contemporary art
creations of Europe and the United States foreshadowed the end
of Europe's artistic hegemony and the beginning of mutual
contributions from one continent to the other; this exchange was
gradually intensified in the second half of the century.
These elements underpinned the artistic epic of the entire 20th
century: although they did not directly generate its major
developments, they opened the path for them before the First
World War. After World War II, the accelerating progress of
production and communication techniques brought about a radical
evolution of society and called all its conceptions of values into
question. Art's parallel development trespassed against all the
criteria that had ever been dictated by occidental tradition and
implied an investigation of art's own nature.

1. *Eugène Dodeigne*
Hand on Thigh,
1965, stone of Soignies,
139 x 72 x 72.5,
inv. 7353.

2. *Jacques Moeschal*
Dorienne,
1950, white marble
(Dionysos),
54 x 50.3 x 28,
inv. 10205.

● EUGÈNE DODEIGNE was
born in Belgium in 1923.
He received his apprenticeship from his father, a stone-
cutter in the North of
France, and an academic
training which led him to
the School of Fine Arts in
Paris. After carving wood,
he shaped carefully gouged
and polished stone into abstract shapes. From 1960, in
the huge studio he has built
near Lille, he resorted to
anthropomorphic represen-
tation in splintered stone
and bronze. On the other
hand—they are not sketches
for his sculptures, but independent creations—he pro-
duces many drawings that
are loaded with powerful
tension.

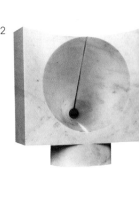

EUGÈNE DODEIGNE

☐ Hand on Thigh

Eugène Dodeigne shapes the stone with a pneumatic
drill, engaging in a single combat against matter. The shape
that emerges from it bears the scars of the confrontation.
The work becomes apparent in the course of the dialogue. The sculptor must decide to bring the work to a
halt when the material has acquired the expressive form.

JACQUES MOESCHAL

☐ Dorienne

The sculptor has carved a shape with subtle asymmetries
from a greek marble block. The cone that focuses the initial gaze is oblique and the rift through the parallelepiped
shows a slight thrust at the rear. The cast shadow of the
piece defines a square with a narrow keyhole. Like with
his signals that welcome the traveller as he enters a country, Moeschal points at the passage towards otherness.
This little work seems to have been devised for medita-
tion and reveals its appeal and its demands.

● JACQUES MOESCHAL (born
in 1913) first studied architecture and worked at Le
Corbusier's. He produc-
ed several public monu-
ments in concrete, of an
extreme elegance and a challenging technical audacious-
ness. At the Brussels World
Fair in 1958, every-
one noticed his Pavillon du
Génie Civil (Civil
Engineering Pavilion) with
its thirty-six metre high triangular spire. Every Belgian

automobilist is familiar with
the gigantic signals he has
erected at the entrance of the
Brussels-Ostend motorway
and on the French-Belgian
border. The thirty metre
signal he has installed for the
Olympic Games of Mexico
in 1968 is probably the most
prestigious among his numerous works in foreign countries—on the Austro-
Hungarian border, in
Houston, in the Negueb
desert.

● OSSIP ZADKINE
(1890-1967), was born in
Russia but settled in Paris in
1908. He was surrounded by
friends such as Pablo
Picasso, Robert Delaunay,
Alexandre Archipenko and
was converted to Cubism.
After an exile in the United
States during World War II,
he returned to France and
conceived the work through
which he achieved fame:
The *Destroyed City*, erected
in Rotterdam.

OSSIP ZADKINE

☐ *Diane*

This monumental Diana still shows the drift of the tree from which the sculptor has shaped her. The work's Cubism comes to the fore in the face, partly half-profile and partly full-face view, in the left arm, dislocated by a hollow cut, and by placing the bust's front to the belly's profile. Like a great virtuoso, Zadkine has unified the silhouette by means of a play with curves that surround it and create a rotating motion in which the spectator is drawn.

DENNIS OPPENHEIM

☐ *Attempt To Raise Hell*

While exercising *Body Art*, Dennis Oppenheim has exposed himself to hazardous conditions on several occasions. In 1970, for example, during a face-to-face performance with a tarantula, his only protection were the tufts of hair he tore off his skull to place them between his face and the spider. He produced an act for his five-year old daughter in 1973, whereby she played the electric organ then dropped down on the keyboard, simulating death. Her body's weight on the keys had to produce a continuous sound two hours long. Oppenheim took the idea over again in 1974, placing the corpse of a German shepherd on the keyboards, involved in a sort of roundabout. The sound evolved with rigor mortis. He replaced this first ersatz human corpse by a puppet, his self-portrait, and placed it in various situations. Here it is seated in a meditative attitude and sporadically bends forward, at random, bumping in the bell with its forehead.

3. *Ossip Zadkine*, **Diane**, *1937, wood, 330 x 103.5 x 80, inv. 6425.*

4. *Dennis Oppenheim*, **Attempt To Raise Hell**, *1974, temporary loan*

● DENNIS OPPENHEIM, was born in Washington D. C. — where his father was an engineer—in 1938, and studied applied arts. He produced his first *Earth Art* work in 1967 and gave a performance within the framework of a collective exhibition of artists from the West coast of the United States. He carried out his first *Body Art* performances in the early seventies, using his own body as material, then introduced machines into his work towards the end of the decennium, like Tinguely. Dennis Oppenheim is in permanent motion and refuses to halt at a specific style or technique.

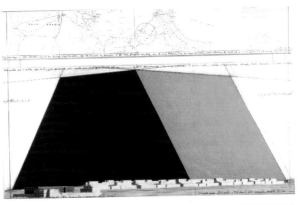

1. *Pol Bury*
Nineteen balls on three curved steel planes,
1967, 124.3 x 30.3 x 39.5, inv. 7579.

2. *Christo,*
The Mastaba of Abu Dhabi,
1981, ink and pencil on paper, (39.5 + 108.5) x 245.5, temporary loan

● POL BURY was born in 1922 on the outskirts of La Louvière (Hainaut), where he later founded an active Surrealist heard. He joined it in 1939, and his painting was geared to Magritte's work for some ten years. He participated in the CoBrA movement from 1949 to 1951. The turning point of his career can be pinpointed in 1953. Under Alexander Calder's influence (cfr. p. 214), Bury stepped away from painting and began his "mobile planes" — abstract coloured surfaces set in motion by an engine and rotating horizontally. His work henceforth evolved with successive discoveries of structures and new techniques, of which random motion is the common denominator. After the "erectile punctuations" appeared in 1959, came the "kinetizations", magnetically animated metallic sculptures, and the hydraulic sculptures.

POL BURY

☐ Nineteen balls on three curved steel planes

The time of contemplation varies from one spectator to the other and corresponds to the time of appropriation of the observed subject. If this subject changes, additional time is required to perceive its modulations. Pol Bury sets a trap of systems to the onlooker, although at first sight the mechanism appears simple to identify and the number of potential variations seems finite. However, he lets the almost imperceptible displacements occur in unforeseen locations, so that these escape from a gaze that wastes its patience by trying to spot them elsewhere. Moreover, he modulates these changes in such a way that the required time to see the item in all its various states is unforeseeable. A doubt arises about what has just been observed, about one's own capacity of keeping the memories of what one has seen. Pol Bury describes the effect of his work as a dilation of time: it is situated in a time that is no longer measurable. His installations literally are figures of eternity.

CHRISTO

☐ The Mastaba of Abu Dhabi

Christo's artistic production begins with the project's drawings, of which he sometimes executes a large number of proofs (three hundred drawings and collages for the Umbrellas project). These carefully finished, fair copies are an intrinsic part of the work. They often occur several years before the actual application on site, and since the latter is ephemeral, the drawings survive them. Certain projects never see the light, like e. g. the *Mastaba of Abu Dhabi,* of which the first sketches date back to 1977. The idea was—to celebrate the oil power of the United Arab Emirates—to erect a 150 m high mastaba in Abu Dhabi, covering a surface of 65,700 m^2 and consisting of 390,500 barrels of oil. The inevitable comparison with the mastabas of Ancient Egypt, that have survived some five thousand years whereas this project, like all Christo's work, was doomed to be dismantled on a short-term basis, induces a reflection on the timelessness of the objet d'art.

4

3. *Vic Gentils*
Vik King,
1964, wood, ivory, metal and felt, 197.3 x 129 x 18.1, inv. 11173.

4. *Vic Gentils*
Rua de amor,
1969, polychrome wood, 207 x 120 x 69, inv. 7770.

● CHRISTO JAVACHEFF, known as CHRISTO, born in Bulgaria in 1935, arrived in Paris in 1958. His first 'packages', in the spirit of New Realism, offered no aesthetic attractivity whatsoever. He settled in New York in 1964 and from then on his career was highlighted with a series of spectacular productions. He presented his first air package in 1966 and wrapped up a public building for the first time in 1968: the Kunsthalle in Berne. He acquired world fame with the *Valley Curtain*, an orange nylon curtain of 110 m high by 394 m long which was spanned across a Colorado valley in 1972. He repeated this type of *Land Art* intervention four years later with the *Running Fence*, a 5.49 m high white curtain, attached to stayed posts and running across 39 km of the Californian countryside. Two famous examples amongst several other wrappings were the Pont-Neuf in Paris (1985) and the Reichstag in Berlin (1995), a project he initiated in 1972.

VIC GENTILS

☐ **Vik King** (GOLDSCHMIDT BEQUEST)

The golden mouldings of huge dismantled frames stand like organ pipes. Diverted from their initial function, the keys of old dismembered pianos have been rearranged in a refined mosaic, adjacent to the dull shades of weathered wood, the faded greens of felt, the black colour of ebony. In the centre, the silhouette of the artist as a *Vik King* (pun on the forename), capped with a milliner's block. All these elements, adulterated by their new implementation, perfectly combine to integrate in this dazzling relief.

☐ **Rua de amor**

With his blunt, ironic manner, Vic Gentils depicts a memory of a brothel alley in Bahia, Brazil, where one side is reserved for coloured prostitutes and the other for the white ones. The white, adipose whore, who provocatively flaunts herself on the one side, peculiarly contrasts with the slender, somewhat enigmatic black girl; the customer pats her buttocks with a coarse laugh. In his series of remarkably expressive likenesses, Vic Gentils has developed a caricatural, sometimes even trivial style, most daringly exemplified by *Rua de Amor*. It definitely confirms the astute and spirited mastery of the artist to integrate such dissimilar elements in utterly expressive figures.

● VIC GENTILS (born in 1919) was trained in Antwerp, and he first painted in an Expressionist style between 1943 and 1957, then kindred to Surrealism. He began to introduce objects in his paintings in 1954 and produced his first reliefs in 1959. They are large assemblages, scanned by vertical wooden elements placed next to one another. He then added broad golden mould ings stemming from large frames and whatever can be retrieved from old pianos. The next stage included milliner's blocks, orientating him towards sculpture in the round, in which he integrated furniture elements. His compositions were complex and representational, and sometimes likenesses emerge from them, whose resemblance is striking in spite of the heterogeneity of the materials.

● HENRY MOORE (1898-1986) trained at Leeds School of Art then at the Royal College of Art in London. He stayed six months in Italy in 1925 and travelled to Paris almost every year until World War II. The influence of the work of Brancusi, Laurens and Zadkine constituted the underpinning of his own work. His human figures from around 1935 were kindred to Surrealism and his non-representational research links him to the abstract Constructivists. Henry Moore found his originality in a style where voids and masses echo one another and balance each other out in a gradually more monumental conception. He obtained the Prize of the Biennale of Venice in 1948. Since then, he has collected honours and has become the world's most exhibited living sculptor.

● FRANCIS BACON (1909-1992), originated from Dublin and moved to London in 1925. He first worked as an interior designer then took on painting towards 1930. He was a demanding autodidact and has destroyed the better part of his early work. His manner asserted itself in 1944 with *Three Studies for Figures at the Base of a Crucifixion* (London, Tate Gallery) and its shockingly distorted figures. He continued in that direction and produced tortured images of the human body and face, filled with extreme tension, sometimes hallucinatingly expressive. He was acknowledged in an artistic realm where informal art seemed to prevail, and became a forerunner and leading figure of the new representational art of the sixties.

1. *Henry Moore*
Draped Woman On Steps,
*1957-1958, bronze,
187 x 207 x 154,
inv. 6856*

2. *Francis Bacon*
The Pope with the Owls,
*1958, oil on canvas,
198 x 142,
inv. 7355.*

HENRY MOORE
☐ Draped Woman On Steps
This imposing seated woman expresses the tension of expectation, toned down by the way the head is fixed to the cylindrical neck, poised like that of an attentive bird. The drapery of the dress stresses the sculpture's lines of force: two parallel lines descending from the breasts to the knees, almost at a right angle with the legs, conferring its seat to the figure. Between the thighs, the broader drapery softens the slender, nervous creases of the waist and of the torso, making the breast swell. Henry Moore worked in unison with nature and treated drapery like a landscape: "... the contrast of the folds, graceful and delicate here, full and unwieldy there, [that] evoke the shape of the mountains that are the creased skin of the earth."

FRANCIS BACON
☐ The Pope with the Owls
Francis Bacon often produced series. From 1947 to 1967, he painted thirty-five popes, more or less faithfully inspired by Diego Velasquez's portrait of Pope Innocent X, dating back to c. 1650. The *Pope with the Owls* amalgamated the Renaissance model and the figure of Pius XII, who still reigned in 1958 and whose photograph Bacon had in his studio. The throne could be the *sedia gestatoria* in which the pope was carried during the Holy See's solemnities. He indeed seems to move forward along a diagonal that leaves the painting. However, in spite of all etiquette, the apparently worried pope stares to his right, in the same direction as the owls. He is plunged into absolute darkness and like isolated in a glass cage with a strangely distorted perspective. When asked why he reverted to this obsessional motif, Bacon just answered that this was a simple pretext to use purple without falling in Fauvism. Nevertheless, it seems likely that it was the artist's pleasure to subvert a venerated representation by a fiercely Expressionist treatment.

3. *Roel D'Haes,* **Dicky as the Christ of Prague**, *1965, bronze, 119.5 x 40 x 36.8, inv. 11138.*

4. *Gaston Bertrand* **Portrait of Alla Goldschmidt**, *1951, oil on canvas, 54 x 45, inv. 11071.*

The following works are exhibited in the gallery that begins on the left hand-side of Francis Bacon's canvas.

ROEL D'HAESE

☐ **Dicky as the Christ of Prague** (GOLDSCHMIDT BEQUEST)
Bénédict Goldschmidt had closely followed the evolution of Roel D'Haese for ten years and purchased several drawings and sculptures from him. They had become friends, which explains why he used his patron's nickname in the title of this work. It has not been proven that the Goldschmidt had a remote Czech lineage, but the artist liked to believe it; and he had seen a reproduction of a small statue, venerated in a Prague church: a stately Jesus, forty-six centimetres high, splendidly dressed and wearing a gold crown set with jewels and topped by a sphere. Roel D'Haese imagined this way out portrait for his friend, combining deferent tenderness and derisive spirit. The sphere of Jesus has changed in a triumphal pear and Dicky's body in a hollow tree, on the trunk of which a twig still grows, although the main branches are broken.

GASTON BERTRAND

☐ **Portrait of Alla Goldschmidt** (GOLDSCHMIDT BEQUEST)
This portrait's facture is guided by the firm will to boil the figure down to geometrical forms. The left shoulder's rectangle is opposed to a non-representational parallelogram on the other side. A truncated pyramidal plane outlines the nape of the neck on one side and resolves in an oval accompanying the curve of the hand and the arm. The outline of the face is divided up in a Cubist way. Alla Goldschmidt's expressive likeness powerfully shows through these

● THE GOLDSCHMIDT BEQUEST.
Bénédict Goldschmidt and his wife Alla Safieva have gathered a first rate collection of Modern art. Upon her demise in 1989, Alla Goldschmidt left the collection to the Royal Museums on the condition that works which were not exhibited permanently would be sold to constitute a fund to purchase works of living artists. A selection commitee has chosen hundred seventy-four works that have enhanced the museum's collection.

● ROEL D'HAESE (born in 1921) attends drawing courses at the academy of Aalst from his eleventh year. At the age of fourteen, he became the apprentice of a smith, then of a sculptor who made devotion statues. From 1938 to 1942, he was a pupil at La Cambre, in the class of sculptor Oscar Jespers. Once his training completed, Roel D'Haese carves stone, using direct cut until 1953. He then switched over to wrought iron and to work with steel and copper sheets, from which he shapes a strange bestiary. He started up a foundry, where he worked alone until 1964, taking up the challenge of considerable works. Since 1957, Roel D'Haese uses the lost wax process for hollow casting, a technique which enables him to unfurl a never slackening talent and imagination.

1

2

3

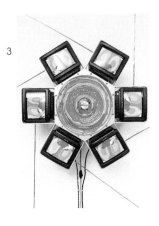

1. *Reinhoud*
Migraine VI,
*1967-1968, coppered
lead, 41.4 x 24.5 x 22.5,
inv. 7664.*

2. *Rik Wouters*
Head of Jean Krickx,
*c. 1910, plaster of Paris,
28 x 19 x 22.5,
inv. 11620.*

● NAM JUNE PAIK was born in Seoul in 1932 and lived there till he was eighteen. During the Korean war in 1950, he fled to Japan where he studied art history and philosophy at the Tokyo University. He arrived in Germany in 1956 to study composition and had a decisive encounter with John Cage. Paik soon discovered visual suggestions in the technical media (radio tuners, tape recorders, record players) John Cage added to his prepared pianos, and switched from music to video. During a sojourn in Japan in 1963-1964, he made experiments in this field, then settled in the United States, where he largely developed his video installation work. The most spectacular was welcomed in the Centre Georges Pompidou in 1982 and included three hundred eighty-four monitors and eight video tapes.

systematic distortions. Gaston Bertrand's entire work stands on the border between allusive, very sensitive representational art and pure construction (cfr. p. 199).

REINHOUD

☐ **Migraine VI**
Reinhoud (born in 1928) leaves the use of his surname to his elder brother Roel and merely signs with his forename. In 1950, he settled in the "Ateliers du Marais" in Brussels, opened by Alechinsky to his CoBrA friends (cfr. p. 200). Reinhoud pursued this venture with Alechinsky, Appel, Jorn and Dotremont long after the dissolution of the group. From the beginning, he had chosen a technique and a material: beaten and welded copper sheet out of which he shaped a swarming population of insects and homuncules, or else gigantic voracious flowers. Like anybody does at breakfast, he also kneads the crumb of loaves, but with a particular talent. A series of little creatures emerge from it, and around 1962, he has set them in gold by electrolysis. *Migraine* is the title of a series of fourteen figures shaped from lead sheets, coppered or silvered by galvanoplasty. They form a set of pitiful monsters like this one, shrivelling with pain, holding his head with both hands and pointing his disproportioned fingers at the sky.

RIK WOUTERS

☐ **Head of Jean Krickx**
Rik Wouters had already sculpted for ten years after completing his academic training, and the sensitive works he had produced confirmed his exceptional artistic disposition. Most of these sculptures were cast in bronze (cfr. p. 163). The project of this head was probably given up, and only the original plaster cast remains. However, its expressive force, accentuated by the unfinished facture, singles it out as an audacious creation.

3. *Nam June Paik*
Capella,
1990, aluminium underframe structure, six Sony television screens, a painted hub cap, a Sony laser disk player, Ø 85 (273 with open aerials) x 41, inv. 11323.

4. *George Segal*
The Hustle: The Four-Hand Pass,
1980, plaster, wood, plastic and metal, 244 x 366 x 488, inv. 11015.

NAM JUNE PAIK

☐ Capella

In the same way that cathedrals' stained-glass roses present dazzling images of light and colour to which the churchgoers can gear their faith, this strange device emerging from technological fantasy seems to pick up the images of a primal cosmic energy at the azimuths of its unfurled aerials. The sparkling images that enliven the six monitors of *Capella* have been recorded on a laser disk and perfectly match the suggestion of this poetic item.

GEORGE SEGAL

☐ The Hustle: The Four-Hand Pass

Sidney Janis managed one of New York's most important galleries. He is pictured as a has-been seducer dancing with a very young lady. The white colour standardizes the colour of the skin, the hair and the clothes and, though rendering the detail of the material's texture, gives the couple a ghastly appearance accentuated by their closed eyes. The mirror at the back of the room reflects a shimmering image that seems to move as the spectator steps forward. If several persons wander through the reflection space, then the dancers mingle with the public.

The characters give the impression to have been captured in the midst of action, but they participated in a slow process that required long moments of immobility. As opposed to a model taking the pose for a sculptor or a painter, the subject is literally cast in plaster, and the slightest muscular twitching will be reflected in the statue.

● GEORGE SEGAL was born in the Bronx in 1924, to Jewish parents who had recently emigrated from Eastern Europe. He studied drawing, painting and plaster sculpture in New York. In 1947, he was enthralled by Willem De Kooning's and Jackson Pollock's abstract Expressionism. He stepped away from non-representational expression to join the trend that Allan Kaprow, initiator of the *Happening*, was leading at the time: he arranged heterogeneous materials within compositions that escaped from the canvas' framework to become "environments". The continuation of these practices led Segal to three-dimensionality. He produced his first 'gestural facture' plaster figure in 1958, an alto rilievo of a *Reclining Nude*. Then came the life-size figures, sculpted in the round, roughly modelled in plaster of Paris on a carcass of wire mesh. He made a first experiment of taking plaster casts from life on himself in 1961: as he was seated on a chair, he had himself wrapped up in gauze impregnated with wet plaster of Paris. Once the carapace had set, it was cut up and reassembled, and its surface was superficially remodelled. This figure, sitting at a table, was his first Tableau Vivant. From 1971, George Segal uses the plaster cast as a mould in which he pours a far more solid plaster, enabling him to make much finer figures, where textures are rendered in accurate detail. He applied this technique to the nude figure placed in an intimist setting, like Degas. He started colouring his plaster and also melted bronze pieces.

1. *Rik Wouters*
Lady with Yellow Necklace / Interior D,
1912, oil on canvas,
121.5 x 110, inv. 4741.

2. *Rik Wouters*
The Flute Player,
1914, oil on canvas,
134 x 116, inv. 4742.

● RIK WOUTERS
(1882-1916)
Rik Wouters' father was a furniture manufacturer from Mechlin, and he put his son to work from the age of twelve, encouraging him to carve wood. Rik attended evening courses at the academy of his native town. From 1900 to 1904, he studied sculpture and decorative arts at the Brussels Academy of Fine Arts, where he became acquainted with some of the artists

Fauvism

Paris, 1905. In the Salon d'Automne, the canvases of a dozen painters whose common idiom consisted of a violent juxtaposition of pure tonalities were exhibited side by side: Matisse, Vlaminck, Derain, Marquet and Van Dongen were represented, to mention only the most renowned. In the centre of the room, the work of an academic sculptor could only be perceived as dull and dreary. The scandalized art critic Louis Vauxcelles wrote that it "looked like a Donatello among the wild beasts". 'Fauves' is the French word for 'wild beasts'. The artists used the term as their manifesto because it did not define any aesthetic tenet. The development of Gauguin's and Van Gogh's work had already proven to be at odds with Impressionism and Neo-Impressionism, that had wound up in a dissolution of the shape. The Fauves preferred large contrasting patches of pure tonalities to Divisionism's multiplicity of strokes. They emancipated colour from its descriptive function and used it to develop powerful, simplified forms. The work was not intended to restitute reality anymore, but to create a new and autonomous sensorial equivalent of reality. Fauvism was hallowed at the Salon d'Automne in Paris, in 1906, and it exerted its influence on German Expressionism, featured by the group "Die Brücke" in Dresden. Ferdinand Schirren often travelled from Brussels to Paris, and he introduced these new concepts in Belgium, to which a number of Belgian artists subscribed: the key figure of Rik Wouters, Auguste Oleffe, Charles Dehoy, Willem Paerels, Jean Brusselmans, and a few others. A decisive element for the cohesion of the "Brabantine Fauves" was the way the Georges Giroux art gallery promoted and circulated their work.

RIK WOUTERS

☐ **Lady with Yellow Necklace / Interior D**
Nel has taken the pose next to the window, so as to allow Rik to shade her face with "... these red, green lashes swiped

3

3. *Rik Wouters*
Household Worries,
*1913-1914, plaster cast,
227 x 79 x 79, inv. 11623.*

who would later be the "Brabantine Fauves", like Ferdinand Schirren. He also encountered Nel (Hélène Duerinckx), who posed for the Academy's pupils and was to become his life companion and favourite model. Though the couple had to struggle through several years of material hardships, the young artist's dynamism never slackened. In addition to sculpture, Rik took up painting, initially inspired by Émile Claus' Luminism, then by James Ensor. Auguste Oleffe opened new perspectives to him by the atmosphere he created, but it is likely that Schirren set him on the tracks of his eventual manner by suggesting that Rik should abandon the impasto's of his 1908 canvases. Inspired by dancer Isadora Duncan's show in 1910, he undertook his large bronze nude *Mad Virgin*, at the occasion of which he met Georges Giroux. The latter brought him financial support and a subsequent contract that ensured his career. He worked at a steady pace during the following years: he produced over sixty canvases in 1912, exhibited thirteen sculptures at the 1913 salon of 'La Libre Esthétique', and in 1914, the Georges Giroux Gallery presented sixteen sculptures, forty-five paintings and seventy-six watercolours and drawings for his first one-man show. The war slowed his artistic production down without actually bringing it to a halt. He was made prisoner in Holland from October 1914, but the spent the major part of his time in the military hospital to treat the cancer that ate his face away and eventually overpowered him on July 11, 1916.

on it by the reflections of light". The silhouette is outlined by a fine black brushstroke and stands out against the decorative seedbed of the background. The purple blue mass of the dress, applied in broad stretches with a palette knife, was scraped so as to leave but a thin layer of paint on the canvas. The painter has allowed for gaps between these stretches, so that the blank canvas appears now and then, conferring lightness to the matter and bringing this large dark area to life.

Towards 1910, Rik Wouters had started applying thick layers of pictorial matter with the spatula, like Ensor for his bourgeois interiors. He freed himself from that manner and adopted a more personal technique, using less paint: he scraped the paint on the canvas and sometimes thinned it down with turpentine.

☐ *The Flute Player*
Rik Wouters was subdued by Paul Cézanne, just like he had been enthralled by James Ensor. The very architectural layout of the background in this 1914 canvas hints at this new turning point in the painter's work. The choice of the hues has gained subtlety, the sharp contrasts have subsided, the central motif—in which the drawing asserts itself more forcefully—has been enlivened by a play with transparencies and reflections.

☐ *Household Worries*
Nel was Rik Wouters' wife and favourite model. He pictured her in countless familiar poses, always geared to everyday reality. Here, she sulkily ponders about her household worries. Just like his painting consists of broad, separate patches, he shapes the clay in a series of scattered planes, allowing for deep furrows between relief accidents that catch the light.

1. *Ferdinand Schirren*
**The Woman at
the Piano**,
*c. 1915-1917,
oil on canvas, 136 x 151,
inv. 8955.*

● FERDINAND SCHIRREN (1872-1944) studied sculpture in the class of Jef Lambeaux at the Brussels Academy of Fine Arts, and became acquainted with Rik Wouters, who was ten years his junior. Schirren gave up sculpture for painting round 1905 and discovered the Fauves in Paris. He produced watercolours with allusive shapes, organised in broad, separate patches of pure colour, letting wide stretches of blank paper appear. This opened the way to Brabantine Fauvism, soon chosen by Rik Wouters. Schirren painted mainly watercolours for ten years, and started resorting to oil between 1914 and 1918. He favoured a radically Fauvist technique of expressive, full coloured planes, as exemplified by *The Woman at the Piano*. The Georges Giroux Gallery organised his one-man show in 1917, featuring over a hundred works. After 1918, he toned his hues down and adopted a more structured manner.

FERDINAND SCHIRREN

☐ *The Woman at the Piano*
the volume of the room wherein the scene is staged is not indicated by any form of perspective. In the lower left corner of the painting, the separation between the red floor and the blue plinth does not determine a realistic vanishing line: it only alludes to depth arbitrarily. This also applies to the oblique of a shadow, bearing under the piano. The keyboard's horizontal line is jagged right in its middle. There is no actual drawing in this composition, structured by the coloured masses: the patent brushwork creates the shapes.

"Swiftly jotting down my most harmonious hours of pleasure", wrote the painter, "swiftly enough to let the work come forth from the shudder that electrifies me in such moments. A couple of broad brushstrokes and a few planes will do to recreate the architecture of my emotion." This can be regarded as a definition of the aim and method of Fauvist painting.

AUGUSTE OLEFFE

☐ *August 1909*
This happy family scene in the artist's garden in Auderghem is an accomplished example of synthesis of the Impressionist means he fully mastered. The atmosphere of a warm afternoon bathed with sunlight is sensitively rendered by means of the vivid strokes, letting the light play on the figures and softly shading it off along the pale façade. The black dress of the lady seated at the loom and the laboured blue of the apron of the young girl with the book are reminiscent of Manet. At a later stage, Oleffe's brushwork became fuller and thicker.

2. *Auguste Oleffe*
August 1909,
*1909, oil on canvas,
200 x 200,
inv. 4159.*

3. *Willem Paerels*
Portrait of Georges Giroux,
*1914, oil on canvas,
140 x 105,
inv. 10271.*

3

WILLEM PAERELS

☐ Portrait of Georges Giroux

This painting, produced in the year of the declaration of war, shows the remarkable efficiency of the scarcity of means Paerels had attained in his style. The relief of the features is modelled by the patent juxtaposition of the light zone and the shadow zone, to which the contrasted prevailing colours of the background tapestry are a counterpart: red on one side, blue and green on the other. The dark silhouette perfectly conveys the casual elegance of the character who became a key figure of the Brussels art scene.

● LA GALERIE GEORGES GIROUX.
With his wife Gabrielle, Georges Giroux kept a fashionable milliner's boutique in Brussels. They became acquainted with Rik Wouters in 1910 through a friend and writer. At the time, the young sculptor was working on the *Mad Virgin*: they were enthralled and decided to help him and to create an art gallery. On March 16, 1912, the élite of the Brussels art scene was invited to the opening of the

G. G. G. — the Georges Giroux Gallery. In a mansion of the rue Royale, Giroux sumptuously displayed a group of young artists around the figure of Rik Wouters. He had also invited the prestigious French Nabis Pierre Bonnard, Édouard Vuillard and Ker Xavier Roussel. His well-managed gallery made the brabantine Fauves renowned, and its significant thematic exhibitions pursued the spirit and activity of La Libre Esthétique, that disappeared in 1914.

● AUGUSTE OLEFFE (1867-1931) could initially be regarded as a follower of Gustave Courbet. He was subdued by Auguste Renoir's and Édouard Manet's work during a stay in Paris in 1897, and drew inspiration from them for some time. In 1898, he founded the artistic circle Le Labeur with a few friends like Jef Lambeaux and Ferdinand Schirren. This group exercised free Naturalism and gradually opened up to Impressionism and Luminism, quite fashionable at the time. 1906 was an important year, both for him and for the evolution of Belgian painting: he purchased the house of his dreams in Auderghem, a house that soon became a central meeting point for the Brabantine Fauves, upon whom he exerted a significant influence.

● WILLEM PAERELS (1878-1962)
left his native Holland at the age of sixteen to settle in Brussels. He registered with the Academy of Fine Arts and showed up only once. The canvases he presented at the 1906 "La Libre Esthétique" Salon fell within the Impressionist scope, and he gained some immediate success. He often called at Auguste Oleffe's circle, where he was steered towards the Brabantine Fauves; he was represented at the opening of the Giroux Gallery. Like many of his peers, he oriented his style towards a darker and more structured manner after the First World War.

1. Jean Brusselmans
In the Garden,
1916, oil on canvas,
185 x 200, inv. 4675.

2. Léon Spilliaert
Self-Portrait,
1904, watercolour, India
ink and crayon on paper,
48.8 x 63, inv. 6923.

3. Léon Spilliaert
Woman on the Dyke,
1907, watercolour, India
ink and crayon on paper,
34.3 x 74.4, inv. 6769.

4. Léon Spilliaert
**Airship in its
Hangar**,
1910, India ink, gouache
and pastel on paper,
59.8 x 83.7, inv. 11223.

● JEAN BRUSSELMANS
(1884-1953), studied engraving and painting at the
Brussels Academy. In 1907,
he hired a studio together
with Rik Wouters and made
friends with Auguste Oleffe
and the future Brabantine
Fauves, already sharing their
aesthetic views. However,
when he painted *In the
Garden*, a coloured hymn to
the sweetness of life, his
etchings showed a play with
broad areas of pure blacks
and whites and foreshadowed the clearly more structured style he exercised later
on, under the influence of
Expressionism (cfr. p. 179).

JEAN BRUSSELMANS
☐ In the Garden
The entire scene, staged in Auguste Oleffe's garden in Auderghem, is depicted by a mosaic of oblong strokes of pure hues that cannot be regarded as Neo-Impressionist heritage. The form does not dissolve in Pointillist vibration here, but is firmly structured by a framework of jointed vertical, horizontal and oblique rectangles. These bold strokes integrate in a carcass outlined by a slight line that makes the shapes stand out. The light either plays in the foliage or falls straight on the figures, and is remarkably well rendered by the chromatic contrast between adjacent strokes. Like Rik Wouters, Jean Brusselmans does not shy at the arbitrary nature of colour. He clearly expressed his Fauvist credo himself: "Colour is free, and doesn't obey to any rule. It must be invented by the artist. Colour is light and dramatic feeling." The face of the two women on the left of the painting illustrate this in a dazzling way.

LÉON SPILLIAERT
☐ Self-Portrait
The painter has pictured himself at work. he scrutinizes his mirror, only the rounded back of the seat on which his drawing board lies can be seen, the family-house background around him fades away in the twilight. The faint light of a pinkish moon is reflected by the invisible mirror, catches the objects and moulds the artist's features. The deep-set, dark-circled eyes, the hollow cheeks, the jutting bulges on the forehead and the hairline sculpted by *chiaroscuro* contrasts determine a spectral face, turned towards its own anxiety.
The numerous self-portraits Spilliaert has painted since 1907 all reflect the cruelty of his ill-being. The psychological and morphological analogy between these faces and those Edward Munch had painted some fifteen years earlier—The Shriek is from 1893—underlies the hypothesis of an influence and confirms a mental kinship.

☐ Woman on the Dyke
Spilliaert expresses the absolute solitude of an immobile woman facing the infinity of the sea by means of a synthetic vision, on the border between reality and abstraction. His panoramic centring extolls the feeling of vastness, and he lets the sea, the beach, the breakwater, the promenade and on the right, the slope towards town follow one another under the night sky in a succession of broad, flat, adjacent planes of intensely harmonious arbitrary colours. He arranges them in a perspective with the full moon on the horizon, and with its counterpart, the halo of the lighthouse, at the end of the pier. A flight of

3

4

gulls and the female figure, entrapped in the line of its own mystery, are the only signs of life in this world of unsettled reality.

However, neither this interpretation referring to reality nor the composition, abstracted from it, exhaust the meaning of this work, perhaps the spearhead of Spilliaert's path. It demonstrates how the mystery lies not in things but in the look one casts upon them.

☐ *Airship in its Hangar*
(GOLDSCHMIDT BEQUEST)

A dirigible with a footage of two-hundred and ten and thirty-six feet across must have been deemed astounding at the beginning of the century, when aeronautics were only at their infancy. Spilliaert summarizes it to an epic vision, eliminating every detail, merely outlining the hangar, reducing the two characters to yardsticks, the landscape to a plastic symbol of the world. He focuses the attention on the full shape of the fabulous vessel—a remake of Icarus' dream—about to take off.

Robert Goldschmidt, the father of Bénédict Goldschmidt, was a physician and an art lover and collector (cfr. p. 159). As an engineer, he designed the plans of three airships for the Belgian army. They were built in Auderghem, close to Brussels. In 1910, Robert Goldschmidt invited Spilliaert, whom he knew quite well, to lay down a memory of one these dirigibles. The result was a book of fourteen sketches and a collection of on enhanced India ink drawings.

● LÉON SPILLIAERT (1881-1946) was born in Ostend in 1881, where his father kept a perfumer's shop. He briefly attended the Bruges Academy when he was eighteen, but remained a self-taught painter. In 1903-1904, he was employed by Paul Deman, Émile Verhaeren's and Maurice Maeterlinck's editor. But like for his much admired elder fellow citizen James Ensor, his birthtown became the fertile soil of his visionary art: his innermost anguish changed Ostend's reality into a series of hallucinated views for over ten very inspired years, linking him to Symbolism. He became less tense after his marriage at the end of 1916, after settling in Brussels and having a daughter. His art gradually became more casual. The trees—they had nourished his imagination as much as the marine element—became the prevailing theme of the better part of his later work. He shared his life between the joys of his art and of his family.

Notwithstanding two significant exhibitions (at the Giroux Gallery in 1929 and at the Palais des Beaux-Arts in Brussels in 1944), he passed away in 1946 without gaining international recognition, which has only been granted to him in the eighties.

● RAOUL DUFY (1877-1953), was first attracted by the Impressionists, then discovered Henri Matisse's work in 1905 and began painting in broad planes of contrasting colours. He only acquired his own personal manner in his forties, and remained faithful to it. With his alert style and bright hues, he depicted the mundane pleasures of a light-hearted society—concerts, racecourses, yacht races—and the teeming life of beaches and ports. The famous gigantic decorative scheme *The History of Electricity* for the Exposition Universelle in Paris in 1937 was the highlight of this brilliant period.

RAOUL DUFY
☐ *The Port of Marseilles*

This bird's eye view of the old *Port of Marseilles* seen from a balcony enables the painter to capture the running about on the piers, the fishermen's boats, the masts and spars and the city's buildings in his fluid calligraphic style. The overall work is enhanced by the joyous acidity of the transparent colours and centred by the ultramarine blue on the basin's perspective.

OSCAR KOKOSCHKA
☐ *The Player in a Trance /*
Portrait of the Actor Ernst Reinhold

Oskar Kokoschka (1886-1980) began to paint at the age of twenty. While a student at the School of Decorative Arts in Vienna, he also wrote two Expressionist plays in verse, *The Sphinx and the Scarecrow* and *Assassin, Women's Hope* in which Ernst Reinhold, a young actor and a friend, played. The second play caused such a scandal that the author preferred to leave Vienna and to travel for some time, but not without thanking his friend with this portrait; it was Kokoschka's first portrait, painted in 1908. The sharp contrast between the somber clothing and the pastel blue and rose background, the sinuous stroke, the silhouette's asymmetry, the ill-shaped hand all willingly combine to strengthen the puzzling uneasiness aroused by the steadiness of the model's gaze. Kokoschka named this painting *The Player in a Trance* at a later stage.

This work entered the Breslau Museum in 1919, but was excluded from it due to the artistic purge organised by the 3rd Reich. It was sold in Lucern in 1939, amongst hundred and twenty-five other 'degenerate' works. The Royal Museums of Fine Arts of Belgium purchased the canvas on that occasion.

3

1. *Raoul Dufy*
The Port of Marseilles,
*oil on canvas, 116 x 90,
inv. 4734.*

2. *Oscar Kokoschka*
**The Player in a Trance /
Portrait of the Actor
Ernst Reinhold**,
*1908, oil on canvas,
81 x 65, inv. 6152.*

3. *Marc Chagall*
Me and the Village,
*1912, pencil, watercolour
and gouache on paper,
61.8 x 48.9, inv. 11108.*

MARC CHAGALL

☐ Me and the Village (GOLDSCHMIDT BEQUEST)

The title *Me and the Village* stems from the poet Blaise Cendrars, the artist's tribute to rural life and to the fertility of the milch cow. It is a recurring theme in Chagall's work: he had produced a canvas with a very similar composition a year earlier, although it measured 191 x 150.5 cm and now belongs to the New York Museum of Modern Art. When Chagall first arrived in Paris in 1910, at the age of twenty-three, he was involved with the circles of Cubist painters. Subsequently, his paintings' structure was organised more geometrically, and *Me and the Village* is a breaking point in this series. The two main figures are laid out on the composition's diagonals, and their intersection lies in the centre of a large circle—which appears to be more obvious on the canvas at the New York Museum of Modern Art. The area is divided up in triangles, cut up in turn by several circles. In this painting for example, even the blooming shrub on the foreground is triangular. "The architectural form of Cubism was deemed too important", said Chagall. "I preferred an anti-logical figuration [...]. Illogicality may bring us closer to the truth." In fact, this rigorousness in the composition by no means stifled his imagination. A farmer right side up, a woman upside down; two houses upside down between two houses turned up: these motifs, stemming from absolute fantasy, tally harmoniously with this unbridled geometry. And the way the foreground and the background collide, or the superimposition of his own image, milking the cow, upon the cow's profile, can be regarded as a dazzling poetic and symbolic contribution to Cubism. The three later gouaches, painted between 1926 and 1928, show how Chagall stepped away from all restraints and surrendered to the improvisation of a fantastic imagery.

● MARC CHAGALL (1887-1985), stemmed from a modest Jewish family. He first studied painting in Vitebsk, his home town, then in St. Petersburg. In 1910, a patron of the arts enabled him to journey to Paris. He became acquainted with Cubist painters and a close friend to the two great poets of modernity: Guillaume Apollinaire and Blaise Cendrars. He presented his work at the Salon des Indépendants as soon as 1911, but he had returned to Vitebsk by the time the First World War broke out, then the Russian Revolution in 1917. He was appointed Commisar for Fine Art in Vitebsk in 1918. He stayed in Paris again from 1923 to 1941 and acquired the French nationality. He eventually settled at Saint-Paul-de-Vence in 1948, after living in the United States for seven years. He almost lived to be hundred and was famous across the world when he passed away.

1. *Henri Matisse*
Still Life.
Venice Red Interior,
1946, oil on canvas,
92 x 65, inv. 6412.

2. *Georges Braque*
Grapes /
Fruit Dish,
1919, oil and sand on
canvas, 19.5 x 33,
inv. 11097.

3. *Pablo Picasso*
Guitar and Fruit Dish,
1920, pencil, oily pastel
and gouache on paper,
glued to cardboard,
27.2 x 21.3, inv. 11208.

● HENRI MATISSE
(1869-1954), was a
solicitor's clerk who
took up painting because of
an illness during which he
had practised brushwork.
He settled in Paris in 1892,
attended Gustave Moreau's
class at the School of Fine
Arts and modelling courses
(he exercised sculpture until
1930). He became a friend
of André Derain and
Maurice de Vlaminck
during his training, and presented his works together
with theirs in the Salon
d'Automne in 1905, in the
"wild beasts' cage" (cfr.
p. 162). In 1908, when
Russian and American art
collectors regarded him as
the leading figure of new
French painting, Matisse
opened a studio and published his *Notes of a Painter*,
where he set out his aesthetic principles. He believed
that, rather than concen-
trating on the emotional
contents of a painting, to
unfold and stress the "essential lines" of its architecture
would lead to expression.
Brilliant demonstration thereof is *Dance* and *Music* (St.

HENRI MATISSE
☐ *Still Life. Venice Red Interior*
The Venice red has been applied flatly, barely modulated,
as a background on which the table and the paving are
drawn and indicate the room's perspective. Some zones
have been spared for bright yellows or bluish greys or
even to allow for the white primer to take part in the canvas' harmony, and these are in turn used as the drawing's
support. The nimbleness of the lines and brightness of the
contrasting shades combine to create the harmonious
balance Matisse has ambitioned throughout his work.

Petersburg, Hermitage),
painted for his Russian
patron Shchukin: "Three
colours for a vast dance
panel: azure for the sky,
rose for the bodies, green
for the hill." Matisse resumed his prolific production in
the same spirit of harmo-

nious combination of drawing and colour. One of the
most famous highlights of
his glamorous career may
be *The Dance I, II and III*, a
mural commissioned by the
Barnes Foundation in
Pennsylvania in 1930.

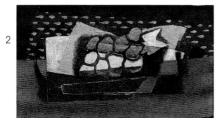

GEORGES BRAQUE

☐ *Grapes / Fruit Dish*
(GOLDSCHMIDT BEQUEST)

The cleaving lines split the stylized bunch of grapes and integrate it in an arbitrary arrangement of planes that also includes the fruit dish. Within a system that unsettles reality, identifiable elements such as the shadows cast to the right or the round segment on the left are delusions. The marks the eye tries to spot refer to the contemplation of an abstract plastic whole. The craftsman's heritage comes to the fore in the decorative technique of mock wood, used to depict a hypothetical table, and in the marbling of the background. They are in the line of the collage technique he had initiated during his Synthetic Cubism period. It is also Braque who had imagined to include sand in the pictorial matter, as soon as 1912.

PABLO PICASSO

☐ *Guitar and Fruit Dish*
(GOLDSCHMIDT BEQUEST)

In the winter of 1920, Pablo Picasso produced seven or eight pastels and watercolours of stylistic kinship to *Guitar and Fruit Dish*, whereby the recurring theme of the still life on a pedestal table he had explored a year earlier is simplified. The representation, fitted into a light arrangement of planes with subtle colours, is tilted towards the front. It announces both versions of the renowned *Three Masked Musicians* of the following year (New York, Museum of Modern Art; Philadelphia, Museum of Art).

● GEORGES BRAQUE (1882-1963), was the son and grandson of house-painters and received a craftsman's apprenticeship. In 1905, under the influence of Henri Matisse and André Derain, he painted as a moderate Fauve. Paul Cézanne's work and Pablo Picasso's *Les Demoiselles d'Avignon* were the two 1907 revelations that oriented him towards Cubism, making him one of the major painters of the beginning of the century, together with Picasso. After a wartime interruption, Braque took up his paint-brushes again in 1917 and produced an abundant and coherent œuvre, largely devoted to still lifes of which the layout was a consequence of his Cubist work. In the last ten years of his life, a recurring bird motif with unfurled wings may hint at the uprising of the still life ascetic's new spiritual concerns.

● PABLO PICASSO (1881-1973) left Barcelona in 1904 to settle in Paris. Until 1906, no trace of concern for the formal issue can be found in his painting. He achieved *Les Demoiselles d'Avignon* (New York, Museum of Modern Art) in 1907, after working on it the whole winter. It marked the dawn of Cubism and opened the way for occidental painting to call everything into question. His blooming protean career developed from there, and the upheaval caused by his numerous major works have turned Picasso into a mythical figure.

1

2

● JULES SCHMALZIGAUG (1882-1917), was born in Antwerp to parents who originated from Germany. He studied painting in the Brussels Academy of Fine Arts, in Isidore Verheyden's class, and applied matter generously like his master. From 1910, he stayed in Paris and was deeply affected by Cubist work. He then read the *Manifesto of Futurist Painters* and—in February 1912 —was influenced by the Futurists' exhibition at the Bernheim-Jeune Gallery. Two months later, he applied these new perspectives while painting in Venice, and presented six works at the *"Primera Espozizione libera futurista internationale"* in May, 1914. He fled to Holland and pursued his work, but the *Portrait of Baron Francis Delbeke* and the unfinished *Portrait of Mrs Nelly Hurrelbrinck* (inv. 7557) were his ultimate works: his unsteady nervous condition, thrown off balance by the war, drove him to commit suicide in 1917.

1. *Jules Schmalzigaug*
Portrait of Baron Francis Delbeke, *1917, gouache and pastel on cardboard, 89.5 x 125.5, inv. 7558.*

JULES SCHMALZIGAUG

☐ Portrait of Baron Francis Delbeke

Around Baron Francis Delbeke, seated at his desk, the sunbeams divide space up in a combination of triangles. As if it were refracted by a series of prisms, the light compels to a syncopated vision that gives the painting its momentum. The vivid pastel cross-hatching stresses that effect. Italian Futurist painters ambitioned to introduce speed and movement in the representation in order to extoll the dynamics of modern life. Schmalzigaug restricts himself to let the light whirl around his model, pictured in an almost naturalist manner.

PROSPER DE TROYER

☐ The Seamstress

The representation of the seamstress, first bent forward, her face in profile, then tilted up again to cast a dark gaze upon us, owes its complexity to being split up into multiple planes that indicate her motion by a subtle play with curves. The kinetic sequence on the ample rising curve on the left side of the painting is even more impressive: three successive images of the same pair of hands fading in one another, one holding the fancywork, the other drawing the needle. An entirely original form of Futurism flows from the way movement is depicted in this dazzling composition, stemming from Cubism but rigorously developed in two dimensions.

● PROSPER DE TROYER (1880-1961) was aged forty-four when he first exhibited his work: it was openly Expressionist. In 1916-1917, he was linked to the Brabantine Fauves. Upon meeting Filippo Tommaso Marinetti and the Italian Futurists, he produced a number of perfectly Futurist works towards 1920, welcomed in several Italian exhibitions. He then stepped away from representational art and his compositions showed exclusive concern for plastic form: strict arrangements of intertwined rectangles, squares and circles on the painting's perpendicular axes. After 1922, he was one of the first of his generation to return to representational Expressionism and depict scenes from daily life or landscapes.

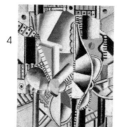

2. *Prosper De Troyer*
The Seamstress,
1920, oil on wood, 150 x 99, inv. 7939.

3. *Marcel-Louis Baugniet*
The Tennis Player,
1926, oil on plywood, 61.5 x 62, inv. 8561.

4. *Fernand Léger*
The Propellers,
1918, oil on canvas, 41 x 33, inv. 6534.

● MARCEL-LOUIS BAUGNIET (1896-1994) was an admirer of Gustav Klimt and Fernand Khnopff till he came out of the Academy. The acquaintance with Cubism during a stay in Paris in 1921-1922 was decisive for his work. He returned to Brussels in 1923 and married dancer Marguerite Acarin, who revealed Raymond Duncan's choreographic concept to Brussels under the name Akarova. Baugniet designed costumes and stage-sets inspired by Cubism for her. In the twenties, he painted moving figures: dancers, sportsmen and labourers. He has also produced a number of abstract paintings, but pulled this trend to its conclusions in the field of interior decoration. As a designer of modern furniture, he set up the "Baugniet et Cie" manufacture in 1930.

MARCEL-LOUIS BAUGNIET

☐ The Tennis Player

The player, captured in the midst of action, is immobilized as if by a snapshot. It is obvious that neither the model's effort, nor his personality nor even his anatomy have impressed the painter. The head is treated as a formal mark. Only the shape this instant of play has created in space is important, and he radically simplifies it in a style kindred to Art-Déco. He summarizes it in a few straight lines extending a triangle. And behind this figure, a fuller volume develops the silhouette's harmonics.

FERNAND LÉGER

☐ The Propellers

To Fernand Léger, the First World War brought about a dynamic deviation of his vision. "I was stunned by the open breech block of a 75mm gun in the sunshine", he wrote, "[it] taught me more for my plastic evolution than all the museums in the world. When I came back from the war, I pursued what I had felt on the front." In the following years—his "mechanical" period—he indeed celebrated the beauty of the machine as a symbol of triumphant modernity. This stylized 1918 canvas, on the verge of abstraction, depicts an engine room, its winding stairs, the machinery's turmoil, the line shafts and helical gears driving the propellers of a hypothetical boat. The Cubist layout and the adjacent, graduated pure colours combine to design these imaginary mechanical devices. The outspoken contrast of the overall yellow tone creates an undetermined space and unifies the composition.

● FERNAND LÉGER (1881-1955) had developed a style—influenced by Paul Cézanne and Fernand Delaunay—in which he broke motifs down from reality into almost abstract forms with highly contrasting colours. During the First World War, he drew his inspiration from the most dynamic aspects of present-day life and gradually reintroduced the human figure into his work, but treated as simple masses. His style progressed right until his last day. After the Second World War, he was concerned with communication with the working classes and worked on huge compositions, amalgamating human figures and abstract elements in series of broad planes with an immediate legibility.

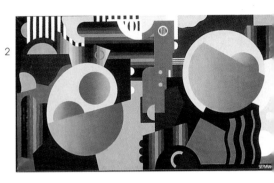

1. *Pierre-Louis Flouquet*
Composition,
*1921, oil on plywood,
71.5 x 56.5, inv. 7645.*

● PIERRE-LOUIS FLOUQUET
(1900-1967) was born in
Paris and settled in Brussels
when he was ten. He studied
at the Academy of Fine Arts
from 1914 to 1919. His first
personal work combines
Cubism and Futurism. From
1921 to 1928, he produced a
most refined plastic art. He
worked in successive
themes, sometimes referring
to reality (*Plastic
Landscapes, Femininities*),
sometimes radically banish-
ing it (*Compositions, Forms,
Constructions*). He then tallied with the "pure plasticity" tenet, supported by the *7
Arts* magazine he had
cofounded. Architect Victor
Bourgeois had clearly defined this concept: "'Pure
plasticity' is a form of decorative painting physically
and objectively obeying to
the process of architectural
composition. Just like a
façade, it does not picture
anything other than a harmony. Its destiny has been fulfilled as soon as, in the form
of a well-proportioned piece
(fulls and empties), it presents a balanced whole of
lines and colours." This is
well exemplified by
the canvas titled *Architecture-
Forms* (inv. 7664).

PIERRE-LOUIS FLOUQUET

☐ Composition

This abstract composition is structured in depth, along
three planes determined by the different tonalities. Three-
dimensional space is organised as a closed location. Due
to the setting out of the two silhouettes and to the relief
of the volumes, the motif on the foreground suggests a
couple of stylized human figures, integrated in a circular
shape; this circle is unified by the play with colours and
centred on the point of intersection of the planes producing it. The painting is ambiguous and attractive: it claims
to refer to 'pure plasticity' but does not completely deny
being representational.

VICTOR SERVRANCKX

☐ Opus 47. Extolling Mechanization

The careful finish of the shapes and the smooth volumes
of this harmonious composition call the accuracy of the
motions of a mechanism to mind, however without picturing a real or imaginary machinery. Sevranckx has
organised a synthesis of alluding forms to pay a tribute to
our industrial era, on which all hope was based at the time.

JOZEF PEETERS

☐ Oil n° 21

This work complies with the strict requirements Jozef
Peeters had set for contemporary painting: as a rigorous
theorist and a sensitive artist, he favoured an exclusively
two-dimensional harmonious scheme of elementary
geometrical forms. Departing from these principles, he
had devised a method to divide the area of the painting
up by means of straight lines crossing it from one side
to the other. Their intersections determined respective
zones of uniform colours. Within this restrictive
framework, he succeeds in producing a fine and sensitive
work. Notwithstanding the absolute evenness of the
drawing, the levels are graduated in depth due to the
contrasts of the coloured zones.

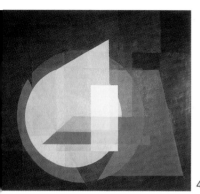

4

2. *Victor Servranckx*
Opus 47. Extolling Mechanization,
*1923, oil on canvas, 113 x 210.5,
inv. 6859.*

3. *Jozef Peeters*
Oil n° 21,
*1924, oil on canvas,
144 x 166.5, inv. 6892.*

4. *Oscar Jespers*
Young Woman,
*1930, wood (limba),
167 x 39.5 x 32.5,
inv. 7228.*

OSCAR JESPERS

☐ **Young Woman**

The overall figure is linked together by a subtle train of simple volumes. The face is treated like a mask and seems added on top of the neck's cylinder. The almost cylindrical arms are attached close to the top of the torso's oblong shape. The grain of the wood, offering a beautiful transition between torso and belly, has obviously determined the place of the belt and the elongation of the abdominal volume. In a similar way, the thighs' ovals are cleverly stressed by the ligneous strokes. The entire piece rests on the massive columns of the calves and the broad base of the feet.

Oscar Jespers has been consequent in submitting this young woman's anatomy to the law of his style and the dictates of the material. He has resorted to direct carving to sculpt a smooth and gracious figure in the close texture of this tropical wood, with an entirely arbitrary morphology but gorgeous with sensuality.

● VICTOR SERVRANCKX (1897-1965), was a pupil of Constant Montald at the Brussels Academy of Fine Arts, and several fellow students became pioneers of the Belgian avant-garde, like Pierre-Louis Flouquet, Marcel-Louis Baugniet and René Magritte, whose début was marked by Cubism. He was prolific between 1921 and 1924; his initial work rested on abstraction, departing from representational elements, then moved towards structures based on mathematical ratios. Towards the end of this fruitful period, he presented hundred and four works at his first one-man show at the Royal gallery in Brussels, in January 1924. He left painting for architecture the next year, but took up his brushes again in 1926 and painted in abstract Surrealist style, as illustrated by his *Opus 18* (inv. 10762), filled with oneiric poetry. He reverted to pure abstraction after World War II.

● JOZEF PEETERS (1895-1960) was born and lived in Antwerp. After several years of groping about, he produced his first radically non-representational work in 1920. He followed this path for five years, also exercising his militant criticism besides editing the review *Het Overzicht*. He designed furniture, textiles and decorative prints. He stepped away from artistic productivity between 1927 and 1937; later, he painted to cover his financial needs.

● OSCAR JESPERS (1887-1970), was the brother of the painter Floris Jespers and the pupil of Thomas Vinçotte at the Brussels Academy. He came from Antwerp, and became closely linked to critic Paul Van Ostaijen, a key figure of the Flemish Modernists who militated for an exclusively plastic conception of art. Between 1918 and 1921, Jespers balanced from Cubism to abstraction. He took part in the Cubist exhibitions organised by the Sélection gallery in 1920. Then he somewhat stepped away from pure abstraction and developed a structured representational style that carried him to the pinnacle of Belgian sculpture.

1. Constant Permeke
The Stranger,
1916, oil on canvas,
173 x 180, inv. 4655.

2. Constant Permeke
The potato Eater,
1935, oil on canvas,
111 x 136, inv. 7022.

3. Frits Van den Berghe
Sunday,
1924, oil on canvas,
138.5 x 163, inv. 4697.

Expressionism

The word "Expressionismus" appeared in the German Magazine Der Sturm in 1911 and was intended to be antinomic to the notion of Impressionism. However, it isn't exactly an aesthetic trend: the artists ambitioned to replace the action of seizing external impressions by the expression of inner emotions. As soon as 1905, the nebula to which the term "Expressionism" refers revolved around the group "Die Brücke" in Germany, including Ludwig Kirchner and Emil Nolde among its members. These artists expressed the tensions of present-day society with forms and colours akin to the Fauves. Some ten years later, in Belgium, Constant Permeke was the first to let the artist's subjectivity mould characters taken from daily life without resorting to an aesthetic dictate.

● CONSTANT PERMEKE (1886-1952), was born in Antwerp and studied in the Brussels and then the Ghent Academy, where he became a friend of his fellow student Albert Servaes (cfr. p. 129). From 1909, he spent the better part of his time in Laethem-Saint-Martin, where Servaes and Gustave De Smet have already settled. His painting was Post-Impressionist then, inspired by Théo Van Rysselberghe and Émile Claus. He settled in Ostend in 1912, became acquainted with James Ensor and lived with Léon Spilliaert. Between 1912 and 1914, the Georges Giroux Gallery (cfr. p. 165) — where Permeke himself took part in a collective exhibition— revealed the German

Expressionists and Italian Futurists in Belgium, the Salon des Indépendants presented French Cubists, and the Kunst van Heden circle organised a major Vincent Van Gogh exhibition. Those two years were decisive for the development of Permeke's style. As he processed those contributions, he drew inspiration for his dormant Expressionism in the daily life of the fishermen's neighbourhood in Ostend. He was drafted in August 1914, injured during the Antwerp siege and transferred to England. He recovered, returned to civilian life and remained there until the end of the war. In 1916, while in exile, he painted *The Stranger*, the painting that

launched Flemish Expressionism, and several other inspired canvases. He came back to Ostend in 1919 and resumed his very personal work, rooted to the truth of his native land, to be regarded as one of the powerful highlights of the art of the first half of the century. Two of the Royal Museums' major canvases are *The Fiancés* (1923, inv. 4868) and *The Potato Eater* (1935). In 1935, he had a huge studio built for him in Jabbeke, close to the Belgian coast; it became a museum after his death. From the late thirties, he exercised both painting and sculpture at the same monumental scale. *Niobé* (inv. 6659), a reclining nude figure from 1951, is his ultimate large sculpture.

3

CONSTANT PERMEKE

☐ *The Stanger*

In the common room of a country house, the arrival of a stranger breaks the rhythm of the family life. He steps inside, set out against the light of the open door, and takes off his hat. He is accompanied by an impressive dog. The men rise to greet him, the women reassure the frightened children. The backlit silhouettes appear massive, their movements slow, the faces remain inscrutable. Not a single detail boils the event and its full meaning down to an anecdote: it's almost a parable. Never mind who is calling: the stranger is welcome.

This dull harmony of ochres and browns around the fiery red hue of the seated woman's silhouette sets the intense image of an emotion out against a bright background of chrome yellow.

☐ *The Potato Eater*

The thickset body is carved out in the light, the heavy head is buried in the massive trunk. The man is bent across the grub he is swallowing in the silence of his immutable fate, he seems to be made of the same earth on which he toils and to which he will return.

At the age of forty-three, Permeke has reached the peak of his inspiration. With an extreme scarcity of means, and with a power that tallies with his theme, he expresses the essence of the life of the peasants he lives with, linked to their soil.

FRITS VAN DEN BERGHE

☐ *Sunday*

Late Sunday afternoon, on the banks of the Leie. On the right, a middle-class couple is strolling behind their son, wearing a sailor suit and a straw hat. In the background, the steeple of the church of Drongen towers above the roof of the Jesuits' convent. Three seminarists are resting on the riverside, watching a couple rowing upstream. Everything is peaceful and sullen.

This composition is organised on either side of the riverbank's diagonal, an entirely reinvented landscape of static geometric masses, determined by the light. The houses, the trees, the strollers, the young priests and the shrubbery at the waterside are all entrapped in closed forms. The rower, his girlfriend and the boy in particular are constructed with assembled volumes.

● FRITS VAN DEN BERGHE (1883-1939) grew up among educated people. After completing his artistic training at the Ghent Academy in 1904, he spent every summer in Laethem-Saint-Martin until 1913. He was joined by his fellow student Albert Servaes, and their manner responded to mild Impressionism. Léon and Gustave De Smet and later Constant Permeke (1909) were also attracted by Laethem. Early 1914, Frits Van den Berghe's trip to the United States brought him in touch with the international artistic avant-garde.
He returned to Europe as the war broke out and headed for the Netherlands with Gustave De Smet, who remained his closest friend until his last day. Their work became outspokenly Expressionist. In 1921, they came home to Belgium and settled in Ostend at Constant Permeke's side. But they returned to the banks of the Leie the next year, in Bachte-Maria-Leerne. Van den Berghe then turned to a lighter palette to celebrate his reunion with his beloved region, and *Sunday* is the finest example thereof. The following years, he developed his new style with the authority of an accomplished artist; but his vision changed again. After 1926, he stepped away from realist Expressionism and experimented with techniques that opened the way to the bizarre. *Choral* typifies that poetic manner, related to Surrealism. However, the economic depression of the thirties compelled him to work as an illustrator to make a living, and this undermined his creative dynamism.

1. *Frits Van den Berghe*
Choral,
c. 1930, oil on canvas,
140 x 120, inv. 7023.

2. *Gustave De Smet*
The Dressing-Room,
1928, oil on canvas,
100 x 81, inv. 6721.

1

● Gustave De Smet
(1877-1943) worked in his
father's workshop for
stage-sets before he settled
in Deurle at Jenny
Montigny's, the passionate
disciple of Émile Claus,
who had invented
Luminism (cfr. p. 134).
They had a lasting influence
upon the young painter. He
moved to Laethem-Saint-
Martin with his wife and
son in 1908, and became a
friend of Frits Van den
Berghe. Constant Permeke
soon joined them. Gustave
De Smet fled to Holland
with Frits Van den Berghe
in 1914, and their work
went through the
same evolution. Stepping
away from Impressionism,
he painted in an
Expressionist style with
Cubist influences.
The two friends returned
to Belgium in 1922 and
joined Permeke in Ostend,
then went back to Laethem
the next year. Gustave De
Smet drove a well-
structured, intensely poetic
Expressionism to its
conclusions. In the thirties,
his concern for a rigorous
formal elaboration
gradually gave way to his
fondness of colour.

☐ Choral

Having emerged from someplace between dream and
nightmare, coarse characters with scant morphologies
chant on their knees, raising their arms. The hybrid creature on the foreground can barely be defined, embodiment of an unbridled phantasmagoria.

Frits Van den Berghe has chosen his ultimate path, letting aside
Expressionism, geared to reality, as he heads for the Surrealists'
universe. He may have been driven there by artists he met at
the Sélection gallery, such as Man Ray or Max Ernst. But he had
a natural inclination towards it. As he put it, "daily life too often
destroys absurd or selfless speculations... The dream is man's
noblest ownership: it underlies the most elevated feelings, the
most generous actions, among which the artist's creation is to
be reckoned." Without being a member of any group or claim-
ing to follow any doctrine, Van den Berghe used his peculiar
genius and extreme artistic boldness to reveal the unexplored
realm of the fantastic to Surrealism.

GUSTAVE DE SMET

☐ The Dressing-Room

A circus artist receives an admirer's compliments in her
dressing-room. although they do not not seem to pay
much attention to each other, the hieratic attitudes make
this scene as solemn as a ceremony and load this suspended moment with constrained emotion. The whole
painting expresses this restraint. However sensuous, the
features are drawn with the objective precision of a
finished plan. The canvas is divided up in overlapping
planes, creating a trompe-l'œil in which all objects are
reduced to simple geometric shapes and the figures are
assimilated to the elements of the composition. The
tempered chromatism does not add any accent to it.

3. *Jean Brusselmans*
The Attic I,
1938, oil on canvas,
131.5 x 125.5, inv. 9236.

4. *Edgard Tytgat*
**The Liquorice Water
Seller / Sunday
Afternoon**,
1927, oil on canvas,
81 x 100, inv. 4695.

JEAN BRUSSELMANS

☐ The Attic I

Between the two world wars, Jean Brusselmans (1884-1953), like most Brabantine Fauves, stepped over from bright optimism (cfr. p. 166) to a very dark vision. Two years before World War II, in a canvas stemming from the same period as Permeke's *Potato Eater*, he expresses the world crisis' distress through this symbolic figure of misery and solitude. The work is related to Expressionism because it resorts to an invented image to convey a feeling. Its technical framework obeys to blunt geometrical harshness. The pyramidal structure encloses the space around the figure; the broad light blue stroke on the background suggests the light of a lamp without actually picturing it. Likewise, the dormer's light defines an ochre triangle on the left side of the painting and determines the planes that make up the face.

EDGARD TYTGAT

☐ The Liquorice Water Seller / Sunday Afternoon

On a Sunday afternoon, a couple of sideshows attract the neighbourhood's strollers. The liquorice water seller carries a huge drum, from which he draws the refreshment he sells for five cents to the thirsty children. This old-fashioned representation is filled with charm and kindness.

Edgard Tytgat depicts the scene with goodhearted mildness and sham ingenuousness. His accurate sense of synthesis led him to exclude unnecessary details. The concise drawing enhances the faint contrasts with dull tonalities.

● EDGARD TYTGAT (1879-1957) already practised draftsmanship and etching in his father's lithographic print workshop. Rik Wouters was his fellow student at the Brussels Academy of Fine Arts. He was quite close to the Brabantine Fauves but never adopted their chromatic bravura. He went in exile in England in 1914 and started painting and producing xylographies, the first step to his illustrator's career. Upon his return in 1919, he settled on the outskirts of Brussels, gave up his Impressionist manner and joined the Expressionists of the Sélection gallery. He was a good-natured dreamer and always stayed on the movement's fringe. His art, typified by the use of halftones, has always been deeply rooted in popular life and tradition.

1. *Marino Marini*
Pomona,
1941, bronze,
156 x 52 x 55,
inv. 6537.

2. *Francis Picabia*
Eclipse,
oil on canvas,
195.5 x 114.5,
inv. 7515.

● MARINO MARINI
(1901-1980) studied painting
and sculpture in Florence
and started teaching
sculpture in Monza, near
Milan, in 1929. He stayed
in Paris several times in the
following years and often
travelled to Germany and
England before World War
II. Horseriders began to
appear in his work in 1936,
a theme he kept developing
and dramatizing more and
more until the end of his
career. In 1968, he
commented: "I seriously
believe we are nearing the
end of the world. The
feeling I mean here is close
to the impression
experienced by the
Romans when the pressure
of barbarian invasions
brought about the collapse
of an age-old order and the
fall of the Empire. My
horsemen's statues express
my distress as I face
present-day events."

MARINO MARINI

☐ Pomona

The gracefulness of the high, slim bosom and the tight,
slender waist gives way to the rich sensuality of the full
hips under the waistline, supported by thickset legs.
Pomona, the goddess of fruit and gardens, is celebrated
here as a symbol of fertility. Marino Marini was thoroughly
impregnated by the classical culture around him, and he
deliberately avoided all autobiographical allusions or hints
at contemporary events when he referred to the forms
of the Ancient. He has explained that his intent was to
react against the bombast of Fascist art, prevailing at the
time; this is the likely reason why the statue has neither
head nor arms, why the bronze is corroded by an artificial
patina, just as if it stemmed from an archaeologic dig.

FRANCIS PICABIA

☐ Eclipse

Eclipse is an imitation of the *Immaculate Conception* of
Bartolomé Esteban Murillo—a Sevillan painter from the
17th century—that Picabia could observe at the Louvre.
It is rather a travesty than a parody. A black mask conceals
the Virgin's features against a nocturnal sky. What could be
interpreted as a mischievous sacrilege tallies with the logic
of the painter's work. This canvas is an exceptional item in
regard of his production, and is a reply to his "mechanical"
period, about which he once wrote: "The machine, a

3

3, *Paul Delvaux*
The Fire,
1935, oil on canvas, 140 x 85, inv. 11541.

● FRANCIS PICABIA (1879-1953), was born in Paris to a French mother and a Spanish aristocrat who had acquired the Cuban nationality. In the course of the century's first three decennia, he stunned the world with the permanent provocativeness of his work and attitude. As a wealthy dandy, he had the opportunity to give free rein to his freedom frenzy. He already gained success in 1905, when he painted in the style of Sisley and Pissarro, but broke the contract that tied him to his dealer. From 1910, his close friendship with Marcel Duchamp had a deep influence on his work.
In 1913, he was present at New York's Armory Show, a huge demonstration that revealed Modern art to America, at which over six thousand works were presented, a third of which stemmed from Europe. Picabia then produced a series of abstract watercolours, exhibited at the Stieglitz gallery. He took refuge in New York in 1915, where he joined Marcel Duchamp who had already produced several 'ready-mades' and currently worked on the *Large Glass*, a synthesis of his "Bachelor machines". Picabia's paintings then began to respond to a machine aesthetic, subversive metaphors of the mechanisms of the human being. Dada activities appeared in Zürich and New York, challenging Rationalism and the values of hidebound Humanism. Picabia joined the movement. He wrote that "reason is a light that lets things be seen the way they are not".

newcomer from man's brain, indeed a daughter born without a mother...". In this perspective, the machine is regarded as a reversed equivalent of Christ, born from an immaculate conception. The eclipse replaces the immaculate with blackness, and is a mere product of a verbal play with subversive logic, an accomplished Dadaïst work.

PAUL DELVAUX

Paul Delvaux was too independent to become an orthodox member of the Surrealist group, and he did not even participate in the movement's activities, just like Magritte. But his uncontested kinship to the Surrealist mainstream is confirmed by the poetry in his painting, arising from alogical associations of irrational images.

☐ The Fire

A woman folds her arms as she silently gazes at an edifice on fire. Its fronton can still be guessed at; perhaps it is a theatre: she would stand at its balcony. The architectural elements on the left hand-side, where a dummy perspective departs from a just above a basement, may merely be a stage-set; in which case the curtain is opened on the background of a scene, and the flames are part of the show. Then the question arises of where the play's spectators are: couldn't they be the same as the painting's spectators?

This canvas is one of the first works Delvaux painted in a Surrealist manner, and it obviously echoes how deeply impressed he had been by Magritte's work. Without concealment, he borrows several characteristic motifs from him: the fire, an element Magritte resorted to frequently at the time (*Tuba on Fire*, etc.), whereas this is the only time Delvaux refers to it; The blazing building's columns, resembling Magritte's balusters; the curtain, withheld by its tieback; the figure seen from the back.

1. *Paul Delvaux,* **Pygmalion**, *1939, oil on wood, 117 x 147.5, inv. 7544.*

2. *Paul Delvaux,* **Evening Train**, *1957, oil on wood, 110 x 170, inv. 6797.*

3. *Paul Delvaux*
La Voix publique,
1948, oil on wood, 152.5 x 254, inv. 7094.

1

2

● LE MUSÉE SPITZNER.
Paul Delvaux recalls having been very impressed by the Spitzner Museum around 1932. Later, he pictured its façade in a painting named after it (presently owned by the Ministry of the French Community of Belgium). It was an educational exhibition, set up in a barrack, intended for teen-agers and mainly devoted to venereal diseases. Life-size coloured wax manikins showed the devastation caused by them with terrifyingrealism. The lush abundance of women surrendered to everybody's stare, blazing images of the forbidden lust with which the artist's paintings teemed for over twenty years, originated from that very vision. *La Voix Publique* is an example thereof.

☐ **Pygmalion**
The legend tells that Pygmalion, king of Cyprus, fell in love with the statue of a young girl he had just sculpted. Aphrodite answered his prayer and blew life into his work. In his interpretation, Delvaux reversed the heroes' gender: The woman attempts to arouse the marble creature's desire. On the ground the shadows are united in a delusive embrace. On the right, a woman blooming with the efflorescence of sensuous delight, staring at the inaccessible, does not see the man engrossed in his erotic dreams as she crosses him.

Surrealists rejected the conscious elaboration in favour of the liberation of the unconscious and largely subscribed to the Freudian theories. Since the parents' ascendancy on the painter is known, the psycho-analytic interpretation of this female *Pygmalion* as a possessive genitor seems particularly relevant. This approach may indeed clarify the conditions of the paint-ing's production, but to restrict oneself to that interpretation would ruin the universal symbolic impact of this image of the unfeasible.

☐ **Evening Train**
The inevitable remoteness of the convoy leaves the little girl bewildered behind a wooden fence. The combined vanishing lines of the perspective accentuate this impression: the rails, platforms, telephone lines and even the bearing shadows of the poles. "These impressions that reappear from childhood—they are never regrets— move me and probably retain my attention due to their suggestive capacity and to that permanent mystery in which all memories dwell", the painter claimed.

☐ **La Voix publique**
A nonchalant Venus poses in front of a 1900 background in which one of those green tramways—that had long disappeared from Brussels at the time—is jolting away. She suggests the showcase windows of the numerous brothels

3

one encountered around the stations. What do her three doubles say to one another, so superbly ostentatious about their dignity? In this realm of memory, Delvaux has gathered the elements of a review that seems dramatically close his teenage fantasies. Magic emanates from it, affecting the onlooker and arousing his own reminiscence.

Francisco de Goya, Ingres and Manet have all resorted to this pose after Titian. Each of them drew a subversive work from it. As opposed to his predecessors, who had just treated the scandalous body, he has extended the subject in the inhabited background. In *La Voix Publique*, the narrative's logic would let us expect that the reclining woman be turned towards the street, the public thoroughfare (*'Voix'* means *voice*, whereas *'voie'* means *way, road, lane*). But we have the impression that we observe the scene from behind her, from the inside. And the plant blooming in an earthenware flowerpot holder at the settee's head is indeed a house plant. Just like in *The Fire*, the representation appeals to the painting's spectator and actually implies him. This subverting of the image confers a dimension of irreality to it.

● PAUL DELVAUX (1897-1994) was born in 1897 in a typical upper middle-class family: the father a solicitor, the mother a musician. They had a tight psychological grip on him for a long time, and it took a lot to convince them to authorize Paul to attend courses at the Brussels Academy of Fine Arts at the age of nineteen. His poetic trends and his fondness of large decorative compositions may well be a consequence of his being the pupil of Constant Montald (cfr. p. 18). The first ten years after his academic years, he was a searching and wavering young artist. In his thirties, he worked in the line of Constant Permeke (*The Couple*, 1929, inv. 7004) and of Gustave De Smet (*Young women dreaming*, 1931, inv. 7340), showing off an obvious colourist's talent and a musing sensitivity. The *Minotaurus* exhibition at the Palais des Beaux-Arts was Brussels' first international Surrealist demonstration. The event brought about Delvaux's genuine artistic conversion: "I then began to produce this Surrealist painting wherein I have attempted to express a deeper feeling, more important than the feeling of pure painting...", he said on a broadcasted interview. Henceforth, he painted in accordance with this final choice. His large wall paintings at the Ostend casino date from 1952. At the time, Magritte and Delvaux were regarded as the most significant Belgian artists alive. In 1969, Delvaux left the outskirts of Brussels to settle in Veurne, West Flanders. His career and fame remained at their peak. He designed a monumental decorative series for the Brussels underground in 1978. A Paul Delvaux Museum opened its doors in St. Idesbald, on the Belgian coast, in 1982. He passed away in Veurne on July 20, 1994, at the age of ninety-seven.

● ARMAND SIMON (1906-1981) was born at the heart of the Borinage region and lived his entire life there. As a teenager, he chose to devote his life to literature, and he was seventeen when the revelation of Lautréamont's *Chants de Maldoror* changed his life. In the early thirties, he gradually gave up writing for drawing. After some wavering, he geared his style to his major project: to translate the fantastic realms of Maldoror in drawing. "The *Chants* abolished all restraints and freed me." It was a time of fruitful exchange with a number of friends who were as enthralled about Surrealism as he was. The Rupture group sprang forth from their meetings; it organised an exhibition of all the major Surrealists in 1935. Armand Simon's work perfectly tallies with André Breton's dictates. It does not transcribe a narrative but conjures up a world to which the drawer is receptive. "All my drawings are automatic", Simon said. "When I take a sheet of paper, I don't know at all what I am about to draw. I begin sketching a form, a circle, an oval... Then I perceive what use I could make from what I have just outlined. [...] I don't have it in my head, it occurs entirely by chance." The thousands of drawings he has allowed his subconscious to produce have fascinated poets and writers. "Far out in the night, as far as another night, The night of his nether world, Armand Simon sees what he invents, he draws with the accuracy of a vision because he is hemeralopic for the most

□ **The Winter or the Engulfed Town**
The space is divided up into concentric enclosures around the *Engulfed Town*'s market-place, organising a maze with a variety of exits. There are gaps in the fence; the doors of the enclosing wall open up on the country-side. The portals in the distance tower above the mountains. Is the purpose of these women wandering through the city, draped in their peplum, to discover the itinerary of some revelation?
Thirty years after his encounter with De Chirico's work, Paul Delvaux remains bewildered by the interrogation of his streets and silent squares. The obstacles to communication and the inhibition of desire are recurring themes in Delvaux's œuvre.

Surrealism
André Breton published the Manifesto of Surrealism *in 1924, defining the fundamental principle of his tenet:"Surrealism: N. m. Pure psychic automatism through which one proposes to express the genuine functioning process of thought in writing or by any other means. A dictation of thought, devoid of any form of control by reason and free from any moral or aesthetic concern." Automatic writing, imagined and exercised by Breton with Philippe Soupault since 1919, remains the appli-*

obscure dreams." (Christian Dotremont).*A selection of drawings by Armand Simon and collages by Marcel Lefrancq is exhibited in the document gallery, above the showcases wherein manuscripts, publications and photographs of Belgian artistic life are presented.*

3. Armand Simon, **Drawing**, 1943, India ink on paper, 27.5 x 18.5, inv. 7782.

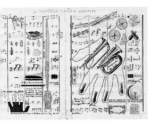

1. *Paul Delvaux,* **The Winter or the Engulfed Town**
1958, oil on plywood, 119 x 152.5, inv. 11565.

2. *Édouard Léon Théodore Mesens*
The Full Score Fulfilled,
*1945, India Ink drawing and collage on paper, 30 x 46,
inv. 6861.*

*cation paradigm of that concept. At a later stage, André Breton
formulated a corollary requirement for painting: "the plastic
work, in order to respond to the need for an absolute revision
of real values [...], shall refer to a purely interior model or shall
not be at all." It must be made clear that Surrealism is neither
an artistic nor a literary doctrine but a way of thinking to which
access can be provided by writing or painting. André Breton
(1896-1966), a French poet and the theorist of the movement
he generated, has drawn many artists on his path, amongst
whom the most significant ones of that period, and their contribution has deeply affected the 20th century's mental scope.
Surrealist activity developed independently in Belgium. In
Brussels, Paul Nougé, the most rigorous theorist of group, initiated this in 1924, soon joined by Édouard Léon Théodore
Mesens and René Magritte, then by Marcel Mariën. As opposed to the automatism prescribed by Breton, Nougé has always
favoured the notion of experimentation, prejudging neither its
discoveries nor its methods. In 1934, a second group was formed in La Louvière (Hainaut) around the figure of the poet
Achille Chavée. Ten years later, a third group gathered around
poet Fernand Dumont. Two key figures asserted themselves in
the artistic field: Armand Simon and Marcel Lefrancq.*

ÉDOUARD LÉON THÉODORE MESENS
☐ The Full Score Fulfilled
E. L. T. Mesens remembers his initial composer's vocation
but "fulfils" his score with written or drawn annotations,
products of his delirious fantasy. Derision ad absurdum is
a powerful mechanism of the Surrealist spirit. Mesens
systematically resorts to this derisive element, from the
preliminary indication "*periculoso*" (sic) to the conclusion
"and everything finishes with an apotheosis of broken
wood". As he himself indicates and illustrates it, "one
identifies the author's hand throughout the score". The
dedication above the title "*for Marcel Duchamp's Band*" is
another example of a widespread Surrealist practice: to
refer to persons or to facts that were significant for the
group. In 1913, as a part of the work for and around the
Large Glass, Duchamp wrote a musical score—with subtitle "Musical Erratum" — according to a digital notation
he had invented, barely more complicated than our sol-
fa. With *The Full Score Fulfilled*, E. L. T. Mesens salutes
Marcel Duchamp, the great initiator of 20th century artistic subversion.

● ÉDOUARD LÉON THÉODORE
MESENS: (1903-1971)
was a key figure of Belgian
Surrealism. As a teenager,
he ambitioned to write
music and met Erik Satie,
whose influence on his early
compositions is obvious.
But he soon abandoned
music. In January 1920, his
friendship with René
Magritte significantly affected Surrealism. Mesens
published his first poems in
1920 and produced his first
collages in 1924. As an
employee of the Palais des
Beaux-Arts of Brussels, he
organised the first international Surrealists' exhibition
in 1934 under the supervision of the *Minotaure*
review, at the time when
André Breton came to
Belgium. The next year, he
managed to gather all the
greater names of international Surrealism at an exhibition in La Louvière
(Hainaut). He settled in
London in 1938 and became
the promotor of the artists of
the Surrealist movement
under the guidance of the
London Gallery and in the
London Bulletin. Mesens
ceased to be an art dealer in
1951 and devoted all his
time to poetry and collage
till he passed away in
Brussels in 1971.

● MARCEL MARIËN (1920-1993)
Marcel Mariën was born in Antwerp to a Flemish father and a Walloon mother. He received a photographer's apprenticeship between his fourteenth and sixteenth year. During that period, he was confronted with two works by Magritte and read André Breton's *Manifesto of Surrealism*. In 1937, at the age of seventeen, he contacted Magritte, then Paul Nougé and Louis Scutenaire. He produced his first Surrealist item that same year: *L'Introuvable*. He was incorporated in the Surrealists' group and from then on he wrote, was controversial, organised magazines, editing and produced collages and assemblages at a never slackening pace.

MARCEL MARIËN

□ **The Common Chord**

Marcel Mariën invented his first assemblage whilst trying to reassemble the remains of his shattered glasses: "spectacles reduced to a single glass, although supported by the two usual branches, genuine Cyclops' glasses that present something like a front view of a profile..." That was in 1937 and materialised under the form of a finished object named *l'Introuvable* ('*nowhere to be found*'). Mariën pursued the subsequent practice until his death. To Mariën, every aspect of the plainest reality becomes the subject of de-stabilizing hypothesis. What if... If a twig grew on the handle of the lumberjack's axe? It would become "*The Dream of a Tree*". If a padlock were used as an earring? — "*The Tomb of the Secrets*". What if the pianist's fingers were contaminated by the black keys of the altered notes? — It would be *The Common Chord*. "These items of the mind", he wrote, "are a product of thought's continuous motion. They depend on chance more than on whims, are less kindred to enigma than to fantasy." Armed with this fantasy, Mariën has questioned images, words, ideas as luck would have it, producing hundreds of objects, collages, photographs, drawings that do not bring answers but upset our certainties.

PAUL KLEE

□ **Mit dem Kometen** (GOLDSCHMIDT BEQUEST)
The passage of the comet in the centre of the skyscape is associated to an astronomical outburst including a radiant sun, a six-pointed star, the moon at each of its stages and a number of unidentified celestial items. The picture is streaked with forked lightning, wrapping up the skies, the earth and the seas in this tormented microcosm. Comets have always fascinated man, who has wanted to read omens in them. Paul Klee however shows no concern for the interpretation of the realms of cosmic figures he has borrowed from universal esoteric tradition: he endows art with the mission of expressing the hidden meanings of the universe by means of new formal epiphanies.

● PAUL KLEE (1879-1940), was the son of musicians and wavered between music and plastic arts for some time before chosing the latter. He received advanced academic training in Berne and Munich, then journeyed to Italy. In 1911, after he had stayed in Munich for four years, he witnessed the rise of the Blaue Reiter and met Wassily Kandinsky and Franz Marc. Klee travelled to Tunisia in 1914 and painted watercolours with urban views, divided up in geometrical planes of an aerial lightness and

intense luminosity due to adjacent contrasting tonalities. He was thirty-five at the time, and discovered the major contribution he would make to modern art. His prolific production includes some nine thousand items, to which his written theories must be added, and his

twelve year long educational career at the Bauhaus then at the Academy of Düsseldorf. His primary concern was for the revelations of the subconscious in artistic creation, and this asserts his kinship to the Surrealists, who have immediately acknowledged him.

RENÉ MAGRITTE

René Magritte's work could be defined as an obstinate quest for "the enigmatic and marvelous light that comes from the world". It appears under the form of a series of experimental images that reveal its hidden mystery, under the patent character of reality. No other public institution in the world owns as many works of René Magritte as

the Royal Museums of Fine Arts of Belgium in Brussels. The collection was started in 1953 through regular acquisitions, and considerably increased by the legacies of Georgette Magritte and, recently, of Irène Scutenaire-Hamoir.

☐ *The Secret Player*

This painting belongs to the very first of Magritte's genuinely Surrealist works. He painted it less than a year after *The Lost Jockey* (1926, private collection), about which he wrote: "This is the first canvas I have truly painted with the feeling that I had found my way...". Moreover, some elements occur in both paintings: this peculiar alley of trees with trunks resembling huge balusters; this slide-like curtain; the jockey coming from the right has been replaced with two elegant baseball players, frozen in the midst of action as a giant tortoise flies over them. On the right, the cupboard's one door opens up on a veiled woman and evokes an illusionist's trick.

The recurring use of the same items staged in various situations became systematic in Magritte's work. This curtain will appear again in the *Mona Lisa*. The balusters—Magritte calls them "cup-and-balls"—are sometimes topped with a snout-like extension (*Natural Encounters*). A manikin by Giorgio de Chirico probably suggested this motif to him. Magritte never avoided the issue: "I could not paint like Chirico, so I looked for something to paint after Chirico's example...". Several hypotheses have been formulated about its meaning, mostly resting on psycho-analysis. Max Ernst has summarized them with the very successful suitcase-word "*phallustrade*". But specific explanations should be handled cautiously. Magritte himself draws our attention on part of the semantics of his paint-ing in general: "...You will have noticed that my vocabulary is quite restrictive: only ordinary, familiar items. What is 'extraordinary' is the link between them..."

1. *Marcel Mariën*
The Common Chord,
1977, cast of a hand, piano keys, velvet and lace in a perspex casing, 43.5 x 23.7 x 12.4, inv. 9194.

2. *Paul Klee*
Mit dem Kometen,
1917, watercolour on cotton gauze, stiffened with gypsum; India ink on cardboard, 24.5 x 22, inv. 11191.

3. *René Magritte*
The Secret Player,
1927, oil on canvas, 152 x 195, inv. 11631.

● RENÉ 1
MAGRITTE
(1898-1967) was
born in Lessines
(Hainaut) on
November 21,
1898. He was a
student at the
public high
school of
Charleroi when
he met young
Georgette Berger
in 1913, whom
he married nine
years later. Victor
Sevranckx (cfr. p
174) was his fel-
low pupil at the
Brussels
Academy of Fine
Arts, where he
registered in 1916. He made
a number of friends who
played a decisive role in his
orientation, particularly E.
L. T. Mesens (cfr. p. 185),
Pierre-Louis Flouquet (cfr.
p. 174) and the poet Marcel
Lecomte. A quest of the self
and a few attempts took a
period of ten years. "In
1921, I wavered between
the desire to paint like the
Cubists, the Futurists, the
traditional painters and the
abstract painters...", he
declared. The *Portrait of
Pierre Broodcoorens (inv.
7801)* was produced in that
year and exemplifies this.
"In 1925", he wrote,
"I found those pleasures
dull and realised how unim-
portant it was to discover a
new manner of painting; for
me, the crux of the matter
was rather to know what to
paint, to know it in order to
bring the mystery to the
fore." He then took part in
the first Belgian Surrealist
group with Paul Nougé and
E. L. T. Mesens. That
orientation was outspoken at
his first personal exhibition
in March 1927 at the
Brussels gallery Le
Centaure. The *Lost Jockey*

2

3

☐ *L'Homme du large*
The character of Fantomas—in
the movie of French director Louis Feuillade—may well
have inspired the character of *L'Homme du Large*, kindred
to that of *The Thief*, painted in the same year. As for the
title, the Surrealist poet Marcel Lecomte recalls the period of the painting's conception: "Magritte and myself
used to read Joseph Conrad's novels aloud. The painting's
title [...] was given by me and stems from this reading."
We know that the English writer's work unfurls around
the sea's reality and symbolic value. Moreover, movie
director Marcel L'Herbier had produced *L'Homme du
Large*, in 1920. The combination of these elements
recreates the climate in which the painting was produced.
The meaning of this work has been subject to interpretations based on the tradition of hermetism and the symbolics of alchemy—Marcel Lecomte was passionately
interested in both.
For none of his paintings did the painter himself try to tear
open the opacity of the mystery to which they lead. A few
months before his death, in one of his ultimate letters, he
still wrote:"I cannot deduct anything from mystery, or I would mis-
judge its essence... For me, it doesn't matter to conquer
secrets [...] but to discover means of painting pictures of which
the unknown cannot be boiled down to the knowable."

☐ *Portrait of Paul Nougé* (IRÈNE SCUTENAIRE-HAMOIR BEQUEST)
Magritte assimilates Paul Nougé, the rigorous theorist of
Belgian Surrealism, to a mythical hero. Like *L'Homme du
Large*, he passes through doors without having to open
them; like him, he wears a strange costume, perhaps that
of music-hall conjurers: doesn't he seem to be in two
places at once, as if by magic?

1. René Magritte
L'Homme du large,
*1926, oil on canvas,
139 x 105, inv. 7221.*

2. René Magritte
**Portrait
of Paul Nougé**,
*1927, oil on canvas,
100 x 73.*

3. René Magritte
Georgette,
*1935, oil on canvas,
64 x 54, inv. 10712.*

4. René Magritte
**The Empire of
Lights**,
*1954, oil on canvas,
146 x 114,
inv. 6715.*

☐ Georgette

Magritte explicitly rules out every form of exegesis of this painting that departs from the portrait of his wife: "There is no explicable mystery in my painting. The inscription of the word 'vague' (also means "*wave*") in this portrait expresses the inexplicable mystery. The objects that go with my wife's face are not symbols, in the same way her face is not a symbol either. The "why?" is not a "serious" question..."

☐ The Empire of Lights

The full daylight sky does not light up the trees that are set out against it, nor the nocturnal landscape under it. This simultaneous occurence of night and day does not prevent either from ruling. Maybe unconsciously, Magritte has produced a demonstration of one of the fundamental Surrealist hypotheses: "Everything leads us to believe that a certain point of the mind exists, where life and death, reality and fantasy, past and future, communicable and incommunicable things cease to be perceived as contradictions." (André Breton, *Second Manifesto of Surrealism*). This particularly inspired canvas shows the image of a second reality, paradoxical and genuinely Surrealist, revealed by the calling into question of daily reality.
The title is said to have been invented by Nougé; the word "empire" should not be understood in its topographical meaning but in the sense of ascendancy, of "power". Magritte may have titled some of his canvases, but mostly left that to friends, such as Nougé or Scutenaire. Those titles have often been created at a later stage and do not explain the painting. They report an association of ideas the work has suggested, but allow for the spectator's own readings.

(1926, private collection), which he has always regarded as his first step into Surrealism, and *L'Homme du Large* were two of the sixty-one canvases presented there. A few months later, Magritte settled in Paris and participated in André Breton's Surrealist group's activities. He returned to Brussels once and for all in 1930. Since he considered painting to be a means to express ideas, he totally neglected questions of pictorial technique, and a consequence of this was that his manner hardly ever changed again, except on two occasions. In 1943, he painted in Impressionist style—sometimes called his "Renoir style" — as a reaction against the pessimism the war had generated; he called it "Surrealism in full sunlight", well illustrated by "*The Fire*" (inv. 10710). Then in 1948, at the occasion of a first exhibition in Paris, he inaugurated the "vache" (at the same time 'cow' and 'mean') style, exemplified by *The Shingle* (inv. 10709), an aggressively provocative portrait of his wife. The exhibition was unsuccessful, and he returned to his own manner for ever. He gradually started gaining recognition in the fifties. This was confirmed by his major 1965 exhibition at the New York Museum of Modern Art. The ultimate peak of his career was the retrospective at the Boymans-Beuningen Museum in Rotterdam, opened on August 4, 1967. René Magritte passed away 11 days later in Brussels.

1. *René Magritte*
The White Page,
1967, oil on canvas,
54 x 65, inv. 10711.

2. *René Magritte*
Discovery,
1927, oil on canvas,
65 x 50.

3. *René Magritte*
Treasure Island,
1942, oil on canvas,
60 x 80, inv. 10708.

4. *René Magritte*
The Return,
1940, oil on canvas,
55 x 65, inv. 6667.

☐ **The White Page**

The same magic operates here through merely reversing the moon's situation and that of the foliage. By showing the impossible, Magritte attests the compatibility of the possible and its contrary.

☐ **Discovery** (Irène Scutenaire-Hamoir Bequest)

To systematically call things and beings into question has driven Magritte to invent metamorphoses for them. In 1927, he wrote the following to Paul Nougé about the painting he named *Discovery:* "I believe I made a discovery..." It was significant indeed. This woman who gradually becomes ligneous initiated a method he would never step away from. Almost twenty years later, in *Black Magic* (inv. 10706), the woman he painted gradually changed into a sky.

☐ **Treasure Island**

The practice of metamorphosis generates cross-breedings between heterogeneous natural kingdoms. "If we imagine young girls in full bloom", Magritte wrote about Treasure Island, "we can also admit the idea of a bird in full bloom."

Never mind if the flower-birds are derived directly from Proust's imagery. It is important to remember that Proust regarded the verbal image and the plastic image as two equivalent means of expression. "Writing is an invisible description of thought and painting is the visible description thereof." One irreducible

difference remains between them: the literary image, used as a metaphor, does not require to be taken literally; whereas the pictorial image asserts itself as a phenomenon.

☐ The Return
A huge bird carries the memory of daylight as it flies over a nocturnal landscape. Does the nest it leaves behind bode the hatching of further images?

☐ The Arnheim Estate
The eagle-mountain is a landscape by itself, a petrified force, powerless as it keeps vigil over the abandoned nest. The recurring themes, such as the metamorphoses of various birds, were sometimes taken up again after many years. They enable us to approach the creative mechanism of Magritte. But it is never possible to allocate a well-determined meaning to any of those images.

☐ The Use of Speech
Several paintings include one or more words, ornamentally and beautifully written, like in *The Use of Speech* or in *Bel Canto*. Those words, Magritte claimed, were "of the same substance as the images". In fact, they are nothing else than images of words. At the same rate as any other image, they constitute a plastic idiom borrowed from the triteness of daily use. However, their privileged mutual relationship casts forth an "extraordinary" image, enriched with a mystery that is presented to the spectator's intuition.

☐ The Forbidden Reading / Siren (IRÈNE SCUTENAIRE-HAMOIR BEQUEST)
Words and images intermingle in this painting. The graphics depart from the forefinger, pointed like an *i*, and change the Christian name of his friend Irène Hamoir into a "siren".

5. *René Magritte*
The Arnheim Estate,
1962, oil on canvas,
146 x 114, inv. 10707.

6. *René Magritte*
The Use of Speech,
1927/1929, oil on canvas,
41.8 x 27.3, inv. 11530.

7. *René Magritte*
The Forbidden Reading / Siren,
1936, oil on canvas,
54 x 73.

1. *Giorgio de Chirico*
**Melancholy of a
Beautiful Day**,
*1913, oil on canvas,
69.5 x 86.5, inv. 11117.*

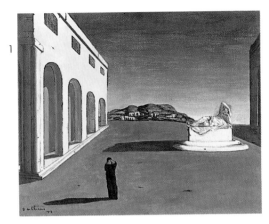

● GIORGIO DE CHIRICO
(1888-1978) was born to
Italian parents residing in
Greece, where he stayed
until his seventeenth year.
His family returned to Italy
when his father died, then
stayed in Munich from
1906 to 1909. Young
Giorgio attended courses at
the Academy of Fine Arts
there and read the philoso-
phers who underpinned his
own thinking, Friedrich
Nietzsche and Arthur
Schopenhauer. He also
became acquainted with the
work of the Symbolist painter Arnold Böcklin and was
deeply marked by it. The
revelation of "metaphysical"
painting occurred to him in
Florence between 1910 and
1911. His first representation of an Italian square,
*Enigma of an autumn after-
noon*, was exhibited at the
Salon d'Automne the next
year. Manikins soon appeared in his paintings. He
developed relationships
with Guillaume Apollinaire,
Pablo Picasso and, at a later
stage, with André Breton.
The latter wrote in
Surrealism and Painting
that, similarly to
Lautréamont's work,
Chirico's "metaphysical"
painting constitutes a "fixed
point" that can be deemed
sufficient to determine the
line of Surrealism. From
1919 on, Chirico takes on a
challenging attitude towards

GIORGIO DE CHIRICO
☐ *Melancholy of a Beautiful Day*
(GOLDSCHMIDT BEQUEST)

The square is lined with palaces, built on running, grassy
soil extending as far as the horizon. It is bathed in a sullen light that stresses the place's irreality. In the oppress-
ive silence, a woman seen from behind stoops under the
weight of a harrowing remembrance. The reclining statue
(recurring in several of de Chirico's canvases) is a reproduction of a Greek sculpture of the Vatican Museum:
Ariadne asleep. Ariadne was the daughter of Minos, the
king of Crete who had imprisoned the Minotaur in a labyrinth; he stemmed from the love of Minos' wife Pasiphae
with a bull. When Theseus came from Athens to kill the
Minotaur, Ariadne fell in love with him and gave him a ball
of thread. He unwound it in the maze to find its exit.
Chirico had a passion for Hellenism, and in his transposition of the myth, he regarded his work as the maze of
which Ariadne possesses the secret.
"By a clear autumn afternoon, I was seated on a bench in the
middle of the Piazza Santa Croce in Florence [...]. A white marble
statue stands at the centre of the square. The mild and loveless
autumn sun lit the statue and the temple's façade. I then had the
impression that I saw all these things for the very first time." This
is how Chirico described the genesis of his first "metaphysical"
work, *Enigma of an autumn afternoon*, that was painted one year
earlier than this one. Disorientation was the access path to the
enigmatic realm his painting opened up to him.

the modern spirit and refers
back to the classical values
prompted by a certain Italian
intelligentsia. He repudiated
the style and the concerns
from which the better part of
his dazzling work had
sprung forth and joined the
Roman group "Valori
plastici", whose ideology

was dangerously close to
rising fascism. That earned
him André Breton's anathe-
ma. In 1965, he wrote: "Is
there a greater madness than
this man's, who is lost
amidst the besieging
party of a city he has
built and made
impregnable."

3

2. *Max Ernst*
The Celestial Army,
*c. 1925, oil on canvas,
80.5 x 100, inv. 7222.*

3. *Max Ernst*
Bird (n° 11),
*c. 1925, oil on black emery
paper glued to wood, with
cork frame, 34.3 x 31,
inv. 11170.*

MAX ERNST

☐ The Celestial Army

Young Max Ernst found his pet cockatoo stone dead just when his father had announced the birth of his little sister to him. The mental association of the two events seems to have given way to a recurring theme in his work, loaded with ambiguous feelings. The bird often appears as an opponent. In *The Celestial Army*, the cluster of birds that gathers round a superior represents a force if not a threat. The stylized head, reproduced somewhat like heraldic furniture in the way that Max Ernst regularly represents birds throughout his work, is intended as a symbol for an aggressive power. The relevance of this type of interpretation—however evasive it may remain—tallies with the attention given by the Surrealists to the suggestive powers of the unconscious, even more so in this canvas where the pictorial technique is based on frottage and resorts to automatism. From a plastic i. e. non-surrealist point of view, it is quite noticeable how the white, gritty paint around the thin layer of transparent matter of the central motif succeeds to lend an additional quality of aerial lightness to it.

☐ Bird (n° 11) (GOLDSCHMIDT BEQUEST)

This small painting belongs to a series of thirty-six, all depicting birds, most of them in a cage. However, this cramped cage set in a cork frame looks more like a trap than like a shelter. Was Max Ernst a bird catcher? He often read a book from the beginning of the 19th century: *French Aviceptology or general treatise on all tricks that can be used for bird-catching*. The technique of outlining the drawing around a gauge to create a sort of totemic figure attests that this hunt is symbolical.

● MAX ERNST (1891-1976) was born in the Rheinland; he started painting in an Expressionist manner in 1910. After the war, he took part in Dadaïst activities in Germany with Hans Arp. He arrived in Paris in 1920 and became the friend of the future Surrealists. That is when he began to prepare his wide range of techniques—painting, collage, frottage, photomontage etc. — by means of which he causes unexpected encounters, filled with poetry, building up his work to an impeccably coherent Surrealist monument. As a German citizen, he was arrested by the French authorities when World War II began, then he fled to the United States with André Breton and Marcel Duchamp. After he returned to France in 1953, he received the Prize of the Biennial Exhibition of Venice, and his approval of the mundane establishment caused him to be excluded from the Surrealist group. However, it never affected the intense sense of poetry in the work he continued till the end of his life.

1. *Max Ernst*
The Crab,
1926, oil on canvas,
81 x 100, inv. 11168.

2. *Joan Miró*
Spanish Dancer /
Olée,
1924, oil on canvas,
92 x 73, inv. 11203.

3. *André Masson*
Woman in a Garden,
1925, oil on canvas,
65.4 x 45.8, inv. 11634.

4. *Yves Tanguy*
The Aeroplane,
1929, oil on canvas,
81 x 60, inv. 8991.

● JOAN MIRÓ (1893-1983)
was the son of a goldsmith
and clockmaker, and he
began to draw when he was
seven. Upon completing his
artistic training in
Barcelona, from 1919 on he
spent every winter in Paris,
where his neighbour was
André Masson. At that time,
he was a representational
painter whose style
responded to accurate realism. He switched to a
graphical style in 1923
and kept on developing
it in his very prolific
œuvre for over
forty years.

☐ **The Crab** (GOLDSCHMIDT BEQUEST)
The golden sand on which the crab appears has been
rubbed in the paint according to a method derived from
frottage, that Max Ernst had imagined to use as a graphics
technique. "On August 10, 1925", the painter tells, "I was
struck by the way a wooden floor, of which every groove
showed up due to manifold scouring, had an obsessive
effect on my irritated gaze." He placed a sheet of paper
on the floorboards and rubbed a blacklead on it, making
a drawing appear beyond his control. "The drawings
obtained like this gradually loose, through a spontaneous
series of hints and transmutations [...] the character of
the interrogated matter (wood for example) and take on
the aspect of unexpectedly accurate images, of such a
nature that they are likely to reveal the initial cause of the
obsession or produce an imitation of that cause." He had
discovered a plastic counterpart to the "automatic writing"
through which Philippe Soupault and André Breton
wanted to reveal a subconscious reality. He relates the
crab to radom graphics and defines this technique as a
ruse: the ruse of a crab that progresses sideways.

JOAN MIRÓ
☐ **Spanish Dancer / Olée** (GOLDSCHMIDT BEQUEST)
In the plane's two dimensions, Miró registers the sign that
conjures up a dancer. Not a figure, not even simplified, but
a mere symbol: an approximated black circle for the head;
a yellow triangle for the flower she holds between her
teeth; a freehand drawing of an oblong shape hints at the
silhouette with a dress flaring out; a right angle, drawn
with a set square, defines the feet and one of them carries a shoe. On the right, a threefold rustling arabesque
indicates the motion. On the left, a dotted line at the end
of which a fan hovers stands for the arm, in an almost abstract way. In the upper left corner, the text of the dancer's

3   4

triumphant cry, a symbol amongst others in this poetic composition.

In 1923, Joan Miró switched from representation to this radical symbolization, close to the riddle. Neither the influence of Paul Klee, who claimed that "to write and to draw are basically identical", nor that of André Breton's friends can be denied. "I often mingled with poets", he said, "because I believed that one had to go beyond the plastic concept in order to attain poetry."

ANDRÉ MASSON

☐ *Woman in a Garden*

This beheaded figure, taken in by the sea, was painted in Antibes in 1925. It is blatantly linked to Cubism, as exemplified by the arabesque that departs from the left wrist to swirl past the shoulder and end at the navel. Another unites the left thigh to the oval of the belly in one single curve. The way the background is divided up is typical, and this painting's fluidity obeys to a rigorous structure. However, the sinuous line of the material draped around the body writhes through this geometry and undermines it. This hybrid composition is a turning point between two contradictory periods of Masson's work.

YVES TANGUY

☐ *The Airplane*

An undetermined object (it would be presumptuous to identify an airplane) and a sort of fleecy meteor hover above a desertic expanse, furrowed by an imprecise layout and fading away in a vague, hazy horizon. This bewildering, suave landscape of a virtual elsewhere is scattered with shingles and inhabited by strange organisms.

For over thirty years, Yves Tanguy has explored the imaginary world created by his paintbrush in a sort of spontaneous, genuinely Surrealist generation. "The painting takes shape before my eyes, unfurling its surprises as it develops", he declared. "That gives me a sense of total freedom, and for that reason, I feel totally incapable of conceiving a plan or designing a preliminary sketch.

● ANDRÉ MASSON (1896-1987) proved to be a precocious gifted child. He settled in Brussels with his family and was admitted at the Academy of Fine Arts at the early age of eleven by special derogation. He attended Constant Montald's class and completed his training at the Paris School of Fine Arts at sixteen. In 1922, his first outspokenly personal orientation led him to restrained Cubism for a few years. But in 1923, he became acquainted with the growing Surrealists' and took part in experiments of automatic writing and drawing, which he transposed to painting. He showed a keen and permanent interest for the manifold possibilities of his art. This put him at odds with André Breton, who reproved his "extra-Surrealist ambitions, i. e. pictorial". Indeed, Masson's work constantly evolved in the course of his long career, and he became one of the most significant French painters of his generation.

● YVES TANGUY (1900-1955), was the son of a sailor from Brittany, and he himself sailed as a pilot for a year before he did his military service in 1920 and became the friend of his roommate Jacques Prévert. In 1924, he painted in a style close to that of the German Expressionists of the group Die Brücke. His concept of painting was shaken by a painting by Chirico, exhibited at the Paul Guillaume gallery in Paris in 1925. His encounter with André Breton confirmed his vocation: he joined Surrealism. He participated in the group's activities from 1925 to 1939, then left France for the United States and never returned, and remained faithful to his choice until he died in 1955.

● SALVADOR DALI (1904-1989) studied art in Spain then settled in Paris in 1928. His collaboration with Luis Buñuel for the film *Un chien andalou* (*An Andalusian Dog*) introduced him into the Surrealist group, where he met Gala, the wife of Paul Éluard. She became his life's companion. The protean work he started developing then was linked to a theorist's thought process based on psychoanalysis. He defined this process as a "paranoiac-critical method", in accordance with which he transformed his own psychic aberrations into creativity. Dali creates intensely disorientating images with a perfectly mastered academic facture, often combined with modern techniques such as *dripping*. He geared his life to his delirious work with a genius for publicity, and soon managed to focus a lot of attention on him. André Breton expelled him from the Surrealist group for reasons of intellectual ethics at the beginning of World War II, spent in the United States by both of them. This by no means deviated Salvador Dali's spectacular path: in 1940, he claimed: "The difference between the Surrealists and myself is that I am a Surrealist."

SALVADOR DALI

☐ *The Temptation of St. Anthony*

Anthony, a founder of monasticism, lived in the 3rd century A. D. Towards the end of his life, he was harassed in his retreat by visions of temptation, often depicted in Christian iconography, e. g. by Hieronymus Bosch. The exaltation with which Dali imagines one of these visions betrays a profound investigation process of his own sexual fantasies, about which he has never been mysterious. The painter pictures him on a beach near Cadaquès he often used as a setting for his canvases: the saint is almost overcome, but still brandishes his crucifix to protect himself from the demon: rearing up above him, a frantic white horse twists his forelegs with excitement, followed by a procession of elephants bearing symbols of triumph of sensual delight. Like monstrous waders, the pachyderms are perched on spider-like legs. These creatures, stemming from an unbridled state of hallucination, recur in Dali's work. In the distance, a tiny group: a man hurriedly bows before the crucifix held by a figure dressed in crimson under the patronage of an angel. High up in the clouds, the Escorial appears as a symbol of divine order forced upon mankind: Philip II, His Highly Catholic Majesty, steeped in austerity there as he ruled all Spains in the 16th century.

In 1946, an American producer prepared a movie after Guy de Maupassant's novel *Bel-Ami*, in which a painting on the theme of the temptation of St. Anthony was to play a prevailing role; so the producer organised a contest. Twelve painters participated, among whom Salvador Dali, Paul Delvaux, and Max Ernst. The latter's work was preferred, but Dali's gained considerable fame when it was exhibited with the eleven others at the Palais des Beaux-Arts in Brussels in 1947.

WIFREDO LAM

☐ *The Soulless Children*

From the heart of the jungle, tangled like the vegetation of the primeval forests, elongated hybrid beings—stemming from man and from fabulous horse-like creatures—appear in tight hordes. As opposed to other Surrealists, eager to

find the sources of their imagination within themselves, Wilfredo Lam was the only one to find the embodiment of his mythology at the roots of his own culture. He unveils these in a stylistic synthesis of primitivism and modernism that forcefully singles his work out.

ROBERTO MATTA ECHAURREN

☐ *Eleven Forms of Doubt /*
Kaleidoscope Aquarium

In 1944, Matta paid tribute to Marcel Duchamp with his canvas titled *Science, conscience et patience du vitreur* (*Knowledge, Consciousness and Patience of the Glazier*). To Duchamp's *Large Glass*, a key to 20th century art, Matta owes the access to the maze-like realms of which he investigated the reflections during his entire life. This venture is not devoid of philosophical and moral background. An anthropomorphic totem entrapped within a delirious cosmic machinery named *The Pilgrim of Doubt* and dated 1947 was the first occurence of this painting's theme, recurring ten years after. In 1956, Matta produced *The Doubt of the Three Worlds* for the Unesco in Paris: a gigantic canvas in which he resorted to the same idiom of translucent screens, traces of dashing breakthroughs, undetermined organisms and virtual machines. "If wanted, one can make out three characters in my canvas. However, only the manifold potentialities of the three characters can be distinguished, and they are so closely linked that they are incapable of breaking away from each other." The human figure has been erased, but not man. In the oneiric devices of this mental laboratory, the activity of an imaginary reflection of human energies can be observed.

● ROBERTO MATTA ECHAURREN, known as MATTA (1911), is a Chilian painter who came to Europe in 1930. He trained as an architect and worked in Le Corbusier's studio. He took on painting in 1937 and was introduced into the Surrealist group by Salvador Dali the next year. He lived in the United States from 1939 to 1948, in company of Marcel Duchamp and the Surrealists in exile. He continued painting in his highly original style after returning to France; his thoroughly Surrealist work often showed ideological involvement.

1. *Salvador Dali*
The Temptation of St. Anthony,
1946, oil on canvas,
89.5 x 119.5, inv. 7223.

2. *Wifredo Lam*
The soulless Children,
1964, oil on canvas,
210 x 249, inv. 7722.

3. *Roberto Matta Echaurren*
Eleven Forms of Doubt /
Kaleidoscope Aquarium,
1957, oil on canvas,
200 x 505, inv. 7095.

● WIFREDO LAM (1902-1982), was born in Cuba to a Chinese father and a mulatta mother, and his godmother was a healer who exercised magic. He attended the school of Fine Arts in Havana and in Madrid, where he studied primitive art. He had fought with the Republicans during the Spanish Civil War and was compelled to leave Spain and flee to Paris in 1938, after they had been defeated. Picasso had finished *Guernica* the year before. He had a permanent influence on Lam's work. The Surrealists welcomed him in their group and, in 1941, he left France for Havana with André Breton, Max Ernst and Claude Lévi-Strauss, the anthropologist. A journey to Haiti in 1945 initiated him to voodoo symbolics. After he left Cuba in 1952, he never ceased to travel and paint.

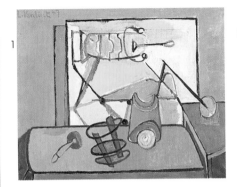

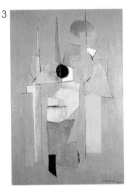

● ANNE BONNET (1908-1960), LOUIS VAN LINT (1909-1986) and GASTON BERTRAND (1910-1994), were fellow pupils at the Academy, and their respective careers ran parallel. Anne Bonnet had her first personal exhibition in the Palais des Beaux-Arts in Brussels in 1941, Louis Van Lint in 1942 and Gaston Bertrand the same year in a Brussels gallery. MARC MENDELSON (1915) studied in Antwerp, and his first one-man show also took place in 1942. All four were co-founders of the "Jeune Peinture Belge" in 1945. Although not simultaneously, their paths led them all to a more or less radical form of abstraction.

Jeune Peinture Belge

On July 3, 1945, the Jeune Peinture Belge association was founded under the honorary chairmanship of James Ensor: it included twelve artists, half of whom are presented here. Robert-Léon Delevoy, manager of the Apollo gallery, became the secretary of the association and proved to be as brilliant an organiser as Octave Maus or Georges Giroux. The program of the association—that later welcomed numerous young artists—was to spread "living Belgian art, without preconceived idea about the school or tendency". Until its dissolution in 1948, Jeune Peinture belge organised personal and group exhibitions in Belgium and exhibition exchanges with e.g. the Galerie de France in Paris. Many Belgian artists were presented there for the first time and became acquainted with artists of the School of Paris. Their example thrust the evolution of Belgian painting ahead after it had been maintained in its provincial remoteness by World War II. In the light of these apertures, several young artists chose the path of abstraction.

LOUIS VAN LINT

☐ Still Life. Lamp Glass

At the time of the Jeune Peinture Belge, Van Lint gradually experiments with the decomposition of representation. In this still life, it can be perceived that he is standing at the crossroads of Cubist influence and Jean Brusselmans' Expressionism. The next year, his encounter with painters from the School of Paris lead him on the path of non-representational art. In the course of his career, he swayed from harsh geometrism to a total autonomy of colour (cfr. p. 213).

MARC MENDELSON

☐ Portrait of Mia

Marc Mendelson induces a strange atmosphere in the realism of this portrait of the young actress Mia, whom he would marry one day. The play with *chiaroscuro* allows the transition from the ambient tonality to the young woman's range of rose shades, treated in a slightly shimmering matter: she has the unwonted presence of a hieratic apparition, gazing into the invisible. The naturalist rendering of the wooden floor, divided up by patches of light, unusually contrasts with the undefined matter of the background.

Mendelson was very impressed with Chirico's Metaphysical painting and could well have developed his poetic approach of reality from where he stood. The trends of the Jeune Peinture Belge drew him towards abstraction after a period inspired by Cubism (cfr. p. 213).

ANNE BONNET

☐ The Golden City

Ten years after her participation in the Jeune Peinture Belge, Anne Bonnet had given her vision the time to become clearer and eventually suggested non-representational urban landscapes. It would be perfectly legitimate to see no more than a refined variation on an exquisite harmony of shades in this *Golden City*, clustering before its towering minarets that point at the sky.

GASTON BERTRAND

☐ Seaview

The painter departed from perception of reality—a seaside resort—and abolished all its anecdotal remains to keep only a sensitive working drawing, thus producing an abstract image: ratios between the distances, incidences of the lines, balance between the colours are the essence of reality, obtained through distillation of the global perception. Gaston Bertrand claimed: "By means of a sensitive transformation of what is real, I want to attain what is unreal or the real truth." From there, his entire work rests on this requirement (cfr. p. 159).

WILLY ANTHOONS

☐ Human Cathedral

The switch from representational to abstract art—which was deemed an irreversible step at the time—went through this symbolic, transitional work by Willy Anthoons: in an accomplished, coherent plastic synthesis, he unites man, the favourite model for art of all times, and the cathedral, the symbol of the art of occidental builders. Henri Laurens' Cubist influence may still be obvious here, but Anthoons pursued towards abstraction, shaping the pure process of the spirit.

4

1. *Louis Van Lint*
Still Life.
Lamp Glass,
*1947, oil on canvas,
80 x 100, inv. 6427.*

2. *Marc Mendelson*
Portrait of Mia,
*1944, oil on canvas,
170 x 120, inv. 7648.*

3. *Anne Bonnet*
The Golden City,
*1955-1956, oil on canvas,
150 x 100, inv. 6765.*

4. *Gaston Bertrand*
Seaview,
*1948, oil on canvas,
81.5 x 63.5, inv. 7483.*

5. *Willy Anthoons*
Human Cathedral,
*1948, wood (elm),
153 x 59.5 x 52.5,
inv. 8215.*

● WILLY ANTHOONS (1911-1982) was the only sculptor amongst the founders of the Jeune Peinture Belge. He settled in Paris in 1948 and took part in the great events of contemporary art. The combined influences of Piet Mondrian and Henry Moore led him to abstraction. Although he has privileged direct cut of marble or wood, he experimented with the mobile, like Alexander Calder (cfr. p. 214).

5

1

1. *Antoine Mortier*
Coloured Transposition / Nude from Behind,
*1952, gouache on paper glued to canvas,
233.5 x 149.5, inv. 6901.*

● ANTOINE MORTIER (1908)
joined the Jeune Peinture
Belge group at the Apollo
gallery in 1946, where his
first personal exhibition
took place. At the time, his
work could be described as
stylized Expressionism and
his figures were stressed by
a vigorous black outline. He
pulled out of the group
because he found it was too
much oriented towards abstraction as it prevailed in the
School of Paris. However,
he personally withdrew
every reference to reality
from his work and asserted
himself as a pioneer of
lyrical abstraction
in Belgium.

ANTOINE MORTIER

☐ *Coloured Transposition / Nude from Behind*
The painter has evacuated the materiality
of the body, its anatomy and sensuality,
retaining nothing more than an ideogram.
He ornaments this raw token of a mental
representation with plastic attractiveness,
like a sensitive contrast between blacks and
light or the dynamism of the monumental
outline. The question arises whether this
emphatic gesture is the expression of
Antoine Mortier's struggle to the limit
against the power of abstraction, immanent
to his work, as if he baulked before a hurdle
he would later jump, when his work would
no longer be transposition but, with the same force,
Harmony (inv. 7516) or *Suggested Volumes* (inv. 7952).

Cobra

*On November 8, 1948, in a Parisian café, Christian
Dotremont wrote down the founding articles of the Cobra
group in presence of the Belgian poet Joseph Noiret, the
Danish painter Asger Jorn and the three Dutch painters
Karel Appel, Constant and Corneille. This text is about
experimentation more than about art. The "CoBrA" acronym,
invented by Dotremont, re-assembles the first letters of
Copenhagen, Brussels and Amsterdam in a single name with
a symbolic echo. Cobra, joined by a number of artists like
Pierre Alechinsky and Pol Bury for Belgium, edited ten issues
of a review in which their experiments—blending plastic
arts and literature —were reported. These artists ambition
to recover the spontaneous powers of expression that have
been asphyxiated by the prevailing standardizing codes, and
refer to chidren's drawings, (particularly Scandinavian) popular
art to give unlimited credit to man's powers of intuition.
Cobra was a reply to the spreading of abstract art and to
Socialist realism. Although kindred to Surrealism, Cobra
opposed the liberation of creative spontaneity faced with
matter to the intellectual implementation of artistic means.
The last issue of the Cobra magazine suspended common
activities in October 1951. Each participant followed his
own path, mostly in the same line like Appel, Jorn, Dotremont,
although some others, like Pol Bury (cfr. p. 156), chose entirely
different directions.*

2. Asger Jorn
The Three Wise Men,
1955, oil on canvas,
65 x 100, inv. 7211.

3. Karel Appel
Reclining Nude,
1957, oil on canvas,
130 x 195, inv. 6823.

ASGER JORN
☐ The Three Wise Men
The three fascinated figures supposedly conjure up the Magi of the Christian tradition, the three wise men who came from the Orient. They appear through and out of the syncopated gesture that models them in the pictorial matter with frantic energy. A tight link is created between them by the echoed hues and the movement of the paste. A clear outline around the bust of the figure on the left and the face of the central figure, applied with a light-handed paintbrush, does not actually structure them: it has been added in order to balance out, in the diagonal, the forceful line finishing the figure on the right. Jorn works without any predefined plan but complies with a perfectly mastered method. Successive additions lead the painting towards its coherence. "To create a work is a process of which the progress and the outcome are unknown [...] Each time I see my finished work, I am quite amazed."

KAREL APPEL
☐ Reclining Nude
The men and animals of Karel Appel's world are cruel, hallucinated, horrified, screaming or roaring with laughter, always at the paroxysm of an emotion. He does not paint screaming beings, he paints the scream itself. In this canvas, meekly named *Reclining Nude*, the sarcasm or complaint is not only expelled by a gaping mouth but savagely bursts from everywhere. The harmony of pure hues combines with the ductility of the matter, powerfully stretched across the canvas to liberate a maelstrom of violence. Karel Appel is probably the most instinctive of all painters branded by the CoBrA spirit.

● KAREL APPEL (1921), is born in Amsterdam, where he studied and sought himself until he was twenty-six: He found his way in 1947 when he spent a few months in Brussels with the artists of the Jeune Peinture Belge. He them thrust himself headlong in the Cobra adventure, of which his fiercely expressive work is an extension. His work became more playful in the sixties, with huge plywood and expanded polystyrene figures, a sort of monumental polychrome toys.

● ASGER JORN (1914-1973) Asger Oluf Jørgensen, known as Asger Jorn, was born in a village close to Silkeborg (Denmark) and painted his first canvases at the age of sixteen. He travelled to Paris in 1936 and worked in Fernand Léger's studio there. When he returned to Denmark in 1939, he took part in the creation of the *Helhesten* (*Hell's Stallion*) magazine that stemmed from a group of young Danish artists who were to join Cobra later on. Jorn played a key role there between 1948 and 1951. In 1953, still in Denmark, he concentrated on ceramics, then continued his work the next year in Albisola, Northern Italy, a sort of central arts and crafts gathering point for a number of European artists. Jorn was prolific till his last day, travelling a lot, publishing significant articles and theoretical essays, and never slackening in the production of his pictorial work. The catalogue of his mature period, covering the period from 1956 to his demise, includes a thousand items by itself.

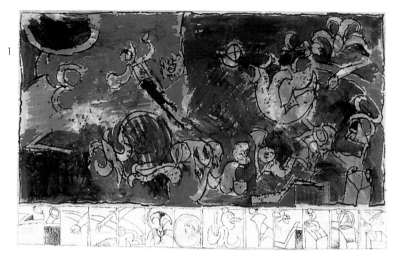

1. *Pierre Alechinsky*
Sometimes it's the Opposite,
*1970, acrylics on paper pasted to canvas (marouflage)
183 x 298, inv. 7938.*

● PIERRE ALECHINSKY (1927) was born and studied in Brussels. In 1949, he met Christian Dotremont, who introduced him to the Cobra group, of which he became one of the most active members. He organised the group's last exhibition in Liège in 1951, then settled in Paris and studied engraving at Stanley William Hayter's workshop. Édouard Jaguer entrusted the production of the first issue of the *Phases* magazine to him in 1953. Alechinsky resumes his career with steady success, building up a striking œuvre among the better work of the second half of the century.

PIERRE ALECHINSKY

☐ Sometimes it's the Opposite

It capers, bawls, frisks about, it dives, it runs and swims in the cheerfulness of an overall turmoil. Where about? Never mind, as long as there seems to be grass and water and the sun has highlighted them both with a touch of vermillion. Please refer to the predella's drawings for further details about the characters: follow a swimmer; find a character with a headdress of feathers, a 'gille de Binche' (traditional costumed figure of the town of Binche) or a Maya dancer; look at this strange creature that hasn't found a way out of the circle in which it is entrapped, or that bawling child. Should doubts remain about what is seen, refer to the title, informing us that '*Sometimes it's the Opposite*'. Alechinsky forces the cheeky freedom he allows himself upon the spectator.

The very casual manner of this splendid work rests on a technique of which the mastery is the result of a patient practice of spontaneity. The artist outlined his drawing with an agile gesture, taught to him by a Chinese painter fifteen years earlier: spread the paper on the floor and, whilst holding the inkpot in one hand and the paintbrush in the other, bend over and involve your entire body in the vivaciousness of the line. Sparing the zones determined by the outline, he then structured the painting with planes of the two other colours. The predella is taken over from Renaissance altarpiece painters: they pictured details from the main narrative on small panels. Alechinsky sometimes added it after an observation period of a few days, a few weeks or exceptionally up to a few years. Drawn on a background of pages of a 17th century register, it seems to offer a comment on the painting.

● CHRISTIAN DOTREMONT (1922-1979), was born on the outskirts of Brussels and published his first collection of poetry in 1940, *Ancient Eternity*, through which he was linked with the Belgian Surrealists. He was the protagonist and founder of the Cobra group in 1948, of which he incarnated the spirit in his work until his last day. Although he was essentially a writer, he approached plastic arts through the logogram, a peculiar technique he resorted to for a prolific and interesting work.

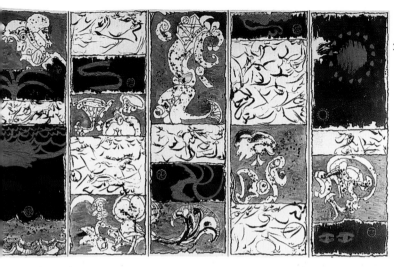

2. *Pierre Alechinsky et Christian Dotremont*
Abrupt Fable,
*1976, India Ink and acrylic
paint on paper (marouflage),
284 x 475, inv. 11418.*

PIERRE ALECHINSKY ET CHRISTIAN DOTREMONT

☐ Abrupt Fable

Christian Dotremont was a poet, a controversial and theoretical author, a writer more than anything else. As early as 1948, he had imagined a dialogue with Asger Jorn on the same medium: Jorn painted and he wrote with a paintbrush in a shared composition. These "word-paintings" became a common practice within the Cobra group and were known as "work for four hands". This huge screen exemplifies the collaboration between Pierre Alechinsky and Christian Dotremont. However, the latter resorted to the "logogram" instead of using roman letters: in 1950, it unexpectedly occurred to Dotremont to observe one of his manuscripts by transparency, perpendicular to the writing's direction. The text had thus become unreadable and had "acquired something chinese", as he put it. He applied this discovery to the logogram in 1962, a sort of writing-painting that entrusts a part of the written matter's elaboration to the hand. He traces poetic texts in an unsystematized stenography, depending on the combination of the gesture's physical inspiration with thought. "I insist on the fact that logograms are original manuscripts. None is a copy [...] I suggest you find the drawing—certainly not naturalistic, neverthless material drawing—of my cry or my song in their exaggeratedly natural and excessively free handwriting [...] Whereafter you may read the text, always written in clear under the logogram."

You may want to use the poem in clear to decipher the logogram:
"abrupte fable
d'être d'herbe de verbe
 de sable de flots
à serpentements d'orage
tendre de fruit
à cheminements presque
 terrestres
à trace de presque pas
à presque rien d'avant
à développements
en roue d'oiseau-lyre
à brusquement voler
de nuances ensemble
à la nuit d'un nuage
doré jusqu'au soleil
à dépliures de cri
à bruissements de jour
à regards de chant"

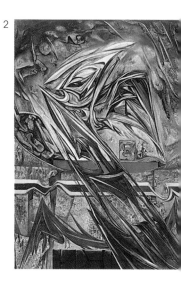

1. *Jacques Lacomblez*
**Funeral Song - For
Albéric Magnard,**
*1965, oil on canvas,
162.5 x 130, inv. 7360.*

2. *Jacques Zimmermann*
**From all sides,
the trace,**
*1967, oil on canvas,
146 x 114, inv. 7930.*

● JACQUES LACOMBLEZ (born in 1934), departed from fantastic representation but switched over to abstract Surrealism under the influence of Max Ernst. His encounter with Édouard Jaguer in 1955 convinced him to join the Phases group and be its organiser in Belgium. The evolution of his work, underpinned by a network of poetic and musical affinities, was very coherent and never deviated.

Phases

Édouard Jaguer was a Parisian poet and art critic who had long been involved in autonomous Surrealist activism when he founded the Phases magazine, around which a genuine movement of artistic research soon developed. Although it was geared to Surrealism, this movement showed a greater concern for the artistic dynamics of plastic or poetic creation than for ideologic speculation. Édouard Jaguer proved to be open to remote contributions from the start, thus creating a cosmopolitan convergence point and giving rise to kindred movements throughout Europe, in South America and in Canada. He organised over sixty international exhibitions under the "Phases" label. In this perspective, Jacques Lacomblez joined the movement upon meeting him and spread its spirit in Belgium, immediately followed by Marie Carlier and Jacques Zimmermann. The results of his activity can be valued in the Edda review, edited by Lacomblez from 1958 to 1965.

● JACQUES ZIMMERMANN (born in 1929), has been Jacques Lacomblez' partner and is still represented nowadays at the Phases exhibitions. He departed from Hans Hartung's heritage and invented a lyricism of the gesture, organically adapted to the feverish landscapes he reinvents in every one of his canvases.

● MARIE CARLIER (1920-1986), was trained as an engraver and exercised drawing and direct cut until 1957. As a consequence of her meeting with Jacques Lacomblez, she switched from representational art to a symbolic approach and to express herself through painting. Her work can be seen at most of the Phases exhibitions since 1958.

3

3. *Marie Carlier*
Thalassa or the Initial Element,
1967, oil on canvas, 90 x 116, inv. 8384.

JACQUES LACOMBLEZ

☐ *Funeral Song - For Albéric Magnard*
In order to celebrate a composer with a magician's name, Jacques Lacomblez has erected a stern mausoleum where the opalescent gem of his memory glistens. All around lies an undifferentiated realm from which the accurate geologist's work of the painter has drawn a fantastic stratified world of cleavages.

JACQUES ZIMMERMANN

☐ *From all sides, the trace...*
For the last forty years, Jacques Zimmermann has never slackened in his investigation of the raging winds and the reply of the landscapes. Notwithstanding the eddying violence and the perilous hazards, he keeps repeating those blissful crash-dives in the turbulent splendour of an oneiric realm. The vehemence of the collected evidence prevents from believing that the venture could be assimilated with symbolic description. Everything here leads to believe that the act of painting occured like an exercise of immediate capture of the invisible, in accordance with the strictest Surrealist tenet.

MARIE CARLIER

☐ *Thalassa or the Initial Element*
In the tracks of Gaston Bachelard's philosophy and poetry in particular, like an ascet, Marie Carlier has persevered in the imaginary exploration of the Primeval elements. Her fondness of deep psychology led her to fathom the symbolic ocean deeps—the maternal element from which all on our planet stems—from where she returned with images of a great poetic density, that can also be regarded as inner self-portraits.

1. *Jean Degottex*
Hana,
1961, oil on canvas, 162 x 114, inv. 6935.

2. *Simon Hantaï*
Painting,
1957, oil on canvas, 181 x 302, inv. 7482.

1

2

● JEAN DEGOTTEX (1918-1988) was born in France. A journey to the Maghreb countries in 1938 inspired him to paint Fauve landscapes. He switched to non-representational art in 1949, mainly sign painting. André Breton organised an exhibition for him in 1955 at the Surrealist gallery l'Étoile Scellée. Degottex deepened his thorough knowledge of zen-tenets and an enquiry about the relationships between gesture, sign and painting. He experimented with various materials—plaited paper, beaten sheet iron—but made it a rule to drastically simplify his work.

Abstraction

The generic name of "abstract art" covers a constellation of trends of which the common factor is to be non-representational. A watercolour painted by Wassily Kandinsky in 1910 is generally credited as the first deliberate act of non-representational painting. He had evolved from an expressive Fauve manner to a representation of reality that gradually became more allusive in its arbitrary distribution of space, titling his work Improvisations. It took him only a small step to withdraw every object and run into abstract poetic lyricism. Piet Mondrian came from Holland and joined him in Paris in 1912, at the age of forty. Cubism opened new perspectives to him and, in the canvases he then painted—sequences with themes such as the tree, the façade, a church, the sea, the dunes, — he literally abstracted shapes within a stylization that gradually dissolved the models. Beyond this metamorphosis that took him two years, he developed a style that eventually led him to Neo-plastic compositions in which he restricted his idiom to surfaces surrounded by lignes cutting each other at a right angle and his palette to flat applications of primary colours, to which he added black, white and grey. Two main divergent tendencies developed from Kandinsky's and Mondrian's pioneer work. On one hand, Mondrian's followers structured their art and based it on rigorous geometry, as drawn to its conclusions in Victor Vasarely's urban development concepts and Nicolas Schöffer's spatiodynamic towers. On the other hand, partly as a reaction to this harshness, the liberation of gesture also generated a profusion of personal manners, often referred to as "informal art", including Hans Hartung's lyrical abstraction as well as Tachism. Artists from the United States have extended these latest investigations in very significant ways, and their research has deeply influenced the further evolution of art in Europe.

JEAN DEGOTTEX

☐ Hana

Without prejudging his spiritual involvement in his approach of zen disciplines, it can be seen by the masterliness of his draftsmanship that Jean Degottex was familiar with the mental concentration techniques prevailing in Japanese martial arts, archery, acting and the art of painting. The gesture can only be the spontaneous spring of banded energy. From within a being's innermost self, a regretless token uncoils and dashes out on the canvas. The title refers to a treatise of theatrical doctrine written in the 15th century by the Nô-actor Zeami: *The Book of Transmission of the Flower of Art*. Hana is the flower, the visual effect created by a style one level above all levels.

SIMON HANTAÏ

☐ Painting

"Once again, probably like every tenth year, a great start", André Breton wrote to hallow Simon Hantaï's first exhibition he had welcomed in 1953 at the Étoile Scellée gallery, the new stronghold of the hard-core Surrealists. Hantaï was born in Budapest in 1922 and had arrived in Paris three years earlier. He induced countless symbols taken over from alchemy and magic in his fantastic representational painting. But from 1955, his orientation deviated towards lyrical abstraction, as exemplified by this very sober canvas showing impeccable masterliness and deep concentration, hinting at the painter's interest for the Far East's spiritual discipline. The spontaneous gesture is kindred to automatism. However, this orientation did not tally with the line of the Surrealist group, hence an in-evitable split. Hantaï has changed his manner several times since.

HANS HARTUNG

☐ Composition T. 1963 - R 40

This composition—one of the better products of his mature period—arranges depth without resorting to perspective. The black median strip with its shimmering, slightly blurred edges, is set out against the refined shades of the background, whereas the dishevelled motif comes to the fore, in relief. This tangle is scraped in the fresh paint with combs or rough brushes in order to free the rosish ochre of the prime layer (that also shows through the streaks of the greyish purple zone at the bottom of the painting). The structured drawing on the canvas' diagonal, superimposed upon this lively release of energy by means of a palette knife, stroke by sroke, expresses the triumph of willpower over the inertia of matter.

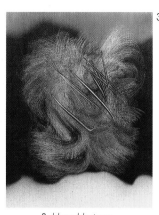

3

3. *Hans Hartung*
**Composition
T. 1963 - R 40**,
*1963, oil on canvas,
180 x 142, inv. 7035.*

● HANS HARTUNG (1904-1989) was born in Leipzig. He is likely to have been the first painter who approached abstraction without a preliminary representational stage. He had not been in touch with recent non-representational trends when he produced his first abstract watercolours in 1922. He was eighteen years at the time, and those first experiments underpinned the plastic idiom he was to develop at a later stage. His first personal exhibition took place in Dresden in 1931, and he settled in Paris in 1935, acquiring the French nationality at the end of the war. As opposed to geometrical abstraction, Hartung developed a dynamic informal style in the thirties, based on the spontaneity of the gesture. "What I like", he declared, is to act upon the canvas", foreshadowing the *Action Painting*, exercised by American artists since 1949. He was soon acknowledged as a key figure in modern art.

● SERGE POLIAKOFF
(1900-1969) left Russia in
1918 and settled in Paris in
1923 after five years of
roving life. He attended the
courses of two free acade-
mies and completed his training in London. Subsequent to
his encounter with Wassily
Kandinsky in 1937, then
with Robert and Sonia
Delaunay, he chose the path
of abstraction and developed
a very personal style from
which he never deviated.

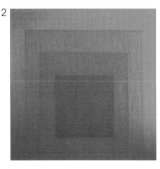

SERGE POLIAKOFF

☐ **Grey Canvas** (GOLDSCHMIDT BEQUEST)
In Poliakoff's work, the shape springs forth from
colour and from the limitation the artist decides
to assign to a coloured zone, depending on his
inner need. From the one to the next, colours
take over free spaces and change into shapes that
adjust to one another without submitting to any
previous drawing. The successive transparent
layers confer a vibrating density to the pictorial
matter, extolling its tactile values.

JOSEF ALBERS

☐ *Homage to the Square, Signal*
Josef Albers (1888-1976) had been a pupil in the
Bauhaus before being a professor there, from 1925
until the Nazis closed it down in 1933. He then
emigrated to the United States, where he resumed
his creative work, and teaching. He undertook the
production of the long programmed series of the
Homage To The Square in 1950. The colours he uses
do not refer to any personal connotation, neither
memory, nor emotion. They report a physical
phenomenon—the interplay of adjacent colours—
the artist perceives as a metaphor of man's
relationship to the world, in which independent
individuals are also interdependent. Colours have
become symbols or even a psychic and spiritual
driving force. Their increasing luminous intensity
corresponds to a symbolic passage from material
to spiritual world, from the terrestrial to the
celestial. The painter manages the series
systematically and, at the back of each canvas, notes
the exact shade and the manufacturer of the paint.
The form is conceived as a vehicle for colour. The
painting's entire composition complies with a strict
metric pattern, whereby one unit equals one tenth
of the side of the initial square; The bases of the
successive concentric squares are separated by
one unit, their sides by two units and their tops by
three, producing an optical illusion. The upper space,
freed by the effect of compression of the figures,
symbolizes spiritual drift.

VICTOR VASARÉLY

☐ *Kerrhon*
Victor Vasarély was born in 1908 in Pécs, Hungary. He
was trained at the Muhely Academy, Budapest's Bauhaus.
When he settled in Paris in 1931, his manner gradually
evolved from a form of Expressionism to a sort of Post-
Cubism. When the time of wavering was over came his

Belle-Isle period, of which *Kerrhon* is one of the later examples. Since 1947, the sea had inspired him a plastic idiom of broad flat planes of colour, divided up in ellipsoidal shapes suggested by the distortion of reflections in water. These stylized, well-balanced forms hint at the elements of the coastal landscape: the oval of the setting sun on the horizon, the waves, the clouds and the shingles, more literally. Despite their outspoken formal and chromatic abstraction, the structure of the paintings of that period generally allows for a dividing line between two zones, like the horizon in a landscape. At the same time, Vasarély leans towards what is to become his Kinetic manner, a major contribution to geometrical abstraction.

Moreover, he challenged the notion of the unique original work: he created "multiples" as soon as 1959, and developed programmed systems of coloured permutations, enabling infinite modulations of a same work. In a most coherent way, his overall aim is to integrate art in the urban landscape.

LUCIO FONTANA

☐ *Concetto spaziale, Attese*

Lucio Fontana (1899-1968) was born in Argentina to an Italian sculptor who taught him the rudiments of his art. He resumed his artistic training in Milan, then returned to Argentina, opened a sculptor's studio and exhibited work inspired by Futurism. He went back to Italy in 1928 and produced his first abstract sculptures in 1934. World War II was the occasion of another stay in Argentina. The *Manifesto Blanco*, which later underpinned Spatialism, was published by him in Buenos Aires in 1946, where he was surrounded by a generation of younger artists. When he finally returned to Italy the following year, he became the main protagonist of Spatialism, revealed at an exhibition of a Milan gallery in 1949 where he presented his first *Spatial Environment*: fluorescent abstract forms, suspended in space and lit by Wood lights. He henceforth named all his works *Concetto spaziale*, whatever the technique. Fontana's innovations open the path for the use of new materials in art, like neon, television, radars. He invented a plastic idiom of perforations and tears, eventually resulting in monochrome canvases incised with a cutter in 1958. At first, they were perceived as a symbolic killing of Western pictorial tradition, although Fontana intended to transcend consecrated categories in order to open new technical perspectives to art, that could generate unprecedented contents. From the beginning of these "*tagli*", he subtitled them *Attese*, expectation, which could be understood as a claim of faith in the future of modernity.

1. *Serge Poliakoff*
Grey Canvas,
1953, oil and tempera on canvas, 116 x 89, inv. 11211.

2. *Josef Albers*
Homage to the Square. Signal,
1967, oil on masonite, 102 x 102, inv. 7736.

3. *Victor Vasaléry*
Kerrhon,
1953-1954, oil on canvas, 120 x 100, inv. 6744.

4. *Lucio Fontana*
Concetto spaziale, Attese,
c. 1968, watercolour on canvas, 61.5 x 50, inv. 11528.

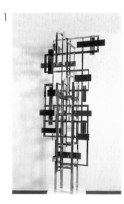

1. *Nicolas Schöffer*
Spatiodynamics 24,
1955-1968, chromed steel
199.5 x 95.5 x 68,
inv. 8686.

NICOLAS SCHÖFFER

☐ *Spatiodynamics 24*

Nicolas Schöffer (1912-1992), a native Hungarian, settled in Paris in 1936. He first produced sculptures inspired by Piet Mondrian's Neo-Plasticism, and his first Spatio-dynamic work dates back to 1948: a dynamizing cutout of space perceived through sculpture. From then on, Schöffer systematically developed a gradually more ambitious œuvre, integrating space and dialectically integrating itself to the city.

In 1954, in cooperation with composer Pierre Henry, Schöffer built a fifty metre tower that could broadcast sound waves. In 1956, his cybernetic sculpture, CYSP I, moved on wheels and reacted to sound and to light; Maurice Béjart chose it as a partner for his dancers. The next year, he added a lumino-dynamic function, integrating light and light projections. In 1961, in Liège, a fifty-two metre tower combined sixty-six rotating mirrors and hundred and twenty floodlights, the whole being controlled electronically. In 1963, eventually, an inordinate project was presented for La Défense, just outside Paris, for the year 2000. A tower of three hundred and seven metres would emit light signals, controlled by a computer that would process and convey meteorological variations, traffic intensity, social and political events. This gigantic utopia was filed, and Nicolas Schöffer dedicated the rest of his life to theoretical aspects of his research and set them out in several written works.

ALBERTO MAGNELLI

☐ *Luminous Voyage*

Alberto Magnelli (1888-1971) began to paint in 1907. He journeyed to Paris in 1914 and met Guillaume Apollinaire and the painters he knew—Picasso, Matisse, Léger and a few others; this oriented him towards abstract Orphism. However, he reintroduced the figure in his paint-ing in 1916. He settled in Paris in 1930 and adopted his eventual manner three months later: he has chosen the realm between geometric abstraction and gestural painting. His shapes do not belong to the geometric vocabulary but do require an accuracy that doesn't tally at all with the spontaneity of the gesture. The perfection of the drawing proceeds from a meticulous development and the balance of the composition from a correct assessment of the mass ratio's. Moreover, there is a foreseen interplay between the coloured zones and their outline. Chance is totally eliminated when the artist takes up his paintbrushes, because regrets are ruled out. And the subtleness of the shades has its say, the imperceptible gradations that

2. *Alberto Magnelli*
Luminous Voyage,
1950, oil on canvas,
97.5 x 130, inv. 7513.

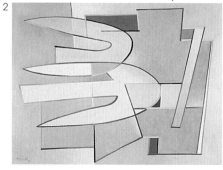

enliven the surfaces, the contrast of colours and slight reflections from which the relief stems. This necessary combination of mastered elements ensure the work's harmonious stability and the eye's pure delight.

AUGUSTE HERBIN

☐ Star

Departing from the Cubist trends developed by the Section d'Or artists, with whom he exhibited his work at the 1913 Armory Show, Auguste Herbin (1882-1960) became one of the pioneers of geometric abstraction. He founded the Abstraction-Création group with Piet Mondrian and Georges Vantongerloo in 1931, and a philosophical concept underlies his work and theirs. He does not consider abstraction as a sterile combination of shapes. He restricts himself to geometrical shapes because they are the substratum of all natural shapes. "When a painter entirely detaches himself from the object, in fact and in spirit, he produces a work in which the shapes, the colours, the ratio's are the purest creation", he wrote in 1945. "This work is perfectly concrete in its relationship from the work to man, since it treats the purest reality, the only reality that wholly stems from man's conscious and unconscious activity."

3. *Auguste Herbin*
Star,
1948, oil on canvas,
92 x 72.8, inv. 7118.

JO DELAHAUT

☐ Peace

Jo Delahaut (1911-1992) was admitted as a member of the Jeune Peinture Belge (cfr. p. 198) in 1946, and that year he was the first member to give up representational art and paint his *First Abstract Composition*, reminiscent of Cubism and of Joan Miró. However, in August he visited the Salon des Réalités Nouvelles in Paris and encountered Auguste Herbin, who converted him to rigorous geometry. In the fifties, he invented this recurring formal element he uses in an infinite variety of combinations. As opposed to Herbin's chromatic scarcity, Delahaut's palette ranges from pure colours to the most delicate pastel shades. He asserted himself as the leading figure of geometric abstraction in Belgium, resumed his research and discovered new shapes, equally devoid of any reference to external hints, but neverthless loaded with a spiritual and poetic content.

4. *Jo Delahaut*
Peace,
1954, oil on canvas,
60 x 184, inv. 8265.

1. *Arman*
Drugs,
c. 1960-1962,
52 x 32 x 6.8, inv. 11064.

ARMAN

☐ **Drugs** (GOLDSCHMIDT BEQUEST)

Armand Fernandez, known as Arman, born in Nice in 1928, painted his first abstract paintings in 1955. He produced his first collection in 1959: used radio lamps, hoarded in a box with a glass side. Arman, who possesses a significant collection of African statues, claims he is driven to collect items by a compelling urge he inherited from his mother; she carefully collected up to bits of string and sorted them in labelled boxes. His artistic process tallies with the spirit of the Nouveaux Réalistes, the group he founded in 1960 with several other artists and art critic Pierre Restany. The latter considers Arman's work as an example of this "new perceptive approach of reality". "A radical method: after a clean sweep has been made of representational painting, the author accumulates "true" objects, and these are neither transcribed, nor drawn, nor reproduced but borrowed directly from the real world."

According to the strict tenet of Nouveau Réalisme, the undertaking should not have any aesthetic aim, but Arman admits he does not constrain the whole of his work within these limits. *Drugs* is one of the first "in bulk" collections he produced in the early sixties. In 1964, he resorted to the technique of including items in transparent polyester; from 1967, with the support of the Régie Renault, he produced very sculptural assemblages of cars' spare parts. In the *Colères* series, he crushes or burns the objects in order to abolish their status of unique piece.

BRAM BOGART

☐ **Blauwvang**

2. *Bram Bogart*
Blauwvang,
1965, mixed techniques
on canvas pasted on
panel (marouflage),
153 x 162, inv. 7364.

Abraham Van den Bogaart, known as Bram Bogart, is born in the Netherlands in 1921. He began to paint at the age of eighteen, under the aegis of Van Gogh and Permeke. He went through a period influenced by Cubism in 1948, then evolved towards Expressionist Tachism where the insistant presence of signs can be noticed. By 1960, he had settled in Belgium and adapted his style to an eruptive pictorial matter that gradually asserted itself and eventually overwhelmed the artist's facture. He gave up the easel and lies huge panels on the ground, lines them with hessian and spreads the flow of muddy matter on it. he works this paste with the trowel and with inordinate palette knives, from fifty centimetres to two metres wide. He has invented the matter himself: an amalgam of carefully grinded pure pigments, bound with a blend of oils and settled for a long time. An equal proportion of watercolour is then added, and sometimes whi-

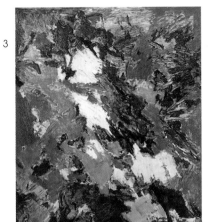

ting to give it a grainy consistency. Up to three hunderd kilo's of matter may be needed for the larger canvases. The tool draws deep furrows in the dense mass, the raw signs of an undecipherable idiom, appearing out of a swollen magma that immediately petrifies. The confrontation of horizontals and verticals, the radical geometry of the shapes that are set out refer to Mondrian. However, the tone is dionysiac and the question arises whether an agreement between two opposite dispositions is possible within the framework of a same idiom.

LOUIS VAN LINT

☐ Autumn Savagery

Broad white impasto's sustain the rising diagonal that guides the drift of the large coloured patches of this warm Tachist composition. Once in his fifties, Van Lint has conquered a steadiness, contrasting with his time of wavering in the midst of the Jeune Peinture Belge (cfr. p. 198).

MARC MENDELSON

☐ Spanish Landscape

Between 1953 and 1956, Marc Mendelson was fascinated by the numerous scratches and anonymous marks on the weathered walls of Catalonia, and these inspired his new manner. He amalgamated powdery materials—plaster and sand—with the uniform colour he has coated his canvas with, and this confers the roughness of a wall surface to it. He then plots an abundance of lively graffiti with an agile hand.

After evolving from Poetic Realism (cfr. p. 198) to abstraction, Marc Mendelson returned to representation, including a great deal of fantasy and humor.

3. *Louis Van Lint*
Autumn Savagery,
*1960, oil on canvas,
200 × 151.5, inv. 6917.*

4. *Marc Mendelson*
Spanish Landscape,
*mixed techniques and
oil on canvas, 162 × 114,
inv. 6966.*

1

2

● ALEXANDER CALDER (1898-1976) was born in Philadelphia. He simultaneously received a sculptor's artistic training and studied for mechanical engineer. Departing from sketches he had made from the Barnum Circus, he conceived his first kinetic work in Paris in 1926: a series of animated puppets made of wire and wood. His visit to Mondrian's studio in 1930 aroused the "shock that started it all", as he put it himself. He decided to produce "Moving Mondrian's". The following year, he exhibited several non-representational sculptures in Paris, forms cut out of steel sheets that were still immobile but foreshadowed motion: the "stabiles". In 1932, an electric engine brought his sculptures to life, and they were the first version of the "mobiles". Two years later, he gave up the motors and entrusted them to the wind. The "mobile" and "stabile" techniques were combined in single works in 1942. He had gained fame

ROEL D'HAESE

☐ *The Lieutenant*

The body of this strange officer is built up of accurately adjusted hollow elements, like a suit of armour. On top of his skinny legs, the waistpiece—named belt or *braconnière* by the smiths—has a bizarre concave fly and is hinged to a puny corselet. The simplified facture of the arms concentrates the character's energy in his gesture of refusal, in spite of the flabbiness of the podgy hands. Does he conceal his face to hide away or to escape the unbearable sight of reality? Could it be that this sickly, faint-hearted man secretly cultivates a flattering image of himself? Does he dream that he is the conceited character whose bloated head with bulging eyes, swollen like a bladder that is about to burst, seems to escape from the helmet? As in *Dicky as the Christ of Prague* (cfr. p. 159), the spherical element on top of the character's head, whatever its meaning may be, arouses a sense of irony.

ALEXANDER CALDER

☐ *Mobile* (GOLDSCHMIDT BEQUEST)

Twelve forms, cut out of aluminium sheets and astutely balanced through a play with counterweights and respective rod lengths, hover in space as they dangle from a single suspension point. As a whole, the light sculpture surrenders to the whims of the slightest winds to offer an infinity of variations. Due to the undetermined amount of possible figures to be created by the combinations of the elements, the mobile provides an inexhaustible supply of formal virtualities. The names Calder has sometimes given to his mobiles lead us to believe that a poet's dreams rustle through this metallic foliage: *Red Petals* or *Twenty-One White Leaves*, or even this astronomer's fantasy, possibly the name of the mobile presented here, in which two starry triangles softly hover up there: *Two Three-Pointed Stars*.

by then and was commissioned for large-scale public orders such as the the gigantic "mobile" for Kennedy Airport in New York in 1957, the spiral for the UNESCO in Paris in 1958, the *Whirling Ear* for the Brussels World Fair—part of the Royal Museums collections today—and, in 1973, the *Flamingo*, a monumental "stabile" erected in Chicago.

DONALD JUDD

☐ *Untitled*

Each of the ten rectangular elements is made up of two copper plates linked by a strip of red perspex. They are piled upon each other, and the respective distance between them is equal to their width. The artist prescribes that at least seven elements be installed, should the room not allow for more, for the work to be complete. By integrating space in its structure, it forces its patent presence upon the spectator without the need for any interpretation or comment. As opposed to Donald Judd's other work exhibited in this room—adjacent horizontal elements of which the respective increasing (or decreasing) lengths are inversely proportional to the distance between them—the vertical repetition of homologous units creates a sensation of upward motion, multiplied ad infinitum by the play of reflections between the horizontal planes.

The work of Donald Judd (1928-1994) is based on the elementary principle of ruling out every element that could refer to artistic practice received before the sixties, even implicitly. His intention was to radicalize the new tendencies — "New Work" — that asserted themselves in the United States. By that time, his work never carried a name, not even the mention "untitled" (added here to respect the customs of museography), lest they might hint at the content. He disclaimed painting, except strictly monochrome painting, because every painted element, restricted by a medium, somehow represented a subject or item situated in an environment. That is why he preferred an undetermined three-dimensional space and avoided sculpture, of which he thought it was loaded with anthropomorphic connotations. Donald Judd has defined his works as "specific objects" that are, within artistic creation, equivalent to natural objects which do not carry any reference.

RICHARD LONG

☐ *Utah Circle*

These superb sand-coloured rocks with wine-coloured veins have been selected by Richard Long in Utah, a mountainous region where the earth's skeleton outcrops. They convey how he communes with a landscape he does not just cross, but through which he slowly wanders

1. *Roel D'Haese*
The Lieutenant,
1966, bronze,
184 x 57.5 x 58.5, inv. 7458.

2. *Alexander Calder*
Mobile, *c. 1953-1954,*
painted sheets, metal rods,
steel thread,
51.5 x 130 x 25,
inv. 11106.

3. *Donald Judd*
Untitled, *1988, copper*
and perspex, 10 elements,
15 x 69 x 61, inv. 11544.

3

4. *Richard Long,* **Utah Circle**, *1989, rocks from Utah, United States, Ø 600 x 28, inv. 11335.*

4

1. *Dan Flavin*
Untitled, Jan. 22, 1964,
1964, frames and neon tubes, 11.4 x 762.5 x 9.5, inv. 11361.

● DAN FLAVIN (born in 1933) studied art history at Columbia University from 1957 to 1959 and produced his first drawings. He dwells in New York's artistic circles and built his first item including a light source in 1961; *Icon 1* was box-like volume of 64 cm high by 64 cm wide by 11 cm deep to be fixed to a wall like a painting. The face side was fiery cadmium red and a fluorescent tube was fastened to the top side. Next step: Flavin attaches a 2.40 m golden TL to his studio's wall at a 45° angle. "An ordinary lamp becomes a technological totem that can absolutely be reproduced to infinity but has a striking peculiarity right now." That was *Diagonal of May 25, 1963*, underpinning of the entirety of Flavin's subsequent work. Departing from the standard tube as unit, he combines them without any other props, playing with their number, their colour and their layout to create multiple installations for which he only has to conceive the diagram. He freely admits that, since 1963, his work does not evolve according to a gradual process aiming at perfection, but as a series of variations of a same system. He even believes that art as a whole is likely to submit to similar determinations.

to immerse himself in it. There is no conflict between the boulders and the artist: he collects fragments as nature has split them and assembles them in a perfect shape. He has no other prerogative than to form a cercle of six metres in diameter. He shows no concern for installing it himself or for any form of organization inside the shape. All he requires is that it should become an object of contemplation, bringing the analogy to the fore between the time of man, who looks and who creates, and the geological time.

In 1967, Richard Long produced *A Line Made By Walking*, acknowledged as his first accomplished work of *Land Art*, created during a walk in England. He followed the same path several times, walking in his own steps to imprint the mark of his passage in the earth. His long solitary strolls from the English countryside to the Sahara or the Himalaya and across the five continents are the foundation of his work. He regards art as "doing something normal for a different reason". He also made straight lines or simple shapes—squares or circles—in the landscape, like branded by his footsteps. Here and there, he scatters less ephemeral landmarks on his path: with stones he has collected along the way, he arranges sculptures, often straight lanes that are several dozens of metres long and under a metre wide. He takes photographs of everything he has restituted to nature after a minimal intervention, mentioning the place and time of his action; he also plots down his itinerary on geographic maps with great accuracy. In galleries and museums, he exhibits arrangements of rocks he has collected on his journeys as an echo to his work in nature. Richard Long is acknowledged as a leading figure of *Land Art*. His thought process is related to Conceptual Art, and to the Minimalist tenet by the scarcity of his handling.

DAN FLAVIN

☐ *Untitled, Jan. 22, 1964*

Five 65 Watt fluorescent tubes are lined up end to end and topped by the same number of 20 Watt tubes, all give out a light of which the colour temperature varies from cold to warm and from left to right: successively cold white, day light, warm white. As it gleams through space, the light focuses the attention and becomes the actual work of art, whereof the tubes and frames are merely a support.

MARCEL BROODTHAERS

After giving up the chemical training he had barely begun, Marcel Broodthaers (1924-1976) dwelled in the Brussels literary circles of the Surrealist trend. He met the poets Marcel Lecomte and Paul Nougé in 1945, then René Magritte. He settled as a second-hand bookseller the following year. He wrote and published several collections of poetry and produced his first object at the age of thirty-nine, thus marking the beginning of his meteoric career. Between 1964 and his demise, Broodthaers held more than twenty major exhibitions in Belgium, Germany, Paris and London; each of these is conceived as a creation, announcing a further stage in his work. He published a collection of poetry in 1963, named *Pense-Bête*. He glued geometric shapes cut out of coloured paper on parts of the text in most of the copies. The following year, he integrated some fifty unsold copies in a sculpture: to him, this meant a transition from literature to plastic arts. An exhibition of casts by George Segal (cfr. p. 161) in Paris had given him the impulse. On the bristol of his first personal exhibition in the Galerie Saint-Laurent in Brussels in 1964, his declaration was a kind of manifest: "I also asked myself whether I could not sell something and be successful in life [...]. Eventually the idea of inventing something insincere crossed my mind and I immediately got down to work." These cynical words determined the position he would assume until his last days. His work never stopped challenging every ideological bias of artistic production, replacing the ideas of the perennial and the natural with the ephemeral and the artificial. At the same time, he integrated the social-economical factor that changes the work of art into sales goods.

Eggs, Mussels, etc.

The undertaking does not disclaim aesthetics. It's just the way Broodthaers "diverts" objects, eggshells or mussels' shells, overlapping them by the thousands on huge panels, where they unfurl a mother-of-pearl palette of ochres and blues on a glazed black background, or presenting them in overflowing casseroles, seasoned with critical humor aimed at the consumption patterns of his own country. However, he refuses to see his thought process assimilated with New Realism because the latter only ambitions the progress of the traditional notion of a work of art.

Museum of Modern Art - Department of the Eagles

In 1968, in the context of the challenge to the structures of authority, Broodthaers developed a personal action platform, presented as a fictitious museum: the "Museum of Modern Art - Department of the Eagles". From this mock institution, he organizes exhibitions and expresses his position about the prevailing ideology in Museums

2

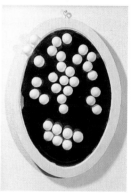

3

4

2. *Marcel Broodthaers*
Eggshells and a pin,
*1965, 19.5 x 19.5 x 6.3,
inv. 11100
(Goldschmidt Bequest).*

3. *Marcel Broodthaers*
**White Frame Mirror
with Eggs**,
*1966-1967,
73 x 50.4 x 70, inv. 11101
(Goldschmidt Bequest).*

4. *Marcel Broodthaers*
**Red Mussels
Casserole**,
*1965, 32 x 34.1,
inv. 11099
(Goldschmidt Bequest).*

1. *Marcel Broodthaers*
**Museum of Modern
Art. D^{ept} Of the Eagles**,
*1971, plastic plate with
hollow print, 84.5 × 121,
inv. 7996.*

2. *Marcel Broodthaers*
**Un Coup De Dés
Jamais N'Abolira
Le Hasard. Image**,
*1969, book, 32.6 × 25,
inv. 9554/10.*

3. *Marcel Broodthaers*
**Un Coup De Dés
Jamais N'Abolira
Le Hasard. Image**,
*1969, 1 plate out of 11 of
a series that should have
counted 12, anodized alu-
minium, ink, 32 × 50 each,
inv. 11548.*

and about the status of art in society. The eagle emblem stems from one of his own poems, written in 1947:

> Ô tristesse envol des canards sauvages
> Vol d'oiseaux au grenier des forêts
> Ô mélancolie aigre château des aigles.
> *(O sadness taking wing of the mallards*
> *Birds' flight in the forests' granaries*
> *O sour melancholy eagles' castle.)*

Marcel Broodthaers later explained: "It can easily noticeable that I wanted to neutralize the customary value of the symbol of the Eagle and boil it down to grade zero in order to introduce critical dimensions in the history and the use of this symbol."

Literary Exhibition Around Mallarmé

Broodthaers was twenty when Magritte gave him a copy of the poem *Un coup de dés jamais n'abolira le hasard* (*Never will a throw of the die abolish chance*), composed by Stéphane Mallarmé with total disregard for all typographical dictates, according to "an exact spiritual stageing of the text". Broodthaers paid tribute to the writer in 1969, considering him as "the source of contemporary art [...]. He unconsciously invented modern space." For his *Literary Exhibition Around Mallarmé* in the Antwerp gallery Wide White Space, the plastician creates three editions of the '*Coup de dés*': the first is presented as a series of abstract engravings on anodized aluminium plates and superimposes black strokes on the original layout of the text. The second is a print of the same figures on transparent listing paper. Last but not least, an edition on paper with a cover identical to that of the original edition, except for the author's name, the editors' name and the subtitle *Image* to replace the original one: *Poem*.

MICHELANGELO PISTOLETTO

☐ Green Curtain

A green curtain opens up on a scene in which a moment of the spectator's life is staged: he came to watch but finds himself acting, framed in a mirror, cut away from reality. From Van Eyck to Magritte, mirrors have fascinated painters. When Pistoletto painted his first Mirror-Painting in 1961, it was only a painted mirror he titled *The Present*. In his eyes, it meant the capture of the reflection of the painting's onlooker "in an eternally present moment, absorbing the past and the future in such a way that their existence was called in doubt: it was the dimension of Time". For over thirty years, Pistoletto (who was born in 1933) has repeated this process under various forms, multiplying mirrors or adding the serigraphy of other characters to the face of the curious visitor, his companions of a brief moment. To fall in the trap set by his paintings is to lead a reflection on reflections with him.

CARL ANDRE

☐ *4 x 25 Alstadt Rectangle*

Consists of hundred steel tiles—50 centimetres by 50—positioned four by four: that would be an objective description of this rectangle measuring 12.5 metres by 2 metres, set out on the room's floor. However, neither the material nor the configuration makes it a work of art. In fact, its status

4

5

results from the plates' arrangement in a museum area. Its artistic nature is conditioned by the relation between the object and the space of the room, which it splits up into clearly defined zones; by the orientation vector it instils into that space; and by the reaction induced in the visitor, who can walk around the ground sculpture, cross it or walk over it lengthwise. Every one of those random behaviours gives rise to a different perception of space. If the *Alstadt Rectangle* were laid out on a different location, it would become a different work of art. In addition, the present arrangement of the steel plates is but one out of five variants proposed by the artist. The tiles can be lined up in a single file and thus create a fifty metres long path. They can be positioned two by two, five by five or form a square measuring five square metres. This set of variations, produced in 1967, was the first of Carl Andre's compositions based on large metal plates.

Carl Andre was born in Quincy, Massachusetts, in 1935. The shipyards and granite quarries of his native town deeply struck his imagination. As a child, he had closely watched how metal, wood and stone were being processed and, at a later stage, they became the materials of his choosing. In 1958, the self-taught artist moved to New York and focused on making sculptures.

In 1959 came a turning point. Carl Andre started producing works inspired by Brancusi's steel *Endless Column*: the *Last Ladder* series, a set of upright wooden beams with three sides left untouched. He used a chisel to carve, in the depth of the wood, five superposed rectangular cells with an oblique bottom. From there, he challenged the relevance of sculpting pieces of wood, which were self-sufficient in their occupation of space, and developed a new concept for sculpture. Instead of carving the material, he started using the raw material to cut up space.

CHRISTIAN BOLTANSKI

☐ *Shrine: Murders*

Boltanski has selected the images for this work in a Spanish magazine specialized in accounts of all sorts of crimes. Behind a fine wire mesh, lit in a crude way by nine electric spotlights, nine enlarged photographs are framed

4. *Michelangelo Pistoletto* **Green Curtain**, *1962-1965, paint on paper, glue on stainless steel, 150 x 120, inv. 11535.*

5. *Carl Andre* **4 x 25 Alstadt Rectangle** *1967, 100 steel plates, 05 x 50 x 50 (each); 0. 5 x 200 x 1, 250 (as a whole) inv. 12025.*

6. *Christian Boltanski* **Shrine: Murders**, *1989-1990, 261 + 9 tin cans, metal wire mesh, lamps, black and white photographs, 249.5 x 211.5 x 67.5, inv. 11038.*

6

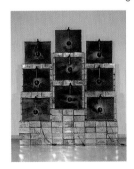

● CHRISTIAN BOLTANSKI was born in Paris in 1944, in a family of middle-class liberal jews. He began a long process of fictitious remembrance in 1963, departing from photographs and elements stemming from various origins, and often borrowed from the present, to reconstruct a past and picture it. In fact, it is a personal vision of a collective memory of a period. For example, in the early seventies, he gathers children's clothes and toys in *Vitrines* (*Showcases*). In 1973, he proposes to sixty-two museum curators to present "elements who have surrounded a person in her lifetime and remain after her death as the evidence of their existence." Since 1985, installations of a subjective liturgy dedicated to death have appeared. That is how he erected a sort of altar to the memory of unknown teenagers around an old class photograph of a Jewish high school. Nothing proves or indicates they were victims of the Holocaust this memorial inevitably conjures up. "The only thing we know about them", says Boltanski, "is that they were pupils of the Lycée Chases in Vienne in 1931."

1. Panamarenko
Spiegelschijven,
1980-1981,
2 sculptures, mixed
media, Ø 192 x 26
+ Ø 95 x 25,
inv. 11053.

in nine biscuit tins, themselves set up on a rusty base of tin cans. The mediocrity of the materials stresses the poignant feeling brought about by this sinister cenotaph to the memory of victims about whom we shall never learn anything else, reminding us that every life, in its time, can be boiled down to a few relics.

PANAMARENKO

☐ *Spiegelschijven*

The "*spiegelschijven*" (flying saucers) Panamarenko has produced since 1976 succeed to his numerous "aeroplanes", built since 1967. However, while the latter had a mechanical propelling device to be activated by the pilot, the model spaceships should be moved by magnetism, collected by induction coils. Without achieving success for any of them, in spite of the hope which he claims motivates his every attempt. Beyond this outspoken naiveness, the fact he uses his craftsmanship to keep on developing unfunctional devices betray the poetic nature of his venture, reminiscent of the dream of Icarus so rooted in mankind.

1

● PANAMARENKO Henri Van Herwegen, born in Antwerp in 1940, has drawn his pseudonym from the name of the "Pan American Airlines" company. He was a pupil of the Academy of Fine Arts of his native town, and approached science as an autodidact. His process is not at all kindred with Leonardo Da Vinci's engineering—he anticipated the conquests of knowledge. Panamarenko rather makes a deliberate scientific regression that investigates the relationship between art and modern science. "I find it strange that men of science only address their peers. If I had to discover a flying saucer, I would enjoy talking about it in such a way that everybody could start building one."

2. *Bernd Lohaus*
Wandskulpturen,
*1981, 16 wooden ele-
ments, white paper,
288 x 1144 x 200,
inv. 10604.*

BERND LOHAUS

☐ *Wandskulpturen*

At the lowest price, Bernd Lohaus purchases used, weathered wood that has been floated on the Rhine or the
Scheldt. He stores it in the port of Antwerp, sometimes
for several years. He only selects his material when the
place where his work is to be set up has been determined. Then comes the shaping, the cutting to length of the
wood, etc., all according to a plastic order designed to
create relationships between the elements, the environment and the spectator. Through the shapes he develops
in the tradition of the cathedral builders, through the history of the material, Lohaus stages a series of cultural
references that arouse a dialogue. The inscriptions and
marks he carves or paints on his sculptures stress the call
he addresses to the onlooker, who cannot find a standard
response to the questions he may ask:"You must find out
why to find yourself. Find yourself within oneself."

● BERND LOHAUS received
an apprenticeship of stone
cutter from 1960 to 1963,
then attended Josef Beuys'
courses at the Academy of
Düsseldorf. His teacher's
charisma marked him
deeply. In 1963, Beuys
had organized a large
festival, Fluxus, that
put Lohaus on the path
of the happenings he
would later produce.
He settled in Antwerp
in 1966.

DIDIER VERMEIREN

☐ *Call to Arms*

Didier Vermeiren was born in 1951 and undertook his
reflection on the relationships between sculpture,
space and the spectator in 1977: he takes photographs
of the same work, once from a series of various points
of view, or else in different locations. He simultaneously
resumes his sculptor's work. The *Call to Arms* consists of
a massive plaster base, supporting a reinforced plaster of
Paris base mould. The work's title evokes the warriors'
heroism celebrated by memorial statues, the origin of
which dates back to Ancient times though they still occupy the squares. The public monuments, exhibited to the
masses, largely contribute to the way a society sees the
sculptor's art. Just like *Sculpture 1982 (inv. 10230)*, super-
imposing two bases in reverted positions, this piece puts
the question of the relationship between the base and
the statue it is intended to extoll: the base and the place
where the statue is exhibited are determining elements
of the social acknowledgement of the status of a work of
art. The substitution he has operated here calls the value
of the support and the supported object into question.

3. *Didier Vermeiren*
Call to Arms,
*1992, plaster and metal
framework
(2 elements),
245.3 x 156.5 x 177.2,
inv. 11421.*

Index of artists and movements